Encounters of Mind

SUNY series in Chinese Philosophy and Culture

Roger T. Ames, editor

Encounters of Mind

Luminosity and Personhood in Indian and Chinese Thought

Douglas L. Berger

SUNY PRESS

Published by State University of New York Press, Albany

© 2015 State University of New York

All rights reserved

Printed in the United States of America

No part of this book may be used or reproduced in any manner whatsoever without written permission. No part of this book may be stored in a retrieval system or transmitted in any form or by any means including electronic, electrostatic, magnetic tape, mechanical, photocopying, recording, or otherwise without the prior permission in writing of the publisher.

For information, contact State University of New York Press, Albany, NY
www.sunypress.edu

Production, Diane Ganeles
Marketing, Michael Campochiaro

Library of Congress Cataloging-in-Publication Data

Berger, Douglas L., author.
Encounters of mind : luminosity and personhood in Indian and Chinese thought / Douglas L. Berger.
pages cm. — (SUNY series in Chinese philosophy and culture)
Includes bibliographical references and index.
ISBN 978-1-4384-5473-3 (hardcover : alk. paper)
ISBN 978-1-4384-5474-0 (pbk. : alk. paper)
ISBN 978-1-4384-5475-7 (ebook)
1. Buddhist philosophy. 2. Buddhism—India—Doctrines. 3. Buddhism—China—Doctrines. I. Title.

B162.B42 2014
181'.043—dc23 2014008113

10 9 8 7 6 5 4 3 2 1

Contents

Acknowledgments

I would like first of all to thank Roger Ames, editor of the SUNY series in Chinese Philosophy and Culture, for all the work he did in making the appearance of this volume possible. Thanks also go to Nancy Ellegate, senior acquisitions editor, and Diane Ganeles, senior production editor, at State University of New York Press, for their most helpful assistance.

I have been working on the issues brought together in this book for the past eight years and so owe a debt of gratitude to all the sources of intellectual inspiration that have informed it. These not only include, obviously, the works of centuries of South and East Asian philosophers but also those of more recent scholars as well. Foremost among these have been Professor J. N. Mohanty of Temple University, Professor Chakravarthi Ram-Prasad of Lancaster University in Great Britain, Professor Tao Jiang of Rutgers University, Professor Dan Robins of the University of Hong Kong, Professor Sor-Hoon Tan of Singapore National University, and Professor Roger Ames of the University of Hawai'i. Whether found explicitly in these pages or not, their ideas have had great influence on me as I made the long and winding journey of putting this work together. I also owe my graduate students at Southern Illinois University in Carbondale enduring thanks for their contributions to the last eight years of seminars that have helped shape what ended up in these pages.

I must note that the sabbatical I was granted from Southern Illinois University in the fall of 2012 gave me the time that was necessary to write this manuscript.

A special note of gratitude must go to the wonderfully kind and cheerful staff of the Just Us! Coffee Roasters Co-op on the 5800 block of Spring Garden Street in Halifax, Nova Scotia, Canada. Most of the book was written in this cozy place, and the patience and friendliness that were shown to me by the people who worked every daily shift here always kept my spirits up during all the hours I was at my keyboard. I've not ever been at a better place to write, and that was because of the good folks there.

My most profound thanks to Ying Zhang, for her love, support, and help. This volume is dedicated to her.

—Douglas L. Berger
Halifax, Nova Scotia

Introduction

One can only wonder about how hopeful the first Buddhist monks from South Asia, who traveled along the mountainous trading routes to the Central Kingdom around the turn of the first millennium CE, were about their mission. They carried with them a legacy of reflection, arisen out of ongoing centuries of debate with *brāhmaṇa*-s, ascetics, and secular South Asian thinkers, on consciousness, the makeup of the human person, and the need to overcome desire. That legacy was of course deeply rooted in a world of language, institutions, and values that prevailed in their more native ambits. They wandered into a culture with a radically different language, with relatively more worldly philosophical and sociopolitical commitments, as well as distinctive conceptions of what persons were, how they were constituted, and what their most important aims should be. Indeed, it would take centuries of itinerant searchers making forays back and forth along the Silk Road paths, sprawling transliterated texts, pitched conflicts with Confucian classicists, and tumultuous changes in imperial fortune before Buddhist ideas and practices would take a strong hold in China. But take a strong hold they did. And they transformed, in fundamental and lasting ways, how Chinese philosophers of both Buddhist and non-Buddhist persuasions would come to regard the nature of human consciousness, and what consequences the nature and capacities of consciousness had on what being a person means.

Those of us who participate in cross-cultural philosophy in the early twenty-first century sometimes fancy ourselves as being hermeneutic pioneers of a sort, better informed than people of previous ages and with unprecedented opportunities to learn from and more sensitively critique other cultures. We may be tempted to suppose that, with our virtual libraries, translation tools, and the opportunity to communicate globally in an instant, we are among the first ones to wonder about a certain case of textual corruption, a disagreement of socially embedded presuppositions, or even a cultural imperialism of ideas. Of course, such temptations are conceits, especially for a generation of academics who often have much less at stake in cross-cultural philosophical debates than generations and eons of immensely learned, and probably less distracted, peoples that have gone before us. There are far too many rich, and sometimes even miraculous, instances of sustained cross-cultural philosophical encounter in human history to meet with such attitudes. And the encounter between Indian and Chinese thought that was facilitated by the migration of Buddhism must surely be counted as one of the grandest of those instances. We are only still beginning to rediscover the treasures of that engagement. And, because we are only at a relative beginning point in mining these treasures, our attempts to philosophically engage with them ourselves over the past three or so centuries and seriously reflect on what implications these traditions of thought and their own dialogue may have for the various dilemmas of the Western tradition and the crossroads at which we presently find ourselves have been, though faltering, also intriguing and provocative. This study proposes to take its own part in these ongoing processes of learning and engagement.

The chapters of this work propose to follow what over time became a progression, in a variety of South and East Asian schools of thought, of debates about the relationship of concepts of mind or awareness to the constitution of personhood. These developing debates eventually resulted first in the appropriation of South Asian Buddhist thought into China and, after that, in impressively synthetic efforts to understand this relationship in Chinese Buddhism and the legacies their efforts worked on the medieval Confucian approach to learning. We begin with an examination of pre-Buddhist Chinese thought, with special attention to the texts of the *Mozi, Mengzi, Xunzi, Analects,* and *Zhuangzi,* in order to comprehend some prevalent perspectives on mind and personhood prior to the arrival of Buddhism in China. Despite the vastly different aims and worldviews of these texts, some shared assumptions will reveal themselves about the vital energies that nurture and propel the body to action; the functioning of the sense organs; the widely variant conceptions of the functions of the heart as the center of feeling, judgment, and moral inclination; and, in the case of the *Zhuangzi*, the provenance of "spirit" in grounding the ultimate core of human "genuineness." We will then turn to two of the most influential frameworks for formulating the relationship between embodied personhood and conscious, ultimate selfhood in the foundational Brāhmiṇical treatises and commentaries of Sāṃkhya and Nyāya in South Asia in order to glean what matrix of views helped to contextualize and in some ways shape the approaches of South Asian Buddhist philosophy. Next, we undertake a detailed examination of the Buddhist school of Vijñānavāda, both in its textual and commentarial articulation in the early generations of its development and also as it is represented in the Chinese interpretation of Paramārtha. This pivotal chapter will elucidate how Brāhmiṇical associations of a unique form of "luminosity" with the awareness of the innermost self is, in this tradition of Mahāyāna, located first not in the self but in a specifically occurrent enlightened awareness. However, in the works that made this school influential in China, the vocabulary of the "luminous mind" was transformed into a notion of a basic capacity of awareness that enables, in the larger sense, certain kinds of physical beings to be sentient, and in the consequential sense what makes it possible for still desirously attached human beings to attain to complete wisdom. It is this reformulated notion of the "luminous mind" that would have such profound and far-reaching effects on both Chinese Buddhist conceptions of cosmology and imperatives of action, and medieval Confucian ideals of learning and moral potential. In the following chapter, therefore, we will see how these influences unfold in the Tang and Song dynasty Huayen and Chan text of the *Yuan Ren Lun*, which argues that no complete account of the foundations of either human nature or the differentiated possession of awareness by various beings in the world can be causally accounted for without the idea of the "luminous mind." We will then address how the Hongzhou Chan *Linji Yu Lu* deploys this very idea in its demands that people manifest their human "genuineness" and fully engage with their natural and social environments. In the fifth chapter, we will move to the works of the Song and Ming dynasty Confucian reformers Zhu Xi and Wang Yangming, who respectively base our capacities for moral learning and insight and unerringly immediate moral action on their contested views of the relation between the embodied mind and the natural "coherence" that gives it its shape and abilities. We will then take stock of the meaning and significance of this long-standing attempt by centuries of South and East Asian philosophers to fully comprehend the character of consciousness, the limitations and possibilities attended to persons by their physicality, and their variously idealized but common hope that human beings could, through mediation and deeds, make themselves perfect.

As happens with any truly worthwhile attempt at scholarship and reflection, this work proved for its author to be a process of discovery as well as a great challenge. In a number of ways, the results of this study were not what I had originally expected. There were primarily two outcomes of my work on this book that led me in directions and to conclusions that, in the strict sense, I was not fully prepared for. And, even after its completion, I am not yet certain how to philosophically evaluate these conclusions.

My initial training was, in one of its foci, devoted to classical South Asian Brāhmiṇical and Buddhist thought and immersed in the metaphysical, epistemological, and linguistic arguments that the singularly brilliant heritage of debates between their schools produced. Clearly, two of the most prominent areas of contestation between these schools were whether there was at the core of human existence an eternal and irreducibly spiritual "self" (*ātman*), or "person" (*puruṣa*), or nothing but an ever-changing and ultimately impermanent stream of psychophysical stuff and experiences, and whether the ability of consciousness to fully and unlimitedly manifest the world had to be grounded in such an ultimate self or not. Obviously, then, all the basic themes of importance to this study were taken up by these centuries-long encounters between South Asian thinkers. However, about ten years ago, though I had already gained some familiarity with and experience of teaching pre-Qin Chinese philosophy and Tang-Song Buddhist thought, a more sustained effort of reading these texts coupled with an attempt to garner better competency in the classical Chinese language offered me unexpected and refreshing forms of inspiration. My studies in these areas held out the possibility that personhood, cognition, and communication could be rooted in a comprehensively more naturalistic framework than was prevalent in ancient South Asian debates. They also provided for the view that people, their identities, and their actions could be given meaning through a more organic relational framework, where we are constituted through our dynamic interactions with our physical environment and our social context. In the face of pre-Qin thought, then, the classical South Asian Brāhmiṇical arguments about personhood and awareness began to strike me at this point as being, in spite of their logical sophistication, rigor, and precision, too abstract. Furthermore, insofar as both ancient "Hindu" and Buddhist practitioners idealized release from rebirth as the ultimate goal of human pursuits, they suddenly appeared too dismissive of the sorts of worldly and human attachments that, rather than detracting from our existence, enriched our lives and made them worthwhile even in the face off all their fraught difficulties. Initially, even Chan Buddhism seemed in many ways to fall into the pattern of these newly discovered contrasts between South and East Asian thought. And so, when I first began planning this volume, and in the years of teaching graduate seminars at Southern Illinois University in Carbondale in preparation for its composition, I thought the book was going to be about precisely those contrasts.

But, when I began writing, something stood in the way of my initial plans. What stood in the way were the texts themselves. If one follows the trek of Buddhism from the South to the East Asian worlds through the classical textual traditions that construct, at least for us, the bridge of its movement, one finds that the notion of the "luminous mind" and its centrality to the question of personhood is every bit as important to the resultant paths of reflection in East Asia as it was in the cultural complexes of its inception. Specifically, when Vijñānavāda Buddhism is rendered into Chinese in the commentaries of Paramārtha, the idea of the "luminous mind" becomes even more indispensible to that tradition's developing system than it had been in foregoing South Asian texts and commentaries. After all, in the latter there was such a steadfast determination to deny the notion that the "luminosity" of consciousness could be identified as the essential core of spiritual selfhood that only sparse and elusive references were made to the idea as a contingently attendant capacity of translucence in a particular moment of transforming enlightened cognition. Initially, for South Asian Vijñānavāda as well as for foregoing scholastic Buddhism, luminosity was the attainment of a specific moment of enlightenment that fully manifested the world, and decidedly not the enduring and unique mark of a transcendent self as distinguished from the unconscious physical body, as conceived in Brāhmiṇical thought. But in the Chinese Vijñānavāda, namely, in *Wei Shi,* complete and unencumbered enlightenment was thought to be impossible if its cause was considered to be nothing more than an admixture of virtuous and wayward motivations as well as inspired and deluded understandings that were made available from previous experience. There had to be some recess, some store of perfectly tranquil and untrammeled awareness that could be tapped, and not produced, by the right experience that served as the most reliable causal basis for the pinnacle of Buddhist praxis. It was this recess, this store of awareness, that Paramārtha and those lineages that followed him called alternatively the "untainted cognition" and the "luminous mind." And, as the influence of this notion spread, its impact on Huayen and Chan Buddhism and medieval Confucian thought became utterly indelible. And so, in any narrative about the encounter between South and East Asian thought that hopes to be faithful, however fragmentally and imperfectly, to its real textual history cannot but itself fully engage this most pivotal of concepts. That is especially so for a narrative such as this one, which focuses on the development of ideas of personhood in this history. Its significance cannot be denied, its story must be told, and the utter seriousness with which century after century of East Asian philosophers treat it demand that the idea of the "luminous mind" be approached with attentive philosophical circumspection.

In the end, I must confess, the "luminosity of mind" that this work will in considerable measure explore is as fascinating as it is incredibly difficult for me to reconcile with my present estimation of what consciousness is. The representation of the mind as "luminous" confronts us with a conception of awareness that is not really captured by the most widely disseminated philosophical depictions of consciousness in the history of Western thought. It is not, after all, akin to a direct realist idea of consciousness, where the latter is either transparent to, mirroring of, stimulated by, or corresponds to, the world of things in its environment. These metaphors and accounts all seem to make of consciousness something passive, something open to reality, and a reliable mediator of it precisely by virtue of the fact that consciousness doesn't "do" anything, at least in its healthiest of states, to distort reality.

By contrast, notions of consciousness that do picture it as active describe it, among other things, as "constituting," "constructing," "representing," "distorting," or "projecting" its imagined world unto an otherwise unknowable reality as whatever the latter may be "in itself." Any attempt to translate the South and East Asian conceptions of "luminosity" into any of these other vocabularies seems to me to obfuscate rather than clarify its intended senses. The idea that consciousness is "luminous" means that it "lights up" the world, makes it "manifest," "brings it into view." Whether this notion of "luminosity" makes consciousness active or not depends on whether particular schools of thought understand such luminosity as the "essence" of consciousness, meaning that consciousness is somehow thought of as the "light" of awareness itself, or whether the act of casting light on the world is in one way or another the basic activity that we speak of in a nominal form. But, in either case, the most fundamental function of the mind is not to distort or concoct the world but rather to reveal it, to make it something that we can experience and act upon purposefully. Now, classical Asian thinkers, as we shall see, will have much to say about how the various physical sense organs, both those susceptible to external and internal sensation, can in their own rights and according to their own specific makeup and limited capacities be aware of, or obscure, or themselves emphasize through desire or love, or otherwise interact with the world. The sense organs, on this view, account for the various modes and moods of our experience, and the fact that all these organs, in some cases even including the faculties of deliberating and judging, were everywhere asserted to be physical helps create all the perspectives we will encounter on the hindrances and powers of embodiment. But awareness as such, in an even more basic sense than physical light itself, makes the world available for the eyes, ears, skin, and the varieties of our expression. This notion of consciousness as "luminous" therefore obviously invites serious reflection and speculation.

I must admit, if only once and at the outset of this study just to dispense with it honestly, that, though I have only really just begun to grapple with this notion, my current and rather naturalistic inclinations on the idea of consciousness make them difficult to reconcile with the mind's "luminosity." It should be said in this context that, while scientific details are relatively new, the depiction of consciousness as a product of strictly physical and natural processes is not. It was held, for instance, in classical Asian thought in different ways by the South Asian Cārvāka or Lokāyata (materialist) thinkers as well as, it seems to me, by many pre-Qin Chinese philosophers. If current scientific trends and these ancient forms of "naturalism" are right, then consciousness is a product of a very specific amalgamation of biochemical processes within the bodies of certain kinds of living beings; its various capacities are likewise contingent on the circumstances of the bodies in which it subsists; and it is attenuated, disabled, and limited by contingent events and, individually speaking, disappears entirely upon the deaths of those bodies that manufacture it. Perhaps the idea of "luminosity" can serve as an apt philosophical metaphor, as it were, for certain kinds of awareness to be attuned to or even to actively seek, manipulate, mediate, and transmit certain kinds of environmental stimulations within the bodily systems and manufacture a "consciousness" of them that enables organisms to survive, navigate, and thrive in their natural and social habitats. Such a metaphor may even be quite felicitous and even true in ways that I have not yet learned how to express or appreciate. The notion that the "luminosity" of consciousness reveals the world even in spite of our habits, prejudices, and desires might have been, for example, crucial for our survival in the many millennia that witnessed human natural evolution. But this metaphorical sense is certainly not how classical South and East Asian thinkers meant the idea of the mind's "luminosity" to be understood. My task in this study, now that I have been forthcoming about my own present sympathies and beliefs, is to, as much as I can, step aside and allow these traditions to speak on their own behalf. And, it is certainly to be hoped, both the reader and I will have much to gain in the encounter.

But there was another surprising outcome of this project that was even less anticipated when I set out on it, and again it dealt with an even earlier stage of my cross-cultural philosophical research. Along with classical South Asian Brāhmiṇical and Buddhist philosophy, my other co-specialization in graduate school was nineteenth- and twentieth-century European thought, and my doctoral dissertation, what became my first book, was devoted to an assessment of Arthur Schopenhauer's appropriation of pre-systematic "Hindu" and Buddhist ideas, particularly the notion of *māyā* or "epistemic falsification." Though I have in the intervening years continued to contribute various essays on Schopenhauer and Asian thought to different venues, I not only did not believe anything having to do with the "sage of Frankfurt" would intersect with the present volume, but that was the last thing I would have ever wanted to happen. I have in my years as a scholar eagerly sought, in the bulk of my published work, to delve into Sanskrit and classical Chinese texts and divest myself, again as far as hermeneutical inevitabilities and my own personal limitations would permit me, of Western philosophical categories and frameworks and adopt those of the ancients. Indeed, shelving the familiar "conceptual schemes" of Western philosophy and taking up those of the classical South and East Asian worlds is one of the most rewarding things about both my teaching and writing, as they offer the opportunity to think and experience the world anew, despite the antiquity of the materials upon which these opportunities are based. All the same, what dawned on me by the concluding stages of the present work was how incredibly and completely wrong Schopenhauer had been after all in one of his most prominent assessments of Brāhmiṇical and Buddhist traditions. He labeled these traditions "pessimistic." And moreover, of course, he considered the label of "pessimism" a philosophical compliment of the highest order. In his estimation, these traditions were "pessimistic" because they were fundamentally "world-denying"; they enshrined release from rebirth in the natural world as the highest aim of human praxis. And this because life in the natural world is tortured with desires for lasting pleasure-filled happiness that, in fact, can never last; is vulnerable to pain, frustration, disillusionment, disease, and loss; and invariably ends in death, only to be recycled in another round of the same maladies. Schopenhauer believed that, while other religions and philosophies avoided these stark realities, or tried to conquer them with metaphysical fantasies of a nonexistent God and heaven, "Hinduism" and Buddhism courageously accepted the true conditions of our existence, and, having done that, laid down paths of *ascesis* that would enable us to transcend our worldly attachments and "renounce the will-to-live." For those Western philosophers and commentators after him who rejected the "life-denying" axiology of Schopenhauer, his characterizations of the South Asian traditions nonetheless stuck, and thus the "pessimism" of the latter became in their minds a reason to reject the value of Brāhmiṇical and Buddhist intellectual and religious heritages for human beings outright. Of course, Schopenhauer's highlighting of the soteriological views and practices of these traditions must, when set in the proper light of their own textual traditions, as we shall see, be heavily qualified. Even though we would have to acknowledge at the end that he was not incorrect about their respective ultimate imperatives regarding release from rebirth, those imperatives deserve more sophisticated philosophical engagement than his throwaway labels afford them. Still, there is a larger sense in which the stigmatizing label of "pessimism" with which Schopenhauer saddled Brāhmiṇical and Buddhist thought is simply a false one. And its falsity is directly related to the aforementioned theme of the "luminosity of mind" that the classical schools examined in this study differently define. After all, the notion of the "luminosity" of awareness is not merely an abstract metaphysical or phenomenological doctrine forged out of a brand of systematic and detached reflection. The Brāhmiṇical, Buddhist, and later Confucian thinkers that employed the idea did so because of its crucial role in making the possibilities of consummate enlightenment and the heights of moral achievement both live and attainable ones for human beings. The fact, that is, that on some level or in some manner we stand in possession of a kind of consciousness that thoroughly, limitlessly, and faultlessly manifests the world means that, given the requisite disciplines and techniques, we can fully actualize that same awareness in knowing and acting. And more, our physical bodies, despite their impermanence and inheritance of both physical and psychological imperfections, are also equipped with all the powers and capacities needed for such actualizations. In short, for all of these traditions, it is possible for persons, because of what they are and what they are capable of, to become perfect. And this was not simply an idealized conviction but was also the goal of praxis for these schools. In the end, therefore, one of the legacies of classical Asian thought is an incorrigible optimism about human beings. It is hoped that this study will help to express the depth and courage of this optimism, so that it can strike us, in the midst of our own cultural and historical travails, as a philosophical provocation in every sense of the term.

The scope of this work is at once daring and also palpably limited. We are after all skipping over ancient and pre-systematic Vedic thought as well as scores of historically important scholastic traditions. The same judgment could be made of our coverage of Chinese thought and its elision of crucial developments during the Han dynasty, as well as more "orthodox" forms of Daoism and Buddhism than the lineages of Zhuangist and Chan thought covered here. No attempt has been made in this work to be comprehensive, as such a lofty standard is beyond the capabilities of its author. Consequently, I do not entertain the conceit that this project will be in any way "definitive." The book itself will be, I can only hope, of far less value than the goal it hopes to achieve, either by inviting correction, supplementation, and critique or prompting related lines of inquiry. My main hope, that is, is for this work to promote enriched dialogue between representatives of South and East Asian philosophical traditions. For far too long and to far too great a degree, each of these cultural complexes has been played off against one or another thinker or theme from Western philosophy. Inevitably, one of the features of this study will surely also be to occasionally fall into this well-laid hermeneutical trap of articulating classical Asian ideas in Western terms, by virtue of both the language in which it is written and the background of its author. But as yet unplumbed philosophical riches can be derived from a renewed dialogue between the Asian traditions themselves, and evidence for the promise of such a reenlivened dialogue can be found in the East Asian varieties of Buddhism. And so, despite whatever flaws may be found in the following pages, in whatever way that this book can inspire such a renewed dialogue, that success will have made this venture worth all the effort, and then some.

1

Heart and Person

Early Chinese Thought

As with many traditions of thought in the ancient world, it is virtually impossible for us to put together a systematic picture of early Chinese philosophical views of the person. The textual tradition is often fragmented, and long-standing beliefs about when and by whom certain texts were written, for almost all the important relevant documents, have been seriously called into question by recent archeological and historical investigations. What we have long been told about defined "schools" or, more accurately, lineages of philosophical thought (家 *jia*) that date back to the Warring States period in Chinese history (c. 480–221 BCE) is perhaps dodgy at best. The earliest versions of seminal philosophical works like the *Dao De Jing* include materials that seem to bridge what only later would be neatly categorized Daoist, Confucian, and Mohist thought rather than to demarcate them. And much of the actual corpus of received works from early China was likely composed and compiled at various periods during the Western Han (西漢, 202 BCE–9 CE) rather than in the tumultuous civil war of previous decades and centuries. In what follows, therefore, it must be borne in mind that we are dealing with a broad array of assumptions about what constitutes human beings. Some of these assumptions are shared and some are argued over, in the latter case even among philosophers of largely aligned persuasions. That is to say, we are not dealing here with clearly defined scholastic orthodoxies that are always oppositional with respect to other orthodoxies but with overlapping ideas and arguments in dynamically developing traditions of thought.

Nonetheless, it does seem possible to piece together some of these broadly held assumptions about what constitutes human existence for the early Chinese thinkers who exerted the longest-lasting influence through history. This chapter will draw largely upon the received texts of the *Mozi* (墨子), *Mengzi* (孟子), *Xunzi* (荀子), and *Zhuangzi* (莊子). These texts will help us see a constellation of those assumptions that were both most widely shared as well as heatedly argued over, since these texts generally contain the most extended narratives and clearest arguments available that help us flesh out these assumptions. Other significant texts will occasionally be called on to supplement the account as well. But the views extracted from these early texts that will be of crucial significance for this study can by way of brief introduction be summarized as follows.[1]

First of all, the human body, besides being a living, acting, and speaking creature that is thoroughly and dynamically related to its natural and social environments, is, to a significant degree, conscious. It is, to begin with, enlivened by wind (風 *feng*) and vital vapor (氣 *qi*)[2] that respond not merely physiologically to changes in the natural surroundings or to different sorts of food and drink but also in dispositional ways to cultural phenomena like music and various kinds of intentional cultivation. Moreover, the body's sensory organs, particularly the eyes and ears, are fairly universally said to themselves desire (欲 *yu*), love (好 *hao*), differentiate (異 *yi*), and know (知 *zhi*) things with which they actively, and not just passively, engage. Depending on the circumstances, the feelings and awareness of the sense organs can be incapacitated, suppressed, obstructed, transformed, or made more acute. But the fact is that the sense organs have specific and entirely natural capacities for sensuously and emotionally involving themselves with things, even at times quite independently of the activities of the heart. The body is therefore often seen as analogous to a kingdom, with each sensory organ being one of its governing officials (官 *guan*), each with its own specific competencies and responsibilities.

The heart (心 *xin*) is, within this larger framework of the conscious body, only one among the collection of natural organs.[3] It certainly has physiological functions, including the distribution of vital fluids about the body, which is made especially evident by the fact that the ancient graph for the word includes both the heart muscle as well as the aorta blood vessel. However, there is general agreement that, while the heart is hardly the sole source of awareness, its specific capacities of awareness can lend to it alternatively an orientational and moral preeminence that in some, though not all, cases is considered the central mark of our humanity. The heart can survey the dispositions or feelings (情 *qing*) of the other sensory organs and select (择 *ze*) which among these, if any, it will follow. It can also approve or disapprove (是非 *shi fei*) of various desires of the other organs, as well as of principles and patterns of conduct that may be recommended by others. It has the unique ability to tally (符 *fu*) the sensations of the other organs and, by virtue of this process, is able to discern everything from whether a thing really is what it is said to be to whether other persons actually conduct themselves in accordance with their pledges and principles. Like the other sense organs, the heart has things that it specifically and spontaneously desires and loves. While some thinkers claim foremost among these is benefit (利 *li*), the *Mengzi* conspicuously singles out feelings such as inner pity (惻隱 *ceyin*) and deference (辭讓 *cirang*), which provide the incipient beginnings of human moral and social virtue. Based on the presence of these special capacities, many early Chinese thinkers deemed the heart to be the governor (治 *zhi*) of the other sense organs. The *Zhuangzi* however, at least in places, is bold in asserting that the heart only takes turns with the other organs in guiding the person's aims and ideals.

Of course, in ancient China, persons are not just sensors, feelers, and thinkers. They also build personal characters that are highly individuated. Indeed, the very comportment of a person's body or his or her countenance was often thought sufficient to reveal aspects of his or her moral character. But the sure touchstones of character were believed to be a person's actions. While in ideal cases words could match deeds in such a way as to indicate trustworthiness, words or guiding principles themselves could also be false, misleading, or calculated to manipulate others to achieve only the speaker's own advantage. In some contexts, such as deceptive forms of warfare or kinds of statecraft, such deception is recommended by some preferred advisors. But, among other lineages of teaching, inconsistencies between words and practice were considered especially dangerous among would-be teachers, exemplars, and especially in ministers and rulers. Only those could be trusted with governing whose maxims and teachings were demonstrably and successfully put into practice in a way that instituted a widely beneficial and sustainable order for all of society. In addition to such things as the continuity of tradition and varying theories of legitimate rulership, the slowness and modesty of words coupled with virtuosity in conduct were the signs of a person's moral credibility.

However, in some circles of thought represented in the *Zhuangzi*, it was not the consistency of word and deed, nor the ordinary reliability of the body and its senses, nor even the orientational and moral capacities of the heart that could lead one to consummate personhood. For the composers of this almost singularly rare collection of texts, the highest potentials of everyone, from recluse to criminal to craftsman to ruler, lay in spirit (神 *shen*). While words and contesting principles of guidance might lead to endless wrangling, the heart may become fixated and one-sided in its own preferences and 氣 *qi* may become wasted in vain pursuits and disperse at death, the actualization of spirit could make the disabled and the dying into moral models, wheel-makers and butchers into teachers of princes, and recluses into companions of the immortals. While all else may lead to artificiality, spirit enables people to be utterly genuine (真 *zhen*).

The Conscious Body

In her recent work on descriptions of the body in early Chinese thought, Deborah Sommer has identified four distinct but overlapping conceptions that characterized specifically human bodies.[4] These she gives as the 躬 *gong* or ritualized body that is adorned for and performs the deeds of ceremony; 身*shen* or the body that accounts for both socially relational and individually cultivated personhood; 形 *xing* or the bodily form, its visible features, shape, and edges; and finally 軆 *ti* or the "cosubstantial" body, the body as an organic part of the larger natural, ancestral, and social bodies to which one belongs. Obviously, all of these senses of body are elements of one's personhood. In varying ways, all of these bodies are alive, the *xing* body has a lifespan and can either be healthy or mutilated; the *ti* body consumes food and functions within a natural environment; the *shen* body reflects on its own behaviors, disciplines itself, and carries out social interaction; and the *gong* body fulfills ritually required duties. We will focus especially on the notions of body as form and cultivated personhood in what follows, though the other two senses of body will also be addressed.

The *xing* and *ti* bodies are kept alive by vital powers of various sorts and are nourished by the environment as well as one's conduct. But what is conspicuous about these vital powers and energies is that they are responsive to both the physical and aesthetic surroundings, and they are so not necessarily only in human bodies but in the bodies of all things. The best-known passages evidencing this are in the second chapter of the *Zhuangzi*, where Zigong instructs Ziyou about the "piping of heaven" and how all creatures respond to it according to the constitution of their bodies.

> 夫大塊噫氣, 其名為風。是唯无作, 作則萬竅怒呺. 而獨不聞之翏翏乎? . . . 泠風則小和, 飄風則大和, 厲風濟則眾竅為虛。而獨不見之調調、之刁刁乎?
>
> When the Great Clump belches forth its vital breath (氣 *qi*), we call it the wind (風 *feng*). As soon as it arises, raging cries emerge from all the ten thousand hallows. Don't tell me you've never heard of how long the rustling continues, on and on? . . . A light breeze brings a small harmony, while a powerful gale makes for a harmony vast and grand (大和 *da he*). And once the sharp wind has passed, all these holes return to their silent emptiness. Have you not seen all the tempered attunements, all the cunning contentions? (*Zhuangzi* 2:3 [Ziporyn 2009, 9])

What we experience as wind is here the vital vapor (氣 *qi*) of the earth as a whole, and when it is emitted, all things that have orifices respond with sound, thus creating a great harmony in nature.

This natural music is emulated in human music, which for Confucian thinkers also has palpable effects on human psychology and behavior.

> 樂者, 聖王之所樂也. 而可以善民心其感人深, 其移風易俗 . . . 凡姦聲感人 而逆氣應之逆氣成象而亂生焉, 正聲感人而順氣應之, 順氣成象而治生焉. 唱和有應, 善惡相象, 故君子慎其所去就也.
>
> Music is something which the sage-kings found joy in, for it has the power to make good the hearts of the people, to influence men deeply (移風, *yi feng*—literally meaning

> "alters their wind") and to reform their ways and customs with facility. . . . When depraved sounds move a man, they cause a spirit of rebellion (逆氣 *ni qi*, literally meaning "opposing *qi*") to arise in him, and when such a spirit has taken shape, then disorder results. But when correct sounds move a man, they cause a spirit of obedience (順氣 *shun qi*, once again, meaning "compliant *qi*"), and when such a spirit has arisen, good order results. As singers blend their voices with that of the leader, so good or evil arise as a response to the force that calls them forth. Therefore, the gentleman is careful to choose his environment.[5] (*Xunzi* 20:8, 9 [Watson 1963, 118–119])

It is, according to the *Xunzi*, precisely because music has such profound effects on people's winds and *qi* that the ancient sages were so fastidious in codifying the classical odes and hymns. This great attention to music would not have been necessary to begin with were *qi* itself, within the human body, not both physiologically and psychologically responsive to people's environing conditions.

Beyond these facts, of course, *qi* can also be intentionally cultivated in ways relevant both to one's capacities of awareness as well as one's moral comportment.[6] The *Zhuangzi* in places dramatically suggests that *qi* can do a far better job of sensing and guiding people through both tasks and perilous social situations than the sense organs themselves, which normally preside over such functions.

> 若一志, 无聽之以耳而聽之以心, 无聽之以心而聽之以氣. 聽止於耳, 心止於符. 氣也者, 虛而待物者也. 唯道集虛. 虛者, 心齋也.

> If you merge all your intentions into a singularity, you will come to hear with the mind (心 *xin* or "heart" should be understood for all references to "mind" in this passage). Further, you will come to hear with the vital energy (氣 *qi*) rather than with the mind. For the ears are halted at what they hear. The mind is halted at whatever verifies its preconceptions (符 *fu*, the "tallies" of the heart).[7] But the vital energy is an emptiness, a waiting for the presence of beings. The Course (道 *dao*) alone is what gathers in this emptiness. And it is this emptiness that is the fasting of the mind. (*Zhuangzi* 4:8 [Ziporyn 2009, 26–27])

In addition, in an extended dispute with Gaozi, Mengzi is represented as exploring what sort of role *qi* plays in the process of moral cultivation. In the first instance, Mengzi is actually depicted as agreeing with Gaozi that the source of moral behavior cannot be found in the *qi* since, as we shall see and contra the previous *Zhuangzi* passage, the former believes that source is the heart. But that does not mean in the least that, for the *Mengzi*, *qi* is not an important factor in moral cultivation. On the contrary, the success of moral cultivation depends on how one tends to it. After conceding that a person's aims or will (志 *zhi*) may either be overcome by their *qi* or overcome it, Mengzi is depicted as claiming:

> 其為氣, 至大至剛, 以直養而無害, 則塞于天地之間. 其為氣也, 配義與道, 無是, 餒也. 是集義所生者, 非義襲而取之也. 行有不慊於心, 則餒矣 . . . 無若宋人然; 宋人有閔其苗之不長而揠之者, 芒芒然歸. 謂其人曰," 今日病矣, 予助苗長矣. 其子趨而往視之, 苗則槁矣. 天下之不助苗長者寡矣. 以為無益而舍之者, 不耘苗者也, 助之長者, 揠苗者也.
>
> It is a *qi* that is supremely great and supremely unyielding. If one cultivates it with uprightness and does not harm it, it will fill the space between Heaven and Earth. It is a *qi* that harmonizes with righteousness and the Way. Without these, it starves. It is produced by accumulated righteousness. It cannot be obtained by a seizure of righteousness. If some of one's actions leave one's heart unsatisfied, it will starve. . . . Do not be like the man from Song. Among the people of the state of Song there was a farmer who, concerned lest his sprouts would not grow, pulled on them. Obliviously, he returned home and said to his family: "Today I am worn out. I helped the sprouts to grow." His son rushed out and looked at them. The sprouts were withered. Those in the world who do not "help" the sprouts to grow are few. Those who abandon them, thinking it will not help, are those who do not weed their sprouts. (*Mengzi* 2A2 [van Norden 2008, 39–40])

In this construal, we see that *qi* can alternatively sprout "weeds" that will choke a person's character if left untended, or can be ruined by people trying to force it in moral directions, or starve if courses of action persistently unsatisfying to the heart are followed. The only way to cultivate *qi* that will ensure successful moral conduct is to follow the dictates of rightness (義 *yi*), which, as we shall see, Mengzi believes the heart naturally loves and slowly accumulates (積 *ji*) through a pattern of conduct. This process of accumulation will enable the *qi* to "overflow" and connect the human with the natural order by enabling the former to complete its moral potentials.

All these senses of *qi* that we have examined strongly suggest that it must be considered aware in some important ways. To return in this context to my translation of the term above as "vital vapor," the most prevalent associations of *qi* in this early Chinese philosophical literature seem to have to do with activities like breathing, the connection between the atmosphere, odors, sounds, and the comportment of the environment to one's states of health and feeling, as well as internal energies, all of which nurture the body and its collective awareness in significant ways. The body is enlivened by a refined fluid that is dynamically and dispositionally nourished by and responsive to its natural and social environment, and accounts for much in one's temperament, perception, and habits of conduct. The *qi* can also, it is sometimes said, guide our conduct in the world even more reliably than the other sense organs.

These sense organs, for their part, were considered by classical Chinese philosophers to be aware of their own accords in even more distinct ways. It must be noted that, although the sense organs like the eyes, ears, nose, mouth, and flesh are physically susceptible to sensing other material things, that susceptibility does not, in the main, account for their sensing. The engagement of the sense organs with things is consistently described in terms of their specific "desires," "loves," and capacities to "differentiate" and "know" things according to their kinds. Indeed, left to their own devices, the attractions of the sense organs to things operate spontaneously and can even become unrestrained.

> 目欲綦色, 耳欲綦聲, 口欲綦味, 鼻欲綦臭, 心欲綦佚.
>
> The eyes desire the greatest extreme of colors, the ears desire the greatest extreme of sounds, the mouth desires the greatest extreme of tastes, the nose desires the greatest extreme of smells, the heartmind desires the greatest extreme of comfort. (*Xunzi* 11:10 [Geaney 2002, 21])

> 若夫目好色, 耳好聽, 口好味, 心好利, 骨體膚理好愉佚, 是皆生於人之情性者也.
>
> The eyes' love of color, the ears' love of sounds, the mouth's love of flavors, the heartmind's love of profit, the bones, flesh and skin-lines' love of pleasure and ease: these are all born of a person's *qing* (condition, disposition) and nature. (*Xunzi* 23:8 [Geaney 2002, 19])

In addition to this, Confucian philosophers tend to hold a kind of anthropological universalism with regard to the preferences of the sense organs. They believed that all human eyes, ears, and tongues desire and love the same things, lending warrant to their moral ideals that are made possible by the conviction that all human hearts are also the same in their love for goodness.

> 口之於味也, 有同耆焉, 耳之於聲也, 有同聽焉, 目之於色也, 有同美焉. 至於心, 獨無所同然乎? 心之所同然者何也, 謂理也, 義也.
>
> Mouths have the same preferences in flavors, ears have the same preferences in sounds, eyes have the same preferences in attractiveness. When it comes to hearts, are they alone without preferences in common? What is it that hearts prefer in common? I say that it is order and righteousness. (*Mengzi* 6A7 [van Norden 2008, 151])

The *Zhuangzi* of course strongly contests this notion that the sense organs of human beings, most of all the organ of the heart, love the same colors, flavors, and values, but even in this dissent, it agrees that the sense organs are naturally attracted to things of their own initiative. The text drives this point home by comparing the natural attractions of human beings with those of animals but then makes the relativity among human preferences clear by parlaying the point as a criticism of widely held moral virtues. The language that this comparison is put in is most revealing, as it speaks of creatures "knowing" what is best for themselves.

> 民溼寢則腰疾偏死, 鰌然乎哉? 木處則惴慄恂懼, 猨猴然乎哉? 三者孰知正處, 民食芻豢, 麋鹿食薦, 蝍且甘帶, 鴟鴉耆鼠, 四

者孰知正味，猨？猵狙以為雌，麋與鹿交，鰌與魚游. 毛嬙，麗姬，人之所美也，魚見之深入，鳥見之高飛，麋鹿見之決驟. 四者孰知天下之正色哉？自我觀之，仁義之端，是非之塗，樊然殽亂，吾惡能知其辯!

When people sleep in a damp place, they wake up deathly ill and sore about the waist—but what about eels? If people live in trees, they tremble with fear and worry—but what about monkeys? Of these three, which "knows" which is the right place to live? People eat the flesh of their livestock, deer eat grass, snakes eat centipedes, hawks and eagles eat mice. Of these four, which "knows" the right thing to eat? Monkeys take she-monkeys for mates, bucks mount does, male fish frolic with female fish, while humans regard Mao Qiang and Lady Li as great beauties—but when fish see them, they dart into the depths, when birds see them, they soar into the skies, when deer see them, they bolt away without looking back. Which of these four "knows" what is rightly alluring? From where I see it, the transitions of Humanity and Responsibility and the trails of right and wrong are hopelessly tangled and confused. How could I know how to distinguish which is right among them? (*Zhuangzi* 2:8 [Ziporyn 2009, 18])

Despite its skepticism about our ability to articulate what is really better or worse, the passage coheres with the notion that the physical sense capacities of creatures, both animal and human, which seek comfort, flavor, and allure, are conscious, are themselves attracted to things and impel individuals to pursue them.

As the previous *Zhuangzi* passage reveals, in addition to having their own attractions and loves, the sense organs themselves, and sometimes the body as an integrated whole, are widely said to "know." It is highly significant, as Jane Geaney has pointed out, that the textual tradition largely employs the same term, 知 *zhi*, to characterize the knowledge both of the sense organs and the heart.[8] In different contexts, the *Mozi* speaks extensively to the body's and sense organs' direct capacities for knowledge. When condemning ancient, malevolent rulers for indulging their needs for sensual gratification at the expense of the populous, the text speaks of pleasing sounds, sights, flavors, and states of comfort:

> 雖身知其安也, 口知其甘也, 目知其美也, 耳知其樂也, 然上考之不中聖王之事; 下度之不中萬民之利.
>
> Although the body knows they are comfortable, the mouth knows they are gratifying, the eyes know they are delightful and the ears know they are pleasing, yet they are found not to be in accordance with the deeds of the sage-kings of antiquity and not to contribute to the benefits of the people at present. (*Mozi* 32:1 [Mei 1929, 175])

Here it is the naturally and socially relational 身 *shen* body of Sommer's classification that knows comforts. And, in its extended discussions favoring the evidence for the existence of ghosts and spirits and refuting the existence of fate, the *Mozi* takes the hearing and sight of the people, and certainly that of the ancient sages, as sufficient standards (法 *fa*) upon which to base the credibility of such beliefs.

> 是與天下之所以察知有與無之道者, 必以眾之耳目之實知有與亡為儀者也; 請惑聞之見之, 則必以為有.
>
> The way to find out whether anything exists or not is to depend on the testimony of the ears and eyes of the multitude. If some have heard it and some have seen it then we have to say it exists. If no one has heard it and no one has seen it then we have to say it does not exist. (*Mozi* 31:3 [Mei 1929, 161])
>
> 今天下之士君子或以命為亡, 我所以知命之有與亡者, 以眾人耳目之情, 知有與亡. 有聞之, 有見之, 謂之有: 莫之聞, 莫之見, 謂之亡. 然胡不嘗考之百姓之情? 自古以及今, 生民以來者, 亦嘗見命之物, 聞命之聲者乎? 則未嘗有也. 若以百姓為愚不肖, 耳目之情不足因而為法, 然則胡不嘗考之諸侯之傳言流語乎? 自古以及今, 生民以來者, 亦嘗有聞命之聲, 見命之體者乎? 則未嘗有也.
>
> Among the gentlemen of today some think there is fate and some think there is no fate. That I am able to judge whether there is fate or not is by the sense-testimony of the multitudes. If some have heard it and some have seen it, I shall say there is fate. If none has heard it, none has seen

> it, I shall say there is no fate. Why not then let us inquire into the sense-testimony of the people? From antiquity to the present, since the beginning of man, has any seen such a thing as fate, or has any heard the sound of fate? Of course, there is none. If the common people are considered stupid and their senses of hearing and sight unreliable, then why not inquire into the recorded statements of the feudal lords? But from antiquity to the present, since the beginning of man, has any of them heard the sound of fate or seen such a thing as fate? Of course, none of them has. (*Mozi* 36:2 [Mei 1929, 189–190])

There is, of course, also the famous passage in the *Mengzi*, quoting the *Zuozhuan*, where heaven itself is said to use the ears and eyes of the people as indications of whether or not rulers are being benevolent toward them and thus whether or not they are worthy to rule.

> 天視自我民視; 天聽自我民聽.

> Heaven sees as my people see. Heaven hears as my people hear. (*Mengzi* 5A5 [van Norden 2008, 124])

In the process of such direct sensory knowing, the organs have the capacity to "differentiate" (異 yi) among the things to which they are naturally susceptible.

> 形體, 色理以目異;聲音清濁, 調竽, 奇聲以耳異;甘, 苦, 鹹, 淡, 辛, 酸, 奇味以口異; 香, 臭, 芬, 鬱, 腥, 臊, 漏庮, 奇臭以鼻異; 疾, 癢, 滄, 熱, 滑, 鈹, 輕, 重以形體異; 說, 故, 喜, 怒, 哀, 樂, 愛, 惡, 欲以心異.

> Forms, bodies, colors and patterns are differentiated by the eye. Sounds and tones, clear and muddy, modes and harmony and strange sounds are differentiated by the ear. Sweet, bitter, salty, bland, pungent, sour, and strange tastes are differentiated by the mouth. Fragrances and stenches, perfumes and rotten orders, putrid and rancid smells, dank and sour smells as well as strange smells are differentiated by the nose. Illness and wellness, cold and hot, smooth and sharp, light and heavy are differentiated by the form and

> body. Speech and causes, happiness and anger, sadness and joy, loves, hates and desires are differentiated by the heartmind. (*Xunzi* 22:5 [Geaney 2002, 44–45])

Here, while the heart has specific things like dispositional feeling states as well as "speech and causes," the other sense organs directly differentiate among their specific contents without any mediation from the heart at all. It should also be noted that the "form and body" that differentiate among tactile sensations, temperature states, and states of health are identified as what Sommer would call both the body as form and the "cosubstantial body" (形體 *xing ti*). The fact that the body and sense organs distinguish not only between different shades of color, pitches of sound, kinds of texture, and so on, but also whether the sensations are appealing or repulsive in various ways is also indicative of their abilities of both sensation and affect.[9]

From all of the foregoing, we can conclude that early Chinese thinkers generally believed that the body was almost entirely and vibrantly conscious. The basic energies that give it vitality were considered physiologically and even psychologically responsive to the environment and were even amenable to being moved by everything from music to moral cultivation. The sense organs themselves, even independently of the heart, were robustly aware not only of the seen, heard, touched, and felt features of things but of their aesthetic qualities and how these qualities were either naturally attractive or repellent to human sensibilities. Each organ was considered to have its own "office," which it could not, as the *Xunzi* asserts, trade with the other organs. In this framework of thought, the heart was by no means the only seat of awareness in the person but rather was merely considered another bodily organ. Though it has crucial and in some cases uniquely human powers, the heart had to cooperate with the other systems of awareness in the body in order to guide it in the ways that different philosophers idealized.

The Heart: Keeping Tallies and Moral Feelings

Though it cannot be overemphasized that, in classical Chinese thought, the heart is only one of the body's many systems of awareness, it is just as important to realize that the heart's specific modes of awareness, for most philosophers of the period under discussion, make it the ruler of the body and make us persons.

> 耳目鼻口形能各有接而不相能也: 夫是之謂天官. 心居中虛, 以治五官: 夫是之謂天君.
>
> Ear, eye, nose, mouth and form, each has its own contacts (lit., "receptions" or "meetings") and does not do things for the others. Now these are called the heavenly officials. The heartmind dwells in the central cavity and governs the five officials. This is called the heavenly ruler. (*Xunzi* 17:4 [Geaney 2009, 19])
>
> 無惻隱之心, 非人也; 無羞惡之心, 非人也; 無辭讓之心, 非人也; 無是非之心; 非人也.
>
> If one is without the feeling (心 *xin* here can be understood as heart or feeling) of compassion, one is not human ("a person" is probably a better choice for 人 *ren*). If one is without the feeling of disdain, one is not human. If one is without the feeling of deference, one is not human. If one is without the feeling of approval and disapproval, one is not human. (*Mengzi* 2A6 [van Norden 2002, 46])

This predominantly Confucian view renders the heart as the nobleman or leader (君 *jun*) of the body as well as the organ that, by virtue of its possession of certain feelings, makes us into persons. Despite the fact that the text of the *Mengzi* and *Xunzi* famously diverge on how such moral feelings are acquired, whether they are achieved through ritual or are inborn, there is a rather pronounced sphere of agreement between them regarding the heart's special powers relative to the other sense organs. Some of these powers are acknowledged by texts with avowedly non-Confucian philosophical persuasions as well, witnessing to at least some ancient consensus on the heart's constitutive role in our humanity.

First, while the other sense organs can know and be attached to things directly, as we have seen, the heart has what the *Xunzi* calls a "levying knowledge" (徵知 *zheng zhi*) with regard to its contents. It seems that, in the heart's knowledge, two steps occur, the first being the presentation of the other sense organs' awareness to it and the second being the heart's "speaking" or perhaps identifying (說 *shuo*) each of those things.

> 心有徵知。徵知, 則緣耳而知聲可也; 緣目而知形可也. 然而徵知必將待天官之當 簿其類, 然後可也. 五官簿之而不知, 心徵知而無說, 則人莫不然謂之不知. 此所緣 而以同異也.
>
> The heartmind has verifying knowledge. There is verifying knowledge; thus, because of [lit., caused by] the ear, it is possible to know sounds; because of [caused by] the eye, it is possible to know forms. However, verifying must await the heavenly officials' meeting and recording their kinds in order to be possible. If the five officials record without knowing, or if the heartmind verifies without speaking, then people will not fail to pronounce it "not knowing." It is this that causes sameness and difference. (*Xunzi* 22:5 [Geaney 2002, 48])

It is also surely important that the passage mentions at the end the ascertainment of "sameness and difference" (同異 *tong yi*) as a specific result of this process of "levying" or "verifying" knowledge. There are other passages in the *Xunzi* that suggest that the "employment" (使 *shi*) of the heart's special capacities is necessary in order for people to be fully aware of the things that they experience.

> 心不使焉, 則白黑在前而目不見; 雷鼓在側而耳不聞, 況於使者乎?
>
> If the heartmind is not being applied to it, then black and white may be right before one's eyes and not be seen; thunder and drums may be at one's side and one will not hear them. How much more so with one whose heartmind is occupied by something? (*Xunzi* 21:1 [Geaney 2002, 96])

It is perhaps not possible for us to put together an entirely complete picture based on these allusions. We know from the previous passages that the sense organs of sight, hearing, and so on are able to discriminate (辨 *bian*) specific things from their background contexts as well as differentiate (異 yi) between things, so it may at first seem puzzling that in the immediately preceding passage the use of the heart appears to be required in order for people to attend to things and recognize them for what they are. One way to resolve this conundrum might focus on the fact that, while the sense organs themselves may be able to identify things belonging to the same kind (类 *lei*), which is to say that the eyes, for example, can see a specific hue of "blue" as an instance of the color "blue," and the ears can hear a particular peal of "thunder" as an instance of the sound "thunder," they may not, on the *Xunzi*'s account, be able to compare "blue" with "thunder" or "grey" with "drums" by themselves. In the ascertainment of "sameness" and "difference," the heart may be needed to exact the necessary "levy." Elsewhere, the *Xunzi* very elliptically corroborates something like this view with the claim that the sense organs, with regard to the same kinds (类 *lei*) of things, intend just those things (意物 *yi wu*), and, because of this, the ancient sage rulers were able to codify "definite names" (約名 *yue ming*) for things that everyone in society could agree to use.[10] In other words, the sameness (同 *tong*) of things, and thus the possibility of associating similar individual things into "kinds," may be drawn from the sense organs themselves but not difference (異 *yi*), since telling the differences between things requires the knowledge of the heart. This depiction would not by any means deprive the other sense organs of the direct awareness of which they are themselves capable but would only enlist the special awareness of the heart.

In any event, the "levying knowledge" referred to here seems to have to do with the other sense organs' meeting and recording their contents that are registered by the heart, for since the eyes cannot hear and the ears cannot see, the heart weighs the contents of each of the senses and perhaps associates their contents with one another in such a way as to make robust sense of attentive sensation and perception. Once again, the *Xunzi* seems to be alluding to two kinds of knowledge, one being the 知 *zhi* that people normally have through their sense organs, and the other being the 智 *zhi* or "understanding" that is brought about when they are able to "unify" things (所合 *suo he*), the latter of which, presumably, requires the capacities of the heart being discussed.[11]

This may be corroborated by what the *Xunzi* and a few other texts of the classical period say about the heart's ability to "tally" (符 *fu*). In denouncing the views of the *Mengzi* on the inborn character of human nature, the text credits the power with the ability to observe and distinguish between phenomena, determine which characterizations and claims made about them are accurate or inaccurate, and apply those conclusions to conduct in successful ways.

> 凡論者貴其有辨合, 有符驗. 故坐而言之, 起而可設, 張而可施行.
>
> In terms of those who analyze things, there is value in discrimination and matching, as well as tallying and confirming. Those who sit and talk should be able to stand and show that what they say can be established—that it can be enacted over a wide area. (*Xunzi* 23:13 [Geaney 2002, 94])

The heart's tallying here, and in other passages in the *Xunzi*, enables people to determine what things are and classify them accurately. The activity of tallying is in other places associated with the establishment of standard weights and measures, for example. Properly demonstrating that its discriminations and classifications help identify things and make them usable in human interaction, and even transaction, helps to establish social trust (信 *xin*).

> 合符節, 別契券者, 所以為信也.
>
> Uniting the halves of tallies and tokens and separating contracts and deeds are the reason for trust. (*Xunzi* 12:2 [Geaney 2002, 94])

As Geaney pertinently points out, tallies in ancient China were sticks with matched notches that were broken in half, each half given to the parties of an agreement as a token of the contract.[12] With regard to the heart's special kind of knowing, then, tallying appears to classify things correctly and, on the basis of this classification, empowers people to tell correct from incorrect and use things for beneficial social ends. Failed tallies don't match visual sensations and words, kinds with kinds, and such failures not only make proper orientation in the world impossible but also render things unserviceable for reliable social use. It is interesting that the *Zhuangzi*, for as much as it mistrusts the standards of the heart to perhaps an even greater degree than the *Xunzi* trusts them, does not deny that tallying is the function of the heart even while emphasizing that tallying represents the heart's limitation: "The heart stops at tallying" (心止於符).[13]

One broad agreement among early Chinese philosophers appears to be about the heart's capacity to select (择 *ze*) which feelings it will prefer. The other sense organs have their natural desires, loves, and attractions, but the heart can decide which of these, if any, are to be preferred in terms of determining which course of conduct will be followed. This process of selection is represented in various ways as a kind of "pondering" or "reflecting" or "thinking."

> 性之好, 惡, 喜, 怒, 哀, 樂謂之情. 情然而心為之擇謂之慮.
>
> The nature's love, hatred, pleasure, anger, sadness and happiness: [we] call this *qing* [condition, disposition]. Given that the *qing* is like this: the heartmind's acting upon this and selecting, [we] call this pondering. (*Xunzi* 22:7 [Geaney 2002, 86])

The terms 性 *xing* and 情 *qing* in this passage are difficult to translate with precision. While Geaney and many others render the former as "nature," and while there is some justification in this translation, the term 性 *xing* in classical and even modern Chinese is often closely allied with people's mood and temperament, as well as the *qi* that constitutes one's gender (both of these associations are invoked in the *Shuowen Jiezi*). Similarly, 情 *qing* can in many contexts be associated with "feelings" or "emotions," and the fact that this passage lists a series of emotional states beginning with "love" and "hatred" appear to indicate that what is being discussed here is that the heart's activity (為 *wei*) can be described as selecting (择 *ze*) which of these feelings to prioritize. The "pondering" (慮 *lu*) that the *Xunzi* calls this activity of the heart seems also to be what the *Mengzi* has in mind when it speaks of the heart's native ability to "think" or "reflect" (思 *si*).

> 耳目之官不思, 而蔽於物, 物交物, 則引之而已矣. 心之官則思, 思則得之, 不思則不得也. 此天之所與我者, 先立乎其大者, 則其小者弗能奪也. 此為大人 而已矣.
>
> It is not the function (lit., the "office," 官 *guan*) of the ears and eyes to reflect, and they are misled (lit., "obfuscated"

> 蔽 *bi*) by things. Things interact with other things and simply lead them along. But the function of the heart is to reflect. If it reflects, then it will get it. If it does not reflect, then it will not get it. This is what Heaven has given us. If one first takes one's stand on what is greater, then what is lower will not be able to snatch it away. This is how to become a great person. (*Mengzi* 6A15 [van Norden 2008, 156])

One of the preferred motifs of the *Mengzi* is the representation of the heart as the "greater" of all the other sense organs, calling it the greater part of one's 身 *shen* body, than the other parts and esteeming people who prefer its own desires over the desires of the other organs in the very next section. Here, the superiority of the heart over the other organs lies in its power to "reflect" and not simply be "pulled away" as the other organs supposedly are by their immediate desires for and engagements with things. Obtaining the things that are most appropriate to the idealized aims of human existence depends, for the *Mengzi*, on the heart's unique potential to reflect. But notable here also is the fact that the heart is not said to automatically reflect. The activity apparently takes some effort and therefore, in both the *Mengzi* and *Xunzi*, requires training and cultivation in order to reflect in a way that ensures the right moral choices.

For the *Xunzi*, the uneducated, unritualized, and uncultivated heart spontaneously prefers whatever feelings and actions will accrue to its own benefit (利 *li*), and this is primarily why the untrained dispositions of human feeling are judged by the received text to be "deformed," "ugly," or as many somewhat misleading translations have it, "evil" (惡 *e*). The *Mengzi*, by famous contrast, asserts that the heart has incipient feelings of compassion and respect, shame and the capacity to approve and disapprove of environing conditions, and it is only because of these feelings that people can become morally virtuous. Citing its most well-known example of the spontaneous, unpremeditated distress and pity that overtake the heart when one sees a child about to unsuspectingly fall into a well, the *Mengzi* argues:

> 惻隱之心, 仁之端也; 羞惡之心, 義之端也; 辭讓之心, 禮之端也; 是非之心, 智之端也. 人之有是四端也, 猶其有四體也. 有是四端而自謂不能者, 自賊者也, 謂其君不能者, 賊其君者也。

> 凡有四端於我者, 知皆擴而充之矣, 若火之始然, 泉之始達. 苟能充之, 足以保四海; 苟不充之, 不足以事父母.
>
> The feeling of compassion is the sprout of benevolence. The feeling of disdain is the sprout of righteousness. The feeling of deference is the sprout of propriety. The feeling of approval and disapproval is the sprout of wisdom. People having these four sprouts is like their having four limbs. To have these four sprouts, yet to claim that one is incapable (of virtue), is to steal from oneself. To say that one's ruler is incapable is to steal from one's ruler. In general, having these four sprouts within oneself, if one knows how to fill them all out, it will be like a fire starting up, a spring breaking through! If one can merely fill them out, they will be sufficient to care for all within the Four Seas. If one fails to fill them out, they will be insufficient to care for one's parents. (*Mengzi* 2A6 [van Norden 2008, 46–47])

One finds in this connection an almost shocking correspondence in the *Zhuangzi*, where it is said that, of one "restriction" (戒 *jie*) conferred by heaven and the other dictated by propriety, the first, conferred by heaven, is:

> 子之愛親, 命也; 不可解於心.
>
> A child's love for his parents is fate; it cannot be removed from his heart. (*Zhuangzi* 4:3 [Ziporyn 2009, 28])

On this aforementioned construal of the *Mengzi*'s, what makes the heart the "nobleman" or "leader" (君 *jun*) of the person are the incipient beginnings of feeling that, when developed through cultivation and learning and extended to others, become the perfected virtues that can in turn make a person into a "nobleman" (君子 *junzi*). For the *Mengzi* then, the heart, like the other sense organs, has its own desires, its own natural pleasures, which, just like the other sense organs, can be obstructed and denied, but which make the heart superior to the other senses because what the heart loves are feelings that enable people to become moral.

We have seen in this section that rather wide-ranging agreement seemed to prevail among early Chinese philosophers, particularly those with Confucian persuasions but not limited to them, about the heart's powers. The heart could weigh and compare the knowledges of the other sense organs, make people aware of not merely the direct objects of their sensory experience but also of the differences that obtain between things as well as between kinds, and select which inclinations made available to it by the pull of the many senses it might follow. In the case of a few philosophers of the period, a heart that is distinctively human has a stock of preferences all its own, including natural attachment to one's parents and the feelings that ultimately are responsible for enabling us to be social and moral beings. However, despite the fact that, at least in the first of these senses, the *Zhuangzi* would concur with the *Mengzi*, the former would vehemently deny the heart both supremacy over the other organs and the seat of our genuine humanity. We turn to the *Zhuangzi*'s quite unique idealization of what it took to be "genuine personhood" and its basis in "spirit," an idealization that would have a palpable impact on Chan Buddhism many centuries later, shortly.

Personal Cultivation and Sociality

Much has been made in recent English-language scholarship about the degree to which early Chinese philosophy emphasizes the supposedly comprehensive degree to which the person is constituted by their relationships. In the Confucian tradition, the child's virtue of family care (孝 *xiao*), the adult's perfected virtue of "co-humanity" (仁 *ren*), [14] and the expectations that people fulfill their appropriate social roles (正名 *zheng ming*) are said to exemplify this thoroughgoing relationality. For the Mohists, the expectations that people will emulate and conform to their superiors (尚同上) and care for one other inclusively (兼愛 *jian ai*) predominate.[15] In the Daoist tradition, natural models and environing circumstances serve as standards for individual conduct. The present work does not question these seemingly overarching assumptions of classical Chinese thought but seeks only to supplement them. What is actually written, and not merely implicit, in early philosophical works makes a very great deal of the notion that successful sociality hinges on individual contingencies of character and degrees of personal cultivation. These highly individuated contingencies manifest themselves to some degree in people's countenance and bearing but are also very often proven for what they are, depending upon whether a person's deeds match their words or not.

One thing that must be noted at the outset of this discussion, however, is the penchant early Chinese texts have for sometimes attaching normative import to distinctions between those who govern society and "ordinary people" or the "masses" (民 *min*). While it is surely the case that Confucian thinkers took great pains in the textual tradition to represent elevated social offices like those of 士*shi*, 君子 *junzi* and 大人 *da ren* as resulting from classical and moral learning, cultivational achievement, and socially accountable spheres of official responsibility to others, all these terms were originally distinctions of often inherited social class. All throughout the history of the tradition, Confucians would continually struggle with the tendency of such offices held by people with these titles to be inherited by already socially well-established families and ever-renewed calls to make officeholding in local and national governments be based on merit built up through the civil service examination system. Early Confucian philosophers did generally insist, based on legends of the ancient emperor Shun—a commoner from a criminal family who inherited the throne as well as Confucius's own impoverished but most exemplary student Yan Hui—that, in principle, everyone had the potential to become a nobleman and even a sage, as well as, in the case of males, access the social opportunity that was necessary to receive an education that would qualify people for government office. However, moral distinctions are upheld in Confucian texts between those well versed in their own particular literary corpus and ritual regimens and those who were not, distinctions that served as the qualifications for one to take up offices of extensive social power. As the famous, or infamous, passage in the *Lunyu* has it:

> 君子之德風, 小人之德草. 草上之風, 必偃.
>
> The virtue of a gentleman is like the wind, and the virtue of a petty person is like the grass—when the wind moves over the grass, it is sure to bend it. (*Lunyu* 12:19 [Slingerland 2003, 134])

Similarly in the *Mengzi*, a text with some of the strongest universalist moral views of the entire period, there are places where the differences between the moral capacities of rulers and those of commoners are highlighted. After ardently encouraging King Xuan of Qi that all that is required to be good is to extend his natural feelings of sympathy to the entire populous, Mengzi is represented as telling the ruler that ordinary folk need sufficient food and schooling to be virtuous, suggesting different programs of moral improvement for people in different political positions.

> 無恆產而有恆心者, 惟士為能. 若民, 則無恆產, 因無恆心. 苟無恆心, 放辟, 邪侈, 無不為已 . . . 謹庠序之教, 申之以孝悌之義, 頒白者不負戴於道路矣.
>
> Only a noble (士 *shi*) is capable of having a constant heart while lacking a constant livelihood. As for the people (民 *min*), if they lack a constant livelihood, it follows that they will lack a constant heart. No one who lacks a constant heart will avoid desperation and evil. . . . If you are careful that the schools engage in instruction, explaining the righteousness of filiality and brotherliness, then those with grey hair will not carry loads on the roads. (*Mengzi* 1A7 [van Norden 2008, 14–15])

The *Xunzi*, despite famously avowing in the chapter on human nature that every man in the street can become a sage, is more explicit still about the function of ritual, and particularly music, in fixing social distinctions, creating through affect the kind of social "harmony" appropriate to the hierarchy of distinct social spaces.

> 故樂在宗廟之中, 君臣上下同聽之, 則莫不和敬: 閨門之內, 父子兄弟同聽之, 則莫不和親, 鄉里族長之中, 長少同聽之, 則莫不和順. 故樂者審一以定和者也 . . . 出所以征誅, 則莫不聽從; 入所以揖讓, 則莫不從服. 故樂者, 天下之大齊也, 中和之紀也, 人情之所必不免也. 是先王立樂之術也, 而墨子非之奈何!
>
> When music is performed in the ancestral temple of the ruler, and the ruler and his ministers, superiors and inferiors listen to it together, there is none who is not filled with a

> spirit of harmonious reverence. When it is performed within the household, and father and son, elder and younger brothers, listen to it together, there is none who is not filled with a spirit of harmonious kinship. And when it is performed in the community, and old and young people together listen to it, there are none who are not filled with a spirit of harmonious obedience. Hence music brings about complete unity and induces harmony. . . . If one marches abroad to punish offenders in accordance with the way learned through music, then there will be no one who will not obey and submit; if one behaves at home with courtesy and humility, then there will be no one who will not obey and be submissive. Hence, music is the great arbiter of the world, the key to central harmony and a necessary requirement of human emotion. This is the manner in which the former kings created their music. And yet Mozi criticizes it. Why? (*Xunzi* 20:2, 3 [Watson 1963, 116, 117]).

However, the Confucians are hardly the only ones who held to moral distinctions between the ruler and the populace. The *Mozi*, for all its criticisms of the abuses of the Confucian court, also argues that people long ago realized that society would remain in chaos without unified moral guidance and thus since have nurtured the inclination to conform to their superiors.

> 正長既已具, 天子發政於天下之百姓, 言曰: "聞善而不善, 皆以告其上. 上之所是, 必皆是之, 所非必皆非之, 上有過則規諫之, 下有善則傍薦之. 上同而不下比者, 此上之所賞, 而下之所譽也. 意若聞善而不善, 不以告其上, 上之所是, 弗能是, 上之所非, 弗能非, 上有過弗規諫, 下有善弗傍薦, 下比不能上同者, 此上之所罰, 而百姓所毀也." 上以此為賞罰, 甚明察以審信.

> When the rulers were all installed, the emperor issued a mandate to all the people, saying: "Upon hearing good or evil one shall report it to a superior. What the superior thinks to be right all shall think to be right; what the superior thinks to be wrong all shall think to be wrong. When the superior is at fault there shall be good counsel, when the subordinates show virtue there shall be popular recommendation. To identify one's self with the superior

and not to unite one's self with the subordinates—this is what deserves encouragement from above and praise from below." On the other hand, if upon hearing good or evil one should not report to a superior; if what the superior thought to be right one should not think to be right; if what the superior thought to be wrong one should not think to be wrong; if when the superior was at fault there should be no good counsel; if when the subordinates showed virtue there should be no popular recommendation; if there should be common cause with subordinates and no identification with the superior—this is what deserves punishment from above and condemnation from below." The superior made this the basis of reward and punishment. He was clear-sighted and won his people's confidence. (*Mozi* 11:3 [Mei 1929, 56–57])

While the *Mozi* is careful to remind the reader that they should regard heaven (天 *tian*), personified, as establishing the standards of rightness and not primarily the ruler, and while it certainly allows for the possibility that both ministers and rulers can be wrong, as do all traditions of the period, the assumption generally is that the most virtuous are chosen by heaven, and they in turn select from among the most virtuous men to be lords and ministers. And even the *Zhuangzi*, in places superlatively concerned with issues of rulership, witnesses to the fact that the obligations that ministers have to rulers, while not written into their hearts as is the love of children for their parents, are still matters of worldly rightness that simply can't be avoided.

> 臣之事君, 義也, 無適而非君也, 無所逃於天地之間. 是之謂大戒.
>
> An underling's service to a boss (lit., a noble or ruler, 君 *jun*) is responsibility (義 *yi*), the response called for by his position: wherever he goes, he is in service to his boss. It cannot be avoided anywhere in this world. (*Zhuangzi* 4:3 [Ziporyn 2009, 28])

We can see then that there is widespread agreement among early Chinese thinkers that social authority is invested with normativity, and that, while the "common masses" are often, though hardly always, accorded moral potentials that are every bit as far-reaching as those of their rulers, one's very existence as a commoner testifies to expected submission to and conformity with an assumed normative supremacy of one's superiors. Hierarchy is an inescapable element of one's personhood in ancient China, and it is drawn along lines as multifaceted as birth, eldership, education, ethnicity, and most presciently gender. One need look no further than the early Confucian notion of the distinction (别 *bian*) between the "outer" social roles of men and the "inner" domestic roles of women and the Han dynasty metaphysicalization of this notion as representing the superiority of the cosmological *yang* or masculine powers over *yin* feminine powers in the works of Dong Zhongshu for ample evidence of this.[16]

All this being accepted, the textual tradition just as widely asserts that the degree of one's social recognition, esteem, and trust depends on the particulars of one's personality and character, and the seriousness and successes of one's personal cultivation. The received *Lunyu* is filled with examples, though they may have been drawn from different early lineages of teaching, of people adjudged to be of various degrees of fitness for political office and of students of differing inclinations of character and varying levels of understanding and moral self-discipline.

> 子路問: "聞斯行諸?" 子曰: "有父兄在, 如之何其聞斯行之?" 冉有問: "聞斯行諸?" 子曰: "聞斯行之." 公西華曰: "由也問聞斯行諸, 子曰' 有父兄在': 求也問聞斯行諸, 子曰' 聞斯行之.' 赤也惑, 敢問." 子曰: "求也退, 故進之; 由也兼人, 故退之."
>
> Zilu asked: "Upon hearing of something that needs to be done, should one immediately take care of it?" The Master replied: "As long as one's father and older brothers are still alive, how could one possibly take care of it immediately?" [On a later occasion] Ran Qiu asked: "Upon learning of something that needs to be done, should one immediately take care of it? The Master replied: "Upon learning of it, you should immediately take care of it." Zihua [having observed both exchanges] inquired: "When Zilu asked you if one should immediately take care of something upon learning of it, you told him one should not, as long as one's father and elder brothers were still alive. When Ran Qiu asked you the same question, however, you told him

> that one should immediately take care of it. I am confused, and humbly ask to have this explained to me." The Master said: "Ran Qiu is overly cautious, and so I wished to urge him on. Zilu, on the other hand, is too impetuous, and so I sought to hold him back." (*Lunyu* 11:22 [Slingerland 2003, 119–120])

Even in the *Mengzi*, where it is overtly argued that 仁 *ren* ("co-humanity," benevolence) is an inborn feeling of the distinctively human heart, it is also maintained that, without personal cultivation, *ren* will be, though not obliterated, so obscured that it will effectively fail to function.

> 豈無仁義之心哉?其所以放其良心者, 亦猶斧斤之於木也, 旦旦而伐之, 可以為美乎? 其日夜之所息, 平旦之氣, 其好惡與人相近也者幾希, 則其旦晝之所為, 有梏亡之矣. 梏之反覆, 則其夜氣不足以存: 夜氣不足以存, 則其違禽獸不遠矣. 人見其禽獸也, 而以為未嘗有才焉者, 是豈人之情也哉? 故苟得其養, 無物不長; 苟失其養, 無物不消.

> The way they discard their genuine hearts is like the hatchets and axes in relation to the trees. With them besieging it day by day, can it remain beautiful? With the respite it gets during the day or night, and with the restorative effects of the morning *qi*, their likes and dislikes are sometimes close to those of others. But then what they do during the day again fetters and destroys it. If the fettering is repeated, then the evening *qi* is insufficient to preserve it. If the evening *qi* is insufficient to preserve it, then one is not far from an animal. Others see that he is an animal and think there was never any capacity there. But is this what a human is like inherently? Hence, if it merely gets nourishment, there is nothing that will not grow. If it merely loses its nourishment, there is nothing that will not vanish. (*Mengzi* 6A8 [van Norden 2008, 152])

And, a bit earlier in the text:

> 乃若其情, 則可以為善矣, 乃所謂善也.若夫為不善, 非才之罪也 . . . 仁義禮智, 非由外鑠我也, 我固有之也, 弗思耳矣. 故曰: "求則得之, 舍則失之." 或相倍蓰 而無算者, 不能盡其才者也.

> As for what they are inherently, they can become good. This is what I mean by calling their natures good. As for their becoming not good, this is not the fault of their potential. . . . Benevolence, righteousness, propriety and wisdom are not welded to us externally. We inherently have them. It is simply that we do not reflect on them. (*Mengzi* 6A6 [van Norden 2002, 149])

In these passages, there is a strong relationship established between what the *Mengzi* calls "nourishment" (養 *yang*) and the degree to which people can fulfill their "potentials" (才 *cai*). To a certain degree, the text associates nourishment of moral capacity with *qi*, as well as rest, which supposedly does not merely mean nighttime slumber but also respite from actions that would tend to do violence to one's natural capacities for goodness. But these capacities are just that, potentials (才 *cai*) of feeling which, only if cultivated and carried into conduct, will result in the establishment of the sort of person Confucians would see as morally worthy. But it is entirely possible for there to be "people who have no regard (or care)" (無算者 *wu suan zhe*) for virtue and therefore quite actively do damage to both their own characters and the world through their destructive conduct. So, for the *Mengzi*, it is these potentials of feeling that are meant when one's "nature" or "natural dispositions" (性 *xing*) are being spoken of. But without the nourishment of family love, moral guidance, and practice, the potentials that are inbuilt into our dispositions can easily be aborted. This is even more the case for the *Xunzi*, which flatly denies that people are born with virtuous feelings and avows that these must be created through ritual in the same manner that cups and bowls are carved out of wood. Finally, for the Mohists, who regard "inclusive care" (兼愛 *jian ai*) as a pattern of action all thinking people are capable of and *ren* as the most rarified yet preeminent of all virtues, all of it depends on human effort that relies on the contingency of people's active decisions to be moral.

> 志不彊者智不達, 言不信者行不果. 據財不能以分人者, 不足與友, 守道不篤, 偏物不博, 辯是非不察者, 不足與游. 本不固者末必幾, 雄而不脩者, 其後必惰, 原濁者流不清, 行不信者名必秏·名不徒生而譽不自長, 功成名遂, 名譽不可虛假, 反之身者也. 務言而緩行, 雖辯必不聽 . . . 言無務為多而務為智, 無務為文而務為察. 故彼智無察, 在身而情, 反其路者也. 善無主於心者不留, 行莫辯於身者不立.

> His wisdom will not be far-reaching whose purpose is not firm. His action will not be effective whose promises are not kept. He who will not share his possessions with others is not worthy to be a friend. And he who does not stand firm on principles and has neither wide knowledge nor penetrating judgment is not worthy to be a companion. Just as a weak trunk will have but small branches, so, mere bravery without cultivation will result in dissipation. And just as a dirty source will issue in an impure stream, so unfaithful conduct will unfavorably affect one's fame. For, fame does not spring up out of nothing, nor does praise grow by itself. Fame follows upon success and is not obtainable by hypocrisy. He will not be listened to who talks much but is slow in action, even though he is discerning. . . . In speech, not quantity but ingenuity, not eloquence but insight, should be cultivated. If one is not wise and without insight, breeding only dissipation in one's personality, this is just the contrary of what should be cultivated. (*Mozi* 2:4 [Mei 1929, 7–8])

Something both obvious and worthy of pause is afoot in all of this. It is with good reason that Roger Ames and Henry Rosemont have pointed out in their work that personhood in early Chinese thought is an achievement of moral development and not a status conferred by mere virtue of one's bodily form.[17] Various Chinese philosophers, as we have seen, attribute a great deal of potential to the body. Its *qi* is connected to the environment by its own unique kinds of awareness and is susceptible to both natural and cultural influences, its sense organs actively know the world and have their own loves and desires, and, for some, the heart too has feelings—which are also its own desires and pleasures—that are incipiently moral. But without conscious, willful, intentional, persistent, and even endless cultivation (修 *xiu*), a fully human life will not be attained by us. And, as the often-used phrase has it, what is being cultivated is one's 身 *shen* body, of Sommer's classification, the conduct of which can be reflected upon, trained, transformed, and which interacts with others in social relations.

And, given the fact that cultivation is bodily, classical Chinese texts attest to the degree of one's cultivation being observable in features of body and countenance. The collected aphorisms and dialogues of the *Lunyu* and *Mengzi* invoke such connections often.

巧言令色, 鮮矣仁.

A clever tongue and fine appearance are rarely signs of Goodness. (*Lunyu* 1:3, Slingerland 2003, 2)

子夏問孝. 子曰: "色難. 有事弟子服其勞, 有酒食先生饌, 曾是以為孝乎?"

Zixia asked about filial piety. The Master said: "It is the demeanor (色 *se*, the countenance) that is difficult. If there is work to be done, disciples shoulder the burden, and when wine and food are served, the elders are given precedence, but surely filial piety consists in more than this?" (*Lunyu* 2:4 [Slingerland 2003, 10])

夫達也者 . . . 察言而觀色.

Someone who is accomplished . . . examines other people's words and observes their demeanor (色 *se*). (*Lunyu* 12:20, Slingerland 2003, 135)

及至葬, 四方來觀之, 顔色之戚, 哭泣之哀, 弔者大悅.

When it came to the time of the funeral, people came from the four directions to observe. People who gave condolences were impressed with the grief in his expression and the sadness in his crying. (*Mengzi* 3A2 [van Norden 2008, 65])

訑訑之聲音顔色, 距人於千里之外.

A reputation and demeanor (色 *se*—lit., countenance) that is self-satisfied will keep nobles a thousand leagues away. (*Mengzi* 6B13 [van Norden 2008, 169])

Of course, Confucian philosophers, rigorous as they were about ritual propriety, also insisted on the appropriateness of posture and dress for requisite occasions, and attached great moral significance to unerring observations of such norms.[18] There are, all the same, numerous passages in the classical texts that warn against being taken in by superficial appearances, since obviously intentions can be masked or faked, just as easily as words can be deceptive. But the point is nonetheless quite pertinent, for it was widely held that genuine human sincerity, rooted in feelings and cultivated in effective ways, could not fail to manifest in one's face, bearing, and expressions. One may be able to hide bad intentions, the ancient Confucians believed, but could not possibly hide good ones. The *Mengzi* in one instance especially underlines this by focusing on what is revealed through the pupils of a person's eyes.

> 存乎人者, 莫良於眸子. 眸子不能掩其惡. 胸中正, 則眸子瞭焉: 胸中不正, 則眸子眊焉. 聽其言也, 觀其眸子, 人焉廋哉?

> Of what is within a person, there is nothing more genuine than the pupils of the eyes. The pupils cannot hide one's evil. If, in one's bosom, one is upright, the pupils will be bright. If, in one's bosom, one is not upright, the pupils will be shady. If one listens to people's discussions (lit., their speech, 言 *xin*) and looks at their pupils, how can they hide? (*Mengzi* 4A15 [van Norden 2008, 97])

As far as the specifics of the cultivation, or what sorts of moral norms go, they of course varied from one lineage of teaching to another, even when these lineages belonged to the same broadly construed school or family (*jia*) of teaching. However, it would appear that there was broad agreement regarding one principle of personal conduct in particular. While in the political sphere—in the dealings of states with one another or, according to the Legalist school, in the dealings of the ruler with his ministers—there were circumstances where deception was recommended, in the personal sphere of relationships, being trustworthy (信 *xin*) was almost universally prized.[19] What made a person especially trustworthy was the correspondence between their words and conduct.

> 子貢問君子. 子曰: "先行其言."

> Zigong asked about the gentleman. The Master replied: "He first expresses his views, then acts in accordance with them." (*Lunyu* 2:13 [Slingerland 2003, 12])

> 君子恥其言而過其行.
>
> The gentleman is ashamed to have his words exceed his actions. (*Lunyu* 14:27 [Slingerland 2003, 165])
>
> 政者, 口言之, 身必行之. 今子口言之, 而身不行, 是子之身亂也, 子不能治子之身, 惡能治國政?
>
> To govern is to carry out (lit., "to enact with the body," 身必行 *shen bi xing*) what one teaches (lit., "says with the mouth," 口言 *kou xin*). Now you don't behave according to what you teach, this means that you yourself are in revolt. Being unable to govern one's self, how can one govern the country? (*Mozi* 48:23 [Mei 1929, 242])

Furthermore, in this connection, as Jane Geaney once again has aptly pointed out, there are occasional but important passages in the early textual tradition that connect the heart's ability to "tally" with the discernment of whether a person's deeds and words are consistent.

> 當使若二士者, 言必信, 行必果, 使言行之合猶合符節也, 無言而不行也.
>
> These two persons then are opposed to each other in word and also in deed. Suppose they are sincere in word and decisive in deed so that their word and deed are made to agree like the two parts of a tally, and that there is no word but what is realized in deed. (*Mozi* 16:4 [Mei 1929, 90])

This point is quite morally significant indeed. If, as in the foregoing, the heart can be said to know the difference between correct and incorrect ways to interact with things in the world based on its ability to tally or match the sensation of a thing with it proper kind and socially agreed upon label, then by extension and in virtue of the very same power of tallying, it can tell the difference between a good and bad person depending on whether his or her words and deeds match.

Of course, the other widely shared general trend in theories of normativity in early China directed people toward conduct that was beneficent toward others. While the Confucian tradition tended to distinguish itself strongly from the Mohists in their constant charge that the latter's prescriptions for "inclusive care" (*jian ai*) traded the primary and natural love for one's parents for an abstract and impracticable equal regard for all, even cursory readings of the *Mozi* would demonstrate that this Confucian characterization was nothing more than a strawman. In fact, the Mohists depend on the affection people feel for their own family members in one of their central arguments for "inclusive care." The Mohists insisted that if one wanted to ensure that others in the community would tend to their parents and family members if they were called away from home for some other duty, then one in the meantime should care for the families of others as if they were one's own.[20] The Mohists are sharply critical of Confucians on other matters, such as their doctrinal inflexibility, their belief in fate, their supposed ritual extravagances in the court, their supposed simultaneous fastidiousness and superficiality about clothing and appearance, some of which have been cited. But, apart from these differences, the general attitude of the Confucians and Mohists about showing respect and compliance with superiors and tending to the needs of one's family as well as social equals and inferiors often reads as if there is broadly held moral consensus on these baselines of conduct.

> 子貢曰: "如有博施於民而能濟眾, 何如, 可謂仁乎?" 子曰: "何事於仁, 必也聖乎? 堯舜其猶病諸! 夫仁者, 己欲立而立人, 己欲達而達人. 能近取譬, 可謂仁之方也已."
>
> Zigong said: "If there were one able to broadly extend his benevolence to the common people and bring succor to the multitudes, what would you make of him? Could such a person be called Good (仁 *ren*)?" The Master said: "Why stop at Good? Such a person should surely be called a sage! Even someone like Yao and Shun would find such a task daunting. Desiring to take his stand, one who is Good helps others to take their stand; wanting to realize himself, he helps others to realize themselves. Being able to take what is near at hand as an analogy could perhaps be called the method of Goodness." (*Lunyu* 6:30 [Slingerland 2003, 63])
>
> 使天下兼相愛, 愛人若愛其身, 猶有不孝者乎?視父兄與君若其身, 惡施不孝, 猶有不慈者乎? 視弟子與臣若其身, 惡施不慈? 故不孝不慈亡, 有猶有盜賊乎? 故視人之室若其室, 誰竊?視人

> 身若其身, 誰賊?故盜賊亡有. 猶有大夫之相亂家, 諸侯之相攻國者乎?視人家若其家, 誰亂?視人國若其國, 誰攻? 故大夫之相亂家, 諸侯之相攻國者亡有.
>
> Suppose everybody in the world loves universally, loving others as one's self. Will there yet be any unfilial individual? When everyone regards his father, elder brother, and emperor as himself, whereto can he direct any unfilial feeling? Will there still be any unaffectionate individual? When everyone regards his younger brother, son, and minister as himself, whereto can he direct any disaffection? Therefore there will not be any unfilial feeling or disaffection. Will there then be any thieves and robbers? When everyone regards other families as his own family, who will steal? When everyone regards other persons as his own person, who will rob? Therefore there will not be any thieves or robbers. Will there be mutual disturbance among the houses of the ministers and invasion among the states of the feudal lords? When everyone regards the houses of others as one's own, who will be disturbing? When everyone regards the states of others as one's own, who will invade? Therefore there will be neither disturbances among the houses of the ministers nor invasion among the states of the feudal lords. (*Mozi* 13:5 [Mei 1929, 79–80])

But here again, moral treatment of others rests on the decisions and efforts of their agents, and markedly different outcomes and vastly different and more tragic worlds can result from courses of action that take selfishness and self-aggrandizement as their motives as well as failures of cultivation.

From all the foregoing, we can see clearly that, while sociality is for many important early Chinese philosophers the primary goal of moral practice, that goal can only be achieved purposefully, with the practitioner's individual circumstances, merits, unique character, effort, and choices. The possibility of social mobility, the significance of individual differences, the degree of cultivation, and the extent to which individuals are able to put themselves in the service of others are not constitutive givens but rather achievements. Even for thinkers of the period who believed, somewhat uniquely, that the heart naturally intends goodness in community, and that it does not even need that much prompting to cultivate toward that end, one must, by one's own striving, constantly dedicate oneself to this goal and not give up, even in the most adverse of circumstances. The *Mengzi* at one point expresses this quite dramatically.

> 仁之勝不仁也, 猶水勝火. 今之為仁者, 猶以一杯水, 救一車薪之火也, 不熄, 則謂之水不勝火, 此又與於不仁之甚者也. 亦終必亡而已矣.
>
> Benevolence will overcome what is not benevolent just as water overcomes fire. Nowadays, those who practice benevolence are like someone who tries to save a wagonload of burning firewood with a single glass of water. When the fire is not extinguished, they claim that water cannot overcome fire. This aids in what is not benevolent more than anything else does. In the end, all will be lost. (*Mengzi* 6A18 [van Norden 2008, 157])

When Spirit Dethrones the Heart

The *Zhuangzi* "anthology," probably compiled during the early Han in some association with the Huainan court, presents an incredible variety of not always consistent philosophical material.[21] The work's content alternates between fantastically speculative metaphysics to profound skepticism, from passages where death is treated with wondrous agnosticism to stories about dwelling with the immortals, from typical Han dynasty obsession with rulership to praise for a superior reclusive existence. Nonetheless, the text is so unique to the period because of the exceptional philosophical positions that are carved out within it, especially as these contrast with what we have already examined in this chapter. And one of the most conspicuous of those differences concerns precisely the human heart, its role in the body, and its subordination sometimes to the other organs and always to "spirit" in the conduct and experience of human life.

As Sommer has noted in her own research, the *Zhuangzi* tends to prefer to talk extensively of the form (*xing*) and substance (*ti*) conceptions of the body rather than its socially relational and cultivational (*shen*) or ritual (*gong*) aspects.[22] In the collection of texts, she points out, the body as form is what lives a certain span of years and that which can be deformed, often to the existential and even concrete benefit of the person who suffers it, while the "cosubstantial" body is what is nourished by food and that which upon death remerges into the "one body" that is the entirety of the natural process (2010: 218–225). In passages where we encounter the frailty and finitude of the living body addressed, we also find significant references to greater and more subtle powers that bestow its life upon it. In one story, the figure of "Confucius" attests to this.

> 魯哀公問於仲尼曰: "衛有惡人焉, 曰哀駘它. 丈夫與之處者, 思而不能去也. 婦人見之, 請於父母曰 '與為人妻, 寧為夫子妾' 者, 十數而未止也. 未嘗有 聞其唱者也, 常和而已矣. 無君人之位以濟乎人之死, 無聚祿以望人之腹. 又以惡駭天下, 和而不唱, 知不出乎四域, 且而雌雄合乎前是必有異乎人者也. 寡人召而觀之, 果以惡駭天下. 與寡人處, 不至以月數, 而寡人有意乎其為人也: 不至乎期年, 而寡人信之. 國無宰, 寡人傳國焉. 悶然而後應, 氾而若辭. 寡人醜乎, 卒授之國. 無幾何也, 去寡人而行, 寡人卹焉若有亡也: 若無與樂是國也. 是何人者也?" 仲尼曰: "丘也, 嘗使於楚矣, 適見純子食於其死母者, 少焉眴若, 皆棄之而走. 不見己焉爾, 不得類焉爾. 所愛其母者, 非愛其形也, 愛使其形者也."
>
> Duke Ai of Lu consulted with Confucius, saying: "There's this ugly man in Wei named Horsehead Humpback. When men are with him, they can think of nothing else and find themselves unable to depart. When women see him, they plead with their parents, saying they would rather be this man's concubine than any other man's wife—this has happened at least a dozen times already! And yet he's never been heard to initiate anything of his own with them, instead just chiming in with whatever they're already doing. He has no position of power with which to protect their lives and no stash of wealth with which to fill their stomachs, and on top of that he's ugly enough to startle off the world. He chimes in with them instead of presenting anything new of his own, his understanding is limited to his immediate surroundings, and yet the men and women converge around him. I figured he must have

> something special, so I called him to my court to take a look at him. He was indeed ugly enough to astonish all the world. It took a few weeks before I could see him as actually human. But after a few months, I started to trust him. My state had no prime minister, so I offered the post to him. Looking trapped and put upon, he was vague and evasive when he finally responded, seeming to reject the idea. I was embarrassed, but in the end prevailed upon him to accept control of the state. But before long he left me and vanished. I was terribly depressed, as if a loved one had died, unable to take any pleasure in my power. What kind of man is this?" Confucius said: "I was once sent on a mission to Chu, where I saw some piglets still nursing at the teats of their dead mother. After a short while they suddenly looked very startled and bolted away from her. They could no longer see themselves in her, could find no similarity to themselves there. What they loved in their mother was not her physical form (lit., her 形 *xing* body), but what moved that form (lit., the 使 *shi* or the cause of her physical form). (*Zhuangzi* 5:5 [Ziporyn 2009, 35–36])

The passage later elaborates that what caused the *xing* body of the mother pig to move and be animated, as well as the mysterious charisma of Horsehead Humpback, must be "a consummate capability that nonetheless is a power not of the physical body" (是必才全而德不形者).[23] The living body then, its apportionment of *qi* and all of its transformations, including the transformation of death, take place at the behest of a power (德 *de*) that is somehow the source of bodily life.

The *Zhuangzi* hits upon a similar theme when discussing the relation of the sense organs and the heart in ruling the body and guiding conduct.

> 百骸, 九竅, 六藏, 賅而存焉, 吾誰與為親? 汝皆說之乎? 其有私焉? 如是皆有, 為臣妾乎, 其臣妾不足以相治乎. 其遞相為君臣乎, 其有真君存焉. 如求得 其情與不得, 無益損乎其真.

> The hundred bones, the nine openings, the six internal organs are all present here in my body. Which one is most dear to me? Do you delight in all equally, or do you have

> some favorite among them? Or are they all mere servants and concubines? Are these servants and concubines unable to govern each other? Or do they take turns as master and servant? If there exists a genuine ruler among them, then whether we could find out the facts about him would neither add to nor subtract from that genuineness. (*Zhuangzi* 2:9 [Ziporyn 2009, 10–11])

We see here how even the heart, one of the six internal organs, is represented as possibly only taking turns with the other organs in ruling the body, and that we cannot be sure whether or not there really is a "genuine ruler" (真君 *zhen jun*) that guides us. The passage then introduces the possibility, quite unique in early Chinese thought, that the heart may indeed not enjoy a position of preeminence in the constitution and experience of the person.

This is not to say, however, that the position and dispensations of the heart ought to be underestimated. The difference between a heart fixated on a specific and unbending set of preferences and a heart open to the world's constant transformations can be the difference between wisdom and ignorance. The 成心 *cheng xin* is the heart that is "finished"; it is self-conceitedly established in its own worldview, its own judgments of others, its own sense of what is appropriate and what is not. But, in example after example in the *Zhuangzi*, this fixated heart is continually upset alternately by the failure to find objectivity in debates where all sides have implacable biases, in advising unruly rulers who will return moral scolding with execution if tested, to princesses who believed that their capture by an enemy was the worst thing in the world until they found themselves happy in their captor's palace. Departures such as forgetting and wandering are recommended in the *Zhuangzi* as remedies for the fixated heart. But ultimately, the heart is in this collection of texts generally seen not to be the core of our personhood.

That core is revealed in other passages that speak about elevated forms of adeptness, such as the famous passage about the renowned Butcher Ding, describing to his ruler how he has become so adroit at cutting up animals.

> 文惠君曰: "譆! 善哉! 技蓋至此乎?"庖丁釋刀對曰: "臣之所好者道也, 進乎技矣. 始臣之解牛之時, 所見无非牛者. 三年之後,

未嘗見全牛也. 方今之時, 臣以神遇, 而不以目視, 官知止而神欲行.依乎天理, 批大郤, 導大窾, 因其固然.技經肯綮之未嘗, 而況大軱乎, 良庖歲更刀, 割也, 族庖月更刀, 折也. 今臣之刀十九年矣, 所解數千牛矣, 而刀刃若新發於硎. 彼節者有間, 而刀刃者无厚, 以无厚入有間, 恢恢乎其於遊刃 必有餘地矣, 是以十九年而刀刃若新發於硎. 雖然, 每至於族, 吾見其難為, 怵然為戒, 視為止, 行為遲. 動刀甚微, 謋然已解, 如土委地.提刀而立, 為之四顧, 為之躊躇滿志, 善刀而藏之."文惠君曰: "善哉, 吾聞庖丁之言, 得養生焉."

The king said: "Ah! It is wonderful that skill can reach such heights!" The cook put down his knife and said: "What I love is the Course (道 *dao*), something that advances beyond mere skill. When I first started cutting up oxen, all I looked at for three years was oxen, and yet still I was unable to see all there was to see in an ox. But now I encounter it with the spirit (神 *shen*) rather than scrutinizing it with the eyes. My understanding consciousness, beholden to its specific purposes (官知 *guan zhe*, lit., "the office of knowledge"), comes to a halt, and thus the promptings of the spirit begin to flow. I depend on Heaven's unwrought perforations (天理 *tian li*, lit., "natural patterns") and strike the larger gaps, following along with the broader hollows. I go by how they already are, playing them as they lay. So my knife has never had to cut through the knotted nodes where the warp hits the weave, much less the gnarled joints of bone. A good cook changes his blade once a year; he slices. An ordinary cook changes his blade once a month; he hacks. I have been using this same blade for nineteen years, cutting up thousands of oxen, and yet it is still as sharp as the day it came off the whetstone. For the joints have spaces within them, and the very edge of the blade has no thickness at all. When what has no thickness enters into an empty space, it is vast and open, with more than enough room for the play (遊 *you* or "wandering") of the blade. That is why my knife is still as sharp as if it had just come off the whetstone, even after nineteen years. Nonetheless, whenever I come to a clustered tangle, realizing that it is difficult to do anything about it, I instead restrain myself as if terrified, until my seeing comes to a complete halt.

> My activity slows, and the blade moves over it so slightly. Then all at once I find the ox already dismembered at my feet like clumps of soil scattered on the ground. I retract the blade and stand there gazing at my work arrayed all around me, dawdling over it with satisfaction. Then I wipe off the blade and put it away." The king said: "Wonderful! From hearing the cook's words, I have learned how to nourish life." (*Zhuangzi* 3:2 [Ziporyn 2009, 22–23])

We have here an account of adeptness that goes beyond itself by eschewing reliance on the body's sense organs and its other avenues of knowledge and allowing for the emergence of "spirit" (神 *shen*). Spirit is not only what enables people to "go beyond skill" in their arts but is also what really nourishes life (養生 *yang sheng*). Spiritual persons (神人 *shen ren*) are said to hold fast to the essence of life (精 *jing*), and while it is certainly the case that the spirit can protect the *ti* body and in turn be protected by it (神保形軆, 形體保神 *shen bao xingti xingti bao shen*), it is also the case that spirit can forget all about the body and leave it behind.[24]

A text very closely historically and compositionally related to the *Zhuangzi* in the form of another "anthology," the *Huainanzi*, also forges this connection between identification with spirit and superior knowledge and concourse with the cosmological order.[25] The great leader (大丈夫 *da zhang fu*), according to this treatise, acts in accord with *dao* and does so at ease, "using heaven for a canopy, the four seasons his steeds, *yin* and *yang* as his charioteers."[26] Controlling his senses, he is able to preserve his luminosity undiminished (聰明不損 *cong ming bu sun*).[27] The notion that the core of a superior ruler's virtuosity lies in some luminous *dao* essence, "pure and tranquil" (清靜 *qing jing*), and thus makes him capable of detaching from the banal artifice of custom (俗 *su*) and identify with spirit (神 *shen*) is often affirmed.[28] There are even extended passages contrasting the perceptions of spirit from those of ordinary sensory knowledge (知 *zhe*) and emotional response (感 *gan*). The latter creates inner agitation, love, hate, and chaos, while the former merely reflects and appropriately responds to things because, as it is said, "people are born tranquil" (人生而靜 *ren sheng er jing*).[29] The *Zhuangzi* "anthology" therefore seems to exist in a general atmosphere of speculation that significantly attributes to spirit superior capacities to sense and act than are found in the bodily sense organs, and furthermore can affect an alignment of the individual with the cosmic order and, at times, even survive physical death.[30]

We find also a strong connection made in places in the "anthology" between identification with the inner essence of life and the ideal of the "genuine person." However, the "spirituality" of the idealized "genuine person" is not one that brings about a diremption between heavenly and worldly things. Rather, by virtue of the superiority of its knowledge to the partial knowledge of the body and its organs as well as its unity of purpose, it is, while found in embodied life, able to unite these realms.

> "知天之所為, 知人之所為者, 至矣." 知天之所為者, 天而生也: 知人之所為者, 以其知之所知, 以養其知之所不知, 終其天年而不中道夭者, 是知之盛也. 雖然, 有患. 夫知有所待而後當, 其所待者特未定也. 庸詎知吾所謂天之非人乎? 所謂人之非天乎? 且有真人, 而後有真知.
>
> "To understand what is done by Heaven, and also what is to be done by Man, that is the utmost." To understand what is done by the Heavenly, just in being the Heavenly, as the way all beings are born, what it does is bring them into being. To understand what is to be done by the Human, that would be to use what your understanding understands to nurture what your understanding does not understand. You could then live out all your natural years without being cut down halfway. And that would indeed be the richest sort of knowledge. However, there is a problem here. For our understanding can be in the right only by virtue of a dependence on something, and what it depends on is always peculiarly unfixed. So how could I know whether what I call the Heavenly is not really the Human? How could I know whether what I call the Human is not really the Heavenly? Let us say instead, then, that there can be Genuine Knowledge (真知 *zhen zhi*) only when there is such a thing as a Genuine Human Being (真人 *zhen ren*). (*Zhuangzi* 6:1 [Ziporyn 2009, 39–40])
>
> 故其好之也一, 其弗好之也一. 其一也一, 其不一也一. 其一, 與天為徒, 其不一: 與人為徒. 天與人不相勝也, 是之謂真人.

> Thus, what they liked was the oneness of things, but what they disliked was also the oneness of things. Their oneness was the oneness, but their non-oneness was also the oneness. In their oneness, they were followers of the Heavenly. In their non-oneness, they were followers of the Human. This is what it is for neither the Heavenly nor the Human to win out over the other. And that is what I call being both genuine and Human, a Genuine Human Being. (*Zhuangzi* 6:6 [Ziporyn 2009, 42])

Such "genuine persons" are able to attain the heights of being indifferent to life and death, but at the same time, because of their mastery of both the heavenly and the personal, they were supposedly also best suited for being arbiters of human affairs. They are said to maintain affectionate feelings (有親 *you qing*) for people, and yet, because they do not identify themselves with a certain clique (朋 *peng*), can judge people with equity.[31] The genuine person could thus perform the requirements of her specific station (行名失己 *xing ming yi ji*) and yet need "not be regarded as an official" (非士也 *fei shi yue*).[32] The Zhuangist model of the genuine person, that is, shrugs off ego-centered concerns and artifices of social status, maintaining a naturally human heart but "not using their heart to contribute to *dao*, not using their person to assist heaven" (不以心捐道 不以人助天 *bu yin xin juan dao, bu yin ren zhu tian*).

The extraordinarily unique collection that became the *Zhuangzi* then, in very conspicuous contrast to almost everything else in early Chinese thought, while at once affirming widely held tenets regarding the consciousness of the body and the powers of the heart, aligns genuine personhood with the "essential" and "spiritual" in human beings that transcend the body and even sociality. There is a certain degree to which these views amounted to somewhat less of an overall regard for both the ultimate value of bodily existence as well as the ideals of sociality that much of the rest of early Chinese thought, in one way or another, valorized as the highest meanings of human life. And yet, many, many centuries later, the presence of the "Zhuangist" vocabulary and ideals, when combined with a particularly Buddhist rehabilitation of the powers of mind and heart, would help to bring about an unlikely but profound synthesis of South and East Asian thought regarding the makeup and significance of personhood.

2

Two Brāhmiṇical Selves

The larger purpose of this study is to assess the influence of Buddhist conceptions of personhood on some of the major movements in Chinese Buddhism and on Neo-Confucianism thereafter. In the next chapter, we will turn to some of the most important conceptions of personhood from South Asian Buddhism that were appropriated into Chinese philosophical reflection. Before we move on to those conceptions, however, it will benefit us to examine, from the classical period, some of the most prevalent early scholastic Brāhmiṇical depictions of personhood with which the first several centuries of Indian scholastic Buddhists had to contend. These alternative representations of the constitution of persons will help us, in the long run, understand some heretofore little-noticed influences of the Indian philosophical tradition on the Chinese that flowed through Buddhism.

The two Brāhmiṇical *darśana*-s (worldviews or schools of thought) that will be covered in this chapter are those of Sāṃkhya (the school of metaphysical "Enumeration") and Nyāya-Vaiśeṣika (the schools of "Logic" and "Particularism").[1] While the latter remained thriving and trenchant adversaries of Buddhism through the entirety of the latter tradition's golden era on the subcontinent, some words must be said to justify the focus on Sāṃkhya here. Doubt over tarrying with the latter school to the exclusion of Mīmāṃsā, a much more serious, long-standing philosophical opponent of Buddhism in the history of the Indian tradition, may especially be pertinent given the relatively short-lived viability of Sāṃkhya as an independent system of thought. For one thing, there occurred alternative and unique appropriations of the basic Sāṃkhya framework for reflecting on personhood and the "luminosity" of consciousness in the systems of Yoga (though this was hardly an "independent" system for many centuries either), Vedānta, and Kashmir Śaivism, systems to which we will also refer in this discussion. Indeed, the philosophical pedigree enjoyed by the theory is attested to by some of its most conspicuous doctrines in an incredible variety of other systems, from the early *Upaniṣads* and the *Bhagavad Gītā* to the medieval articulations of Vedānta. The wide-ranging influence of the Sāṃkhya theory, then, cannot be doubted. Furthermore, it is the confrontation between these early models of personhood and consciousness found in Sāṃkhya and Nyāya that most lucidly place into relief the most fundamental issues that the Buddhist schools that affected Chinese thought took up. Once again, the present work is not intended to offer a comprehensive account of the entire historical spectrum of Indian and Chinese philosophical views about consciousness and personhood. It is rather devoted to an inquiry into how historically relevant South Asian conceptions of personhood and consciousness influenced the Chinese philosophical tradition in the most prevalent ways. Vijñānavāda Buddhism, precisely the Indian school that was most instrumental in impacting Chinese views about consciousness, flourished in the Central Kingdom from the sixth century CE onward. The major encounters between Buddhism and the systems of Mīmāṃsā and Vedānta, on the other hand, all took place from the seventh to the fourteenth centuries and are not reflected in developments of Buddhist thought in China or in its influence on other Chinese philosophers. It is therefore both appropriate and more revealing to orient ourselves to the early Sāṃkhya and Nyāya debates on consciousness and its constitutive role in grounding personhood, and how Indian Vijñānavāda is both influenced by and departs from both for the specific purposes of this study.

Scholastic Indian depictions of consciousness exhibit often sharp contrast with most of the central tenets of classical Chinese notions of the same covered in the last chapter. Sāṃkhya and Nyāya-Vaiśeṣika, despite their differences from one another, hold some ground-level principles of understanding human existence in common. The first is that the body, despite the fact that it, along with the organs that enable its awareness, is concretely physical and organically interrelated with its environment, was believed by almost all Brāhmiṇical thinkers before the turn of the second millennium CE to be entirely and utterly unconscious. Indeed, one of the most contentious debates that took place between these two schools in particular revolved around implications that the opposing viewpoint led to the supposedly indefensible conclusion that the physical body might itself be conscious. Such a charge, if true, would automatically qualify a self-identified Brāhmiṇical school as nihilist and covertly aligned with the school of materialists (Lokāyatikas, "Adherents of the World," or Carvākikas, "Adherents of Sweet Talk"). Both schools believed that the body was surely responsive to its environment, in the case of Sāṃkhya by virtue of "strands" (*guṇa*-s) of dynamically interactive energy and in the case of Nyāya-Vaiśeṣika because of both its own organic constitution and direct contact with things in the world. All the same, none of these factors implied for either philosophical inclination that the body or any of its activities were, of their own accord, conscious. This principle not only applies to physiological and reactive processes of the body but also to its organs of internal awareness, the *antaḥkāraṇa* of Sāṃkhya and the *manas* of Nyāya-Vaiśeṣika. This perspective would be one of the basic tenets to which the Buddhists, with significant qualifications, would object.

The previous point both involves and brings us to our second important observation regarding a standard Brāhmiṇical principle about personhood that is most-widely known but also very seldom systematically argued for. This is the notion that human bodies, psychological dispositions, social duties, and future prospects transcend individual lifetimes. They are a heritage of one's past lives and, if left unresolved and undissolved, will lead to future worldly lives. According to Nyāya-Vaiśeṣika, this karmic heritage, though invisible, or leaving no trace (*apūrva*) of itself to the naked eye, helps constitute one's memories and lives in one's psychological makeup, and for Sāṃkhya, it even informs the affective preferences of the sense organs and impels the organs of movement. *Karma* is, in this respect, a material feature of human bodies. It is a rarefied moral particle that accumulates in different densities depending on the character primarily of one's intentions and partly as a result of one's actions themselves. And this very materiality is what helps form future bodies in successive lives. Both views also held that this interaction involved initiative on the part of the body, owing to certain psychophysical habits (*saṃskāra*-s) that are built up both during one's karmic past and during the present lifetime. The Buddhists would, as we shall see, appropriate a very great deal of this depiction of *karma* and its constitutive role in personhood into their own philosophical systems, but, dramatically, they would make of *karma* itself the mechanism of rebirth and not something also attached to a persisting metaphysical self.

We shall spend a bit of time in this chapter speaking about the perspectives of these Brāhmiṇical schools on the temporal character of our experience, and we will examine their alternative conceptualization in two respects. In the first respect, we focus on a very specific debate that took place between adherents of Sāṃkhya and Nyāya on whether or not our organ of inner sense, that which enables our awareness of internal pains and pleasures, memories, desires, and ideas acts as a kind of container of our experiences, past, present, and future, as was held by the former school, or whether this internal organ had to be in constant movement in order to account for our experience's temporal flow. Sāṃkhya's position was that the internal organ had a kind of tripartite structure, in which the functions of bare awareness, ideation, and ego-generation interacted in the processing of all of one's experiences such that memories could impinge on the present and the present could be attended to. It was also this internal organ, in its extremely subtle makeup, that was "seen" by the all-conscious self—the seeing that makes present experiences and memories known. For Nyāya, the Sāṃkhya model was an implausible account of our experience, since, if it were true, we should expect to be aware of all our experiences, both past and present, at every single moment. Not wishing to deny that we have persistently unconscious memories or present experiences that don't reach the level of awareness, Naiyāyikas nonetheless insisted that a philosophical explanation of our experience had to take proper account of its successive temporal character. It also argued that it was not any subtle internal organ, with its manufactured sense of ego, that was the possessor and transporter of our karmic past into future lives but instead the persisting metaphysical self. This argument about temporality is important for us, not only because it is a significant artifact of the two major models of personhood in the Brāhmiṇical tradition but also because the issue of the temporality of consciousness, in a related guise, would become crucial in Indian Buddhist thought as well.

Finally, we will explore what for Brāhmiṇical thought, under importantly different variations, was the essence and our being, namely, the spiritual and eternal self. Both of these *darśana*-s agreed, to connect with our first point, that it is the metaphysical self and not the physical body that is the source of consciousness; it provides cognitive luminosity (*prakāśatva*) that "lights up," as it were, the external and internal goings-on of the body and acts as their witness or seer (*śākṣin*). It is certainly the case that these conceptions of metaphysical selfhood both, though to different degrees, descriptively and teleologically abstract it from the body as well as from all individual narratives of any single embodied human being. This self, after all, survives and is quite separable from every individual ego, and it is considered the ultimate goal of any religious practice to free the eternal self from its mysterious bonds to physical and perishable existence. But, in other crucial senses, the self lies at the very heart of our personhood. In Sāṃkhya, this self is called the "person" (*puruṣa*—lit., the "man"), distinguishing the core of our supposedly true spiritual nature from the limiting and world-enmeshed artifice that is our perishable, and actually unconscious, ego (*ahaṃ*). It is also that part of us which, in our engagement with the world, only sees and does not enjoy, enabling us to wrench ourselves free of our obsessions as well as be the audience to the dance-play that the natural world endlessly performs. For Nyāya-Vaiśeṣika, this self or *ātman* is, so long as it is embodied, the owner of our experiences, for our memories, habits, feelings, and actions attach to it, are accumulated by it, and determine its future. In fact, the Naiyāyikas went as far as to say, most controversially in the Brāhmiṇical context, that the self could only be conscious while embodied, and that liberation, while it freed the *ātman* from the anguish and loss with which physical temporality saddled it, also rendered it eternally unconscious. In either case, the metaphysical self in Brāhmiṇical thought must be understood as most basic to and inseparable from our personhood, for without it, we cannot be conscious persons nor achieve the highest aims to which moral and meditational practice call us.

There are two very fundamental respects in which an appropriate measure of these Brāhmiṇical depictions of personhood is necessary for us to understand Buddhism and its eventual impact on Chinese thought. The first is well known to anyone familiar with the tradition. The Buddhists concluded that the Brāhmiṇical formulations of metaphysical selfhood gave a wholly untenable account of our experience. This owed both to the degree to which the former insisted that at least this root of our personhood was not subject to the limits of temporality, to arising and ceasing, and in trying to maintain that it alone was the seat of awareness and not any of the processes of the body. The Buddhists would of course conclude that there is simply no such thing as an eternal metaphysical self, and that human consciousness was both contingently produced as a result of bodily and psychic factors that were most impermanent and, for both social and existential reasons, most welcomingly so. However, in a less-often noticed but most conspicuous way, the Buddhists would ultimately reserve for enlightened consciousness a kind of unbounded luminosity, a luminosity that could not only manifest the world to the enlightened person for what it truly was but also could model and transmit the perfection of enlightened personhood from its initial moment of realization to the future. This notion of the luminous mind (*prabhāsvaraṃ cittaṃ*) would become translated into the Chinese Buddhist tradition as 明心 *ming xin* and would have an indelible influence on both Buddhist and non-Buddhist conceptions of personhood thereafter.

The Unconscious Body

After identifying the evolving constituents of *prakṛti* or the "orginary producer" of visible, material nature, the *Sāṃkhyakārika* begins to describe the constitution of the body and its sense organs.

> buddhi indriyāni cakṣuḥśrotraghrānarasanatvagākhyāni /
> vācaṃpāṇipādapāyūpasthāḥ karmendriyāṇyāhūḥ //
> ubhyayātmakamatra manaḥ saṃkalpakamindryaṃ ca sādharmyāt /
> guṇaparināmaviśeṣātnānātvaṃ bāhyabhedāśca //
>
> The organs of awareness are the eye, ear, nose, tongue, and skin; speech, hand, foot, anus, and genitals are called organs of action. The inner sense (*manas*) is itself of both, (it is) an organ of ideation and (is constituted) of similar properties (as sense organs). It is derived from particular transformations of energy stands, as are external (things).[2] (*Sāṃkhyakārika* 26–27)

What distinguishes the organs of awareness from action, we are told in the following verse, is that the former "merely observe" (*ālocanamātra*) objects while the latter are responsible for various kinds of movement, bodily functions, and pleasure. What is for the moment called the inner sense (*manas*), [3] more often referred to in Sāṃkhya texts and related traditions as the inner agent (*antaḥkāraṇa*), shares functions of both sensory and action organs, insofar as its materiality transforms through dynamic interaction with *guṇa*-s both inside and outside the body and because it produces "synthesized ideations" (*saṃkalpa*). The eleventh-century commentator Vācaspati Miśra tells us that these ideations are the result of the inner sense's ability to collect the "mere observations" of the other sense organs and make of them a robust perception instead of just a vague sensation. But the concrete materiality of the *manas*, along with all the other organs of the body, is due to the fact that it is constituted out of the same basic patterns or "strands" of energetic fluctuation that make up all material things.

> prityapritiviṣādātmakāḥ prakāśapravṛttiniyamārthāḥ /
> anyonyābhibhavāśrayajananamithūnavṛttayaśca gūnāḥ //
> sattvaṃ laghū prakāśakamiṣṭupaṣṭambakam calaṃ ca rajaḥ /
> gūru varaṇakameva tamah pradīpavacchārthato vṛttīḥ //

> The essences of pleasure, displeasure, despair, the objects of illumination, activity, and restraint, effecting the domination, support, production of and pairing with one another; these are the *guṇa*-s: brilliance (*sattva*), (which is) the lightest (of them), made of luminosity, passion (*rajas*), stimulating and in movement, stolidity (*tamas*), heaviness, made of that which obscures; the fluctuations (*vṛttī*) that are the object (*artha*) of their so-called lamp. (*Sāṃkhyakārika* 12–13)

In much of the English-language exegetical literature on Indian philosophy, the term *guṇa* is often generically translated as "quality." While this translation is, with some explanation, appropriate for other traditions of thought such as Vaiśeṣika, it is most unhelpful for understanding its meaning in Sāṃkhya and related traditions of thought. A *guṇa* is often literally a "string" or a "chord," which can be found in various kinds of instruments from the musical to the mathematical.

The fact that it is described several times in the previous definitional verses in terms of "activity" or "fluctuation" (*vṛtti*) and is associated with different intensities of affect, patterns of interaction, and densities of different kinds argues strongly for its being understood as a strand or frequency of dynamic energy.[4] The notion of energy strands as the basic constituents of material things was preferred by Sāṃkhya thinkers over the more "atomistic" view of the Vaiśeṣikas because, for the former, the notion that indivisible, and thus partless (*aṇu*), particles could somehow combine, with no parts to attach to other partless particles, was simply incoherent.[5] These basic strands of energy are in the previous passage said to mutually interact, for they sometimes cause and act as a basis for one another, though they can also at times either dominate or cooperate with one another. They are clearly basic physical configurations, as they are both ranked in terms of their relative densities, with *sattva* being the most rarified and *tamas* the most concentrated, and are several times referred to as objects (*artha*), both of knowledge and activity. But they are at the same time basic kinds of affect, paired as they are with pleasure, pain, and presumably immobilizing dejection. Since all material things are composed out of these basic intensities of energy, the body is said to be also, along with all of its organs of movement and sense. Organs of sensation and perception, for instance, are said to predominate in *sattva*, and owing to the fact that they are rarified and luminous, they can penetrate heavier bodies of corresponding elemental compositions in the process of making the latter known.

However, a significant problem arises when it comes to this very point of awareness and knowledge. On the one hand, the eyes, ears, nose, tongue, and skin are said to be organs of "awareness" (*buddhi*) and the inner sense is claimed to be capable of ideation (*saṃkalpa*), and they are susceptible to things in the world as well as internal bodily states precisely by virtue of the fact that they are made out of similar properties (*sādharmyāt*) as these. However, we are told at the same time in the *Kārika* that the *guṇa*-s are "incognizant" (*acetanaṃ*).[6] This of course leads to the question of how a body that supposedly possesses organs of awareness, feeling, and thought, sensing and acting as it does in a world fundamentally made up of energies of affect, can still be said to be, on its own, unconscious. As it turns out, according to Sāṃkhya, the entire causal system of material nature is directed toward the otherness (*parātatvāt*) of awareness, and thus the causal powers of the sense organs do not produce awareness for the sake of matter, for themselves.[7] However, since we do indisputably have experiences, and those experiences can't be attributed to their physical causes, then those experiences must be undergone by something other than our physical being.

> hetumadinityamavyāpi sarkriyamanekāśritaṃ liṅgam /
> sāvayavaṃ prataṅtram vyaktam viparitamavyaktam //
>
> (Arising) from a cause, impermanent, nonpervasive, active, non-unitary, that which is determined, having parts, a product of unfolding; this is what is manifest; it is the opposite of the unmanifest. (*Sāṃkhyakārika* 10)
>
> saṅghāta parārthatvāt triguṇādiviparyayādhiiṣṭānāt /
> pūruṣo'sti bhoktṛbhāvāt kaivalyārtham prakṛtteśca //
>
> To be a compounded thing is to be for the sake of others, it (spirit) is established from that which is the opposite of the three energy strands, and all else; enjoyment (comes) from the primordial person (*puruṣa*), and its end is being isolated from the "original producer," matter (*prakṛti*). (*Sāṃkhyakārika* 17)

For Sāṃkhya, the non-unitary nature of physical energy, owing to the fact that it undergoes constant interaction and change, disqualifies it as a candidate for being considered an enjoyer (*bhoktṛ*) of experience, since enjoyment of past, present, and future experiences requires the continuity of that which experiences. Therefore, while our bodies may be made of compounded parts and organs that have concretized out of different intensities of energy and cosmologically individuating principles, our true personhood (*puruṣa*), to which consciousness belongs, is clearly distinguished from it. We shall return to further discussion of the nature of such ultimate personhood in Sāṃkhya later. But for the moment we note that the school considers consciousness and material existence to be utter opposites.[8]

In Nyāya-Vaiśeṣika, the body and its organs of sense, including the inner sense, are also concretely physical, and sensory capacities are linked, as they are in Sāṃkhya, to the corresponding elements in nature out of which the sense organs are made.

veśdendriyārthāśrayaḥ śarīram //
ghāṇarasanacakṣūstvak dhrogṅāṇi indriyāṇi bhutebhyaḥ //
pṛthivyāpastejo vāyūrākāśamiti bhutāni //
gandharasarūpasparśaśabdhāḥ pṛthivyādiguṇāḥ
tadārthaḥ //
buddhiḥ upalalbdhirjñānamityanarthāntaram //
yugapajjānānutpattiḥ manaso liṅgam //

The support of appearance, organ, and purpose is the body. Nose, tongue, eye, skin, and ear are organs produced from elements. Earth, water, fire, wind, and sound-space (*ākāśa*) are the elements. Smell, taste, color, touch, and sound are qualities of the earth and (have) their objects. (It is an) error to distinguish from one another awareness, apprehension, and cognition. The non-arising of simultaneous cognitions is the determining mark of the inner sense (*manas*). (*Nyāyasūtra* 1:1:11–16)

Here we also have a distinction between the outer sense organs, which, due to the correspondence in their elemental makeup to the elements, can sense external things, and the inner sense, which is, in contrast to the outer senses, said to be conducive to cognitions (*jñāna*). However, in contrast to Sāṃkhya, the Naiyāyikas claim that it would be wrong to say that, merely because of its own unconsciousness, the inner sense plays no role in producing cognitions. We also have in the previous verses the foreshadowing of another argument we will explore in more detail below that Nyāya has with Sāṃkhya, for here the inner sense is said to make available the experience of only one thing at a time. The arising of cognitions in temporal succession implies, for the Naiyāyikas as well as the Vaiśeṣikas, that the *manas* is mobile and moves about the body, making contact with each of the sense organs as it goes and through such contact being stimulated by the sensations of those organs.[9] The movement of the inner sense is so rapid that we often don't take note of this succession, but since we know that all of our experiences occur in a temporal sequence, we can infer such mobile activity of the *manas* does indeed occur. But this also demonstrates, in the context of specifically Nyāya-Vaiśeṣika metaphysics, that the inner sense is a material substance, since only material substances can move.[10] However, the question arises for Naiyāyikas and Vaiśeṣikas as it did for Sāṃkhya philosophers, if the physical organs of the body, among which the inner sense is included, cooperate to produce awareness, why should they not be said to be themselves aware?

Nyāya texts argue variously that, since the dead body is obviously not conscious, we cannot attribute consciousness to the mere physical elements of the body itself.[11] The senses themselves, they claim, cannot be said to possess consciousness either, since each sense is restricted to specific stimulations of their own kind, such that sight cannot hear. Indeed, the *Nyāyasūtrabhāṣya* of Vātsyāyana expressly considers the possible view, not dissimilar to the classical Chinese view of the conscious sense organs covered in the last chapter but here probably something like the Indian materialist position, that the sense organs themselves, because of their fixed relations to stimulations of certain kinds, should be considered conscious. This position is rejected because, in our everyday awareness, we are not conscious of merely distinct stimulations from each of the sense organs on its own but instead are aware of a whole object through the synthetic activity of a self (*ātman*), witnessed by the fact that a unitary self is aware of the same object through sight, touch, and other available senses.[12] Furthermore, sense organs do not, they say, recollect, since one moment of sensory contact between organ and object is always replaced by a successive one.[13] In addition, since the *manas* is atomic in size, as mentioned earlier, it cannot be thought to contain cognitions, for in that case it would have to be either a compounded phenomenon or a substance that was spatially pervasive, as only in these cases can something serve as a host of qualities.[14]

However, while in principle Nyāya philosophers agree with the basic tenet that the body is unconscious and an indwelling spiritual self is conscious, they produce a fundamentally different argument in support of this than do Sāṃkhya thinkers. For the latter, as we have seen, it is the body's activity, where activity and causality are seen as material processes and therefore as the purveyors of *karma*, that serves as the identifying mark of its physicality, while the primordial person (*puruṣa*) is a spectator only and not an agent of any action. Nyāya texts work out this relationship differently, adducing that the body must be unconscious precisely because it is the instrument (*kāraṇa*) with which cognitions are obtained, and so the agent (*kartṛ*) that uses this instrument must be distinct from it.

> *paratantrāṇi bhutendryamanāṃsi dhāraṇaprerana vyuhanakṛyāsu prayatnavaśān pravartante caitanye punaḥ svatantrāṇi syūriti / prakṛtābhyāgamāccha pravṛttirvābuddhi-śarīrārabhya hati caitanye bhutendryamanasām paravṛntam karmam purūṣeṇābhyujyatahaiti syād śravaitanyetu tatsādhanasya svakṛtakarmaphalopabhogaḥ puruṣasyatyupapadyatadhati /*
>
> (If) you think the other sense organs act in accordance with their possession of inclinations (only), (then) they would by themselves be tethered (to their objects) independently of the activities of cognition. It must be admitted that it (the *manas*) is physical, for cognitions are distinct from the activities of the inner sense and body, as the activities of the organs and inner sense, constituted of elements, are employed exclusively by the inner self, who is the agent. If you say, then, that their flowing out and returning is their own efficient cause, then it would not follow that action, fruit, and enjoyment would be those of the inner self. (*Nyāyasūtrabhāṣya* 3:2:41)

The Nyāya commentator Vātsyāyana is pointing out here that, if we accept the premise that the sense organs, including the inner sense, do indeed have their own dispositions to interact with things, then we are also accepting that these dispositions are not themselves cognitive in nature. This is so because, being physical, just like their objects, the sense organs on their own might be impelled in certain directions, but these impulsions would not be driven by an agent in any discernible way. If, by this same token, we do accept that cognitions have intentional relationships with things, both epistemic and motivational, and if these intended relationships cannot be attributed to the physical activities of the organs themselves, then the agency of our ideas and actions must be attributed to something else, namely, the self.[15]

We have then a pivotal distinction between these two major strands of Brāhmiṇical thought, which we will explore in more detail later, with regard to the nature of the innermost, spiritual self. For one, which has its origins in Sāṃkhya, the self is an a-causal source of luminous awareness, which mysteriously has become entrapped in physical existence, while the body is causally active in a natural environment of energetic and affective forces. For the other, which probably has its origins in Vaiśeṣika but also in Mīmāṃsā thought, the self, while also surely the source of awareness, is itself the initiator, owner, and enjoyer of its embodied experiences. The second self, it can fairly be said, has a much more engaged experience of its own body owing to the fact that its consciousness depends upon contact with the inner sense and the sense organs, an important Nyāya-Vaiśeṣika principle to which we will return. All the same, in the bigger picture of things, both schools agree that the physical body is, on its own, entirely unconscious; it possesses the machinery, the tools, of awareness, but without the light of consciousness that has its abode in the spiritual self, the machinery cannot produce experience.

One of the most fundamental reasons that both *darśana*-s rely on in order to deduce the supposed unconsciousness of the body has to do with the respective ways that each school viewed the causal process. In Sāṃkhya, with its view that effects preexist in their causes (*satkārya*), the "originary producer," or matter (*prakrti*), is responsible for all causal activity whatsoever, while spirit or ultimate personhood (*puruṣa*) cannot give rise to causes because causes never came from it. Causes, from this perspective, must themselves receive their potency from a material basis (*upādānagrahaṇāt*) and everything that happens must arise from its cause (*kāraṇabhāva*).[16] But since matter was not originally conscious, none of its evolutes can acquire or evolve consciousness from it, and so the body, even in its subtlest capacities of internal sense, cannot be considered conscious. In Nyāya-Vaiśeṣika, on the other hand, there is a very strict association thought to hold between the grammatical articulation of a causal relationship and its real constituents. So, when we say that eyes are "used" to see, ears are "used" to hear, and the inner sense is "used" to make one aware or deliberate, these organs would be not only put in the instrumental case in a Sanskrit sentence but would be considered instrumental causes (*nimittakāraṇa*). If these organs are instruments, then they are being used by an agent that is separate from them. It is the agent, and not the instruments that it is employing, that would be the subject term in a sentence with verbs such as "sees," "hears," and "knows."[17] This makes the spiritual self, as just mentioned, a direct agent of knowledge, in contrast to the Sāṃkhya position. However, the larger metaphysical implication is the same, namely, that the self is the conscious substance in an instance of awareness, and not the body.

As we shall see in the next chapter, the Buddhists would sharply resist this Brāhmiṇical representation of the relationship between spirit and body, effectively by denying entirely the existence of an eternal spirit separable from the body as well as by arguing that whatever kind of conscious state we experience is intimately connected with whatever physical organs are involved in it. However, they would largely appropriate a notion that the Brāhmiṇical thinkers believed was implicated in the relationship between spirit and body, namely, the consequences of the intended acts that ensured their continued intertwining from one generation to the next, namely, the workings of *karma*.

Affects, Habits, and New Bodies

Perhaps the best-known classical Indian philosophical depiction of human existence is the doctrine of *karma* and rebirth. But its philosophical articulation and defense is not uniform across traditions of belief and practice, even within different schools. There are, we shall see presently, both important differences and crucial commonalities between the two major models of Brāhmiṇical thought with regard to how the transfer of spirit from one body to the next takes place. In one respect, how the whole process of embodiment of spirit in matter began is only attested to in the vaguest of terms. But the evidence for *karma* needs to be searched no farther for than the habits and desires that we are born with. In addition, the authors of our philosophical treatises are quite self-conscious of and freely admit the degree to which their convictions are grounded in worries about what moral motivations human beings will take seriously if they are deprived of the belief in future retribution or reward.

In the *Sāṃkhyakārika,* after a description of the "internal organ" (*antaḥkāraṇa*) that represents it as divided into the threefold function of *buddhi* (awareness), *ahaṃkāra* (ego-generation), and *manas* (sensory and conceptual ideation), the "internal organs" of different persons are called "bodies marked (by *karma*)" (*liṅgam*) that, from time immemorial, have been caught in rebirth.

> *sūkṣmāḥ mātāpitṛjāḥ saha prabhūtaiḥ trdhā viśeṣāḥ syuḥ /*
> *sūkṣmāteṣām nityatā mātāpitṛjāḥ nivartante //*

> *pūrvapannamasktaṃ niyataṃ mahadādi sūkṣmaparyantam /*
> *saṃsārati nirūpabhogaṃ bhavairadhivāsitaṃ liṅgaṃ //*
> *citraṃ yathāśrayamṛte sthāṇvādibhyo vinā yathā chāyā /*
> *tadvāvinā viśeṣairana tiṣthati nirāśrayaṃ liṅgam //*
> *pūruṣārthahetukamidaṃ nimittamainimittika prasaṅgena /*
> *prakṛtevibhutva yogānnaṭvadavyaviṣyate liṅgam //*
> *saṃsiddhikāśca bhāvāḥ prakṛtikā vaikṛtāśca dharmadhyāḥ /*
> *dṛṣṭhāḥ karaṇāśrayiṇaḥ kāryāśrayiṇaśca kalalādhyāḥ //*
> *dharmeṇa gamanayurdva gamanamadhasthādjavatyadharmeṇa /*
> *jñānena cāpavargā viparyayādiṣyate bandaḥ //*
> *vairagyātprakṛtilayaḥ saṃsaro bhavati rajasādragāt /*
> *aiśvaryādavidato viparyāttadviparāsaḥ //*

> Subtle bodies, bodies born from mother and father, together with the elements, are of three distinct kinds. Of the subtle bodies, there are permanent ones, while bodies produced from the mother and father perish. The everlasting subtle body continues from the past, it is unconditioned and unbounded, from Vastness and the rest, it wanders, it does not enjoy, and acquires the primordial traces of becoming; this is the *liṅgam*. As a painting cannot stand without a base, nor a shadow without that which casts it, so a *liṅgam* cannot remain without a base. By means of conjoining with instrumental causes and effects, and in order to bring about the ends of the primordial person, this liṅgam becomes linked with the power of nature, performing like a dancer. Emerging as completed or incomplete, natural products are seen to be virtuous, caused, carried out, and acquired from the womb. Ascending by means of virtue, descending to lower places by means of vice, and achieving release by means of knowledge, while the contrary will, it is determined, result in bondage. By disassociating from enchantment, there is a dissolving into nature, from passion born of enchantment, there occurs wandering, from power results non-obstruction, from weakness results the opposite. (*Sāṃkhyakārika* 39–45)

Bodies acquire, in the preceding verses, their distinctive characteristics from either their *tamātra*-s, irreducible configurations like fire and water in the case of the elements (*bhuta*-s), or from destructible compounded matter in the cases of bodies born from the womb. But some bodies get their form from their actions and interaction, and such bodies are here called karmic bodies (*liṅgam*). The karmic body is permanent (*nitya*) in the sense that no account can be given of its origination and it is not, like the physical body, destructible either. But it can, when a certain kind of metaphysical knowledge has been acquired, dissolve (*laya*) back into the "original producer" of nature and its abundant powers (*prakṛti*). But, just as the basic capacities of awareness, individuation, and affect cannot exist as free-floating qualities but must reside in a base, namely, the actional body of the *liṅgam*, the actional or karmic body in its turn must also reside in a base (*āśraya*). It therefore, in its ongoing transformation (*parimāṇa*) as an actional body, resides in the web of instrumental causes and the effects they bring about (*nimittamainimitta*). And in the course of this process, it acquires in time the requisite accumulation of *sattva, rajas,* and *tamas* to attach to the developing body in an embryo, and thus begins the wandering (*saṃsāra*) of the karmic body through attachment to perishable animal and human forms. During the lifetimes of the latter, the virtues and vices that accrue from the actions of these beings bring about, alternatively, more or less elevated attachments of the *liṅgam* to perishable bodies. The key to understanding *karma* in the context of Sāṃkhya, then, is comprehending that actions and their results in the causal workings of nature do not just float around, as it were, tied together only by sequences and transfers of energy. Those transfers of energy are exchanged between subtle bodily forms that both transport and receive these actions, their affective interchanges and the attendant benefits or detrimental consequences.[18] Those actional bodies in turn can, in the midst of all this causal and energetic interchange, become affixed to the bodies of human beings as they are conceived and develop in the womb. However, at the death of their physical hosts, these actional or karmic bodies do not similarly die, for they are in a strict sense indestructible, just as physical interaction on the larger scale is eternal and ongoing, but instead take their accumulated potentials and psychic energies and affix them to a new host. The continuation of the karmic body's wandering, given the affective nature of the constant interaction with its environment, hinges, however, on a primordial enchantment or rapture with the world's beauty (*raga*). This enchantment can easily intensify as a result of the interactions of specific beings to which the karmic body is attached and can only be diluted on the basis of a special kind of knowledge.

Now, the *buddhi* or basic capacity of "awareness" that belongs to each karmic body serves as the source of this attached enchantment with the world. But it also possesses the ability to detect the difference between its own fundamental groundedness in *prakṛti* and the true source of the awareness that is, in the final analysis, only reflected through it. Its desirous attachment, in a human body, impels it to use the gross body's organs of sensation as the instruments (*kāraṇa*) through which it can actively seek and attain objects.

> *sānaḥ kāraṇa buddhiḥ sarva viśayamavagāhate yasmāt /*
> *tasmāt trividhan kāraṇam dvāri dvārāṇi śeṣsāṇi //*
>
> Since, together with the instrument, awareness pursues and comes into possession of all objects, the threefold instrument is the entrance and the remaining (organs) are the means of entrance. (*Sāṃkhyakārika* 35)

At the same time, however, this capacity of awareness can also detect the difference between its objects and the luminosity whose light it employs. The ability of the faculty of awareness to detect spirit is enhanced to the degree that its interactions, actions, and rebirths equip it with greater and greater shares of the *sattva* energy strand of brilliance. But the capacity, at any rate, was considered the *buddhi*'s own.

> *sarva pratyūbhogaṃ yasmātpuruṣasya sādhyati buddhiḥ /*
> *saiva ca viśinaṣti prādhanapūruṣāntaraṃ sūkṣmam //*
>
> As awareness accomplishes the enjoyment of all the objects of the primordial person, it alone distinguishes the subtle difference between primary matter and the primordial person. (*Sāṃkhyakārika* 37)

This is the signature distinction we find in the Sāṃkhya system between that function of the inner sense that is termed "awareness," which is said to pursue and impact (*avagāhati*) objects as well as discriminate (*viśinaṣti*) between matter and spirit but not itself enjoy or experience (*bhoga*) these pursuits or ascertainments. The language employed to articulate this is telling, for allusions are constantly made to the fact that the *buddhi* is only the "semblance of a lamp" (*pradīpakalpāḥ*) and only appears "as if it were possessed of cognizance" (*cetanātva iva*).[19] This is, we are told by the commentator Vācaspati Miśra, because of the closeness of the karmic body's faculty of awareness to the individuated spirit that is our true personhood (*puruṣa*). For it is the *buddhi* that directly mediates the objects of the sense organs to spirit, and spirit, being the essence of cognitive luminosity (*prakāśatva*) that makes the *buddhi* appear to itself be the source of that light, while in fact it is only its reflection.[20] It seemed to many thinkers in the Indian tradition, including the Naiyāyikas, that, given the facts that active verbs like "ascertain" and "discriminate" were used with *buddhi* as the subject term in Sāṃkhya texts and that, through the mediation of the other sense organs, objects came to be "seated" in the karmic body's faculty of awareness (*buddhyārūdha*), at which point that faculty took on the objects' shape, Sāṃkhya thinkers simply couldn't avoid the implication that the *buddhi* was itself aware.[21] This prompted Sāṃkhya-model defenders in the Yoga tradition to explore possible theories of "double-reflection" of cognitive light in the *buddhi,* where the faculty of awareness could both use spirit's light to illuminate things and could see itself in spirit's reflection back, thus enabling it to achieve both the false conceit of being the source of awareness and enable it to distinguish between itself and spirit.[22] All the same, it is crucial to keep in mind that, for Sāṃkhya thinkers, the capacities or machinery of awareness under discussion were constituents of the actional or karmic body (*liṅgam*). Therefore, even though the activities of the *buddhi* could be considered both causal and responsive to inbuilt impulses, all this interaction and desirous affect was considered strictly unconscious.

But, in addition to the unconsciousness of the karmic process of Sāṃkhya thought, one other detail cited earlier is worthy of notice, namely, that it is also explicitly said to be a performance, as aforementioned, a dance performed in a dramatic presentation (*naṭa*). Despite all its action and beauty, the continual performance of nature in which the karmic body willfully, as it were, takes part is not undertaken for its own sake, for, as emphasized, there is, almost paradoxically, no enjoyment of it on the part of the participants. The performance only has one purpose, and that purpose is not its own. The purpose of a performance is to be seen. And once it is noticed, according to the *Kārika,* it, with utmost modesty, withdraws and lets its formerly captive audience, the *puruṣa*, go free.

> *raṅgasya darśānyevā nivartate naṭarkto yathā nṛtyāt /*
> *puruṣasya tathātmanāṃ prakāśya vinivartate prakṛtiḥ //*
> *nānāvidhairūpāyairūpakāraṇyanūpakāraṇa pūṃsaḥ /*
> *gūṇavatyugūṇasya satastasyārthamapārthakaṃ carati //*
> *prakṛte sūkūmārataraṃ na kiṅcidastīti me mītirbhavati /*
> *yā dṛṣṭ'samīti punardarśanamūpaimi puruṣasya //*
>
> As a dancing girl, after being seen by the audience, stops the dance, so nature ceases its activity after being seen by the self of the person. Through manifold approaches, the beneficent servile one (*prakṛti*), by means of her beneficence, possessing all the *guṇa*-s pursues *guṇa*-constituted substances as objects without any aim of her own. It is my view that there is nothing more tender than nature, who, after thinking, "I have been seen," approaches the sight of the primordial person never again. (*Sāṃkhyakārika* 59–61)

It is, of course, of considerable significance that powers and attributes of nature are overtly represented here as feminine. Given the fact that *prakṛti* is a feminine noun and *puruṣa* a masculine one, this is never in doubt. But here, it is further said that feminine nature is a servile spirit (*pūṃsa*) to the masculine spiritual person and plays the role of his dancing girl (*naṭarkt*). But spirit does not engage her; indeed, since sprit is thought to be a-causal and inert, he does nothing with her except light up the stage where she dances, and once he has seen her perform, he loses interest in her beauty, and she simply stops dancing and withdraws from his audience. This loss of interest of masculine spirit in feminine nature, followed by the suppression of her activity, is formulated by Sāṃkhya in terms of final liberation from rebirth, resulting as it does in the dissolution of the karmic body that is necessary for its continual attachment to physical bodies to cease. Of course, many centuries later, in both Tāntric systems and the Kashmir Śaivism of Abhinavagupta, this early Sāṃkhya bifurcation between masculine spirit and feminine nature would be decisively eliminated with the insistence that the powers (*śakti*) of nature and the consciousness of the primordial person were of one unified essence, and they accounted for the evolution of the universe with more stages of pre-cosmic transformation than did Sāṃkhya. Nonetheless, for many centuries of the development of Sāṃkhya thought as well as for many systems that appropriated various elements of this school into their own frameworks, such as Yoga and Vedānta, embodied personhood results from a virtually beginningless, impulsively affective, even erotic, bondage of karmic bodies to the enchanting world. But that impulsive attachment was thought to remain compelling only until the moment when our innermost core of personhood, which is purely spiritual consciousness, notices.

Against those who questioned the whole credibility of the notion of *karma* and the process of rebirth, the Naiyāyikas pointed to untaught desirous habits that not only made individual people unique but could also be found in the behavior of infants.

> *pūrvābhyastasmṛtyanūbandhājjātasya*
> *harṣabhayaśokasaṃpratipate* /
> *padmādiṣu prabodhasaṃmīlanavikāravatadvikāraḥ* /
> *noṣṇaśītavarṣakālanimitatvāt pañcātmakīvakārāṇām* /
> *pretyāhārābhyāsakṛtāt stanyābhilāṣāt* /
> *śrayaso'yaskāntābhigamanavatadūpasarpaṇam* /
> *nānyann prakṛtyabhāvāt* /
> *vītarāgajanmādarśanāt* /

> From the previously repeated memories of a newborn, from delight, fear, and grief, that together continuously occur in it (we infer there were previous lives). (The opponent claims that) these facial changes of agitation are like the changes of opening and closing that are found together in the maturation of a lotus flower. No, for heat, cold, rain, and the seasons possess the causal power of transformation over things made of the five elements. The attraction to mother's milk comes from similar activities that carry over from previous lives. (The opponent claims that) the child's delight in acquiring mother's milk is like the iron's being drawn to the loadstone. But is it the case that natural phenomena (like the iron) tend toward no other things? (We are) of the view that newborns are desirous and have delights. (*Nyāyasūtra* 3:1:19–25)

It is observed here that children are born with specific desires that draw them only to certain things, such as the mother's breast, and make them fearful and sad only at certain things and not others. The possession of these dispositions, as opposed to merely physical things that are, as it were, indifferently reactive to their circumstances, convinces the Naiyāyikas that these dispositions in the child have been caused by something other than their mere physical constitution. In this system, affective attractions in human beings are not just energetic impulses that occur in unconscious bodies due to causal relations but instead are accreted specifically out of memories from past experiences and the results to which they led. The fact that memories and accreted dispositions are so closely tied is key, for it led Naiyāyikas, in very stark contrast to Sāṃkhya thought, to conclude that these memories and dispositions were the features or qualitative fluctuations (*guṇa*-s) of the spiritual self (*ātman*), since memories could not, for them, conceivably be qualities of any body, no matter how subtle its physicality was construed. On their account, memories certainly can't belong to the eyes, skin, hair, or nails, since these external organs and features merely come into contact with things in succession and their respective sensations are ever being overtaken by new ones. Neither can memories be qualities of the inner sense, or *manas*, for, as we have seen, they believed the *manas* was atomic in size, and being therefore partless, it could not contain anything, but, like external organs, it only experiences successive sensations, coming into contact with only one of the body's organs at a time. Memories must, for Nyāya, be held or stored somewhere that persists, so that the memories themselves can persist, and they must further reside in a place where they can come to consciousness, for in order for a memory to be experienced as a memory, we must be aware of it.[23] Ultimately, for this *darśana*, the persistence and accumulation of these dispositions and their residence in the self was ultimately responsible for the process of rebirth.

> *śarīrotpatinimitavat saṃyogotpatinimitaṃ karma* /
>
> *Karma* is the instrumental causation of the origin of the body, and is the instrumental cause of the origin of its conjunction (with a self). (*Nyāyasūtra* 3:2:70)

The deeds, intentions, attractions, fears, and memories of life, for Naiyāyikas, do not belong to some additional karmic body (*liṅgam*) that is, so to speak, a stranger to the pure and merely knowing self. Instead, these accreted experiences and dispositions belong to none other than the self. In Nyāya, therefore, the self is not just a knower but is also, so long as it remains embodied, itself a desiring, feeling, thinking, and acting being. Its acts, precisely its *karma*, are what keep it tethered to the world, only to be released from bodily existence, and, as it turns out, consciousness too, once it has been purified of its faults, pain, and incomprehension (*avidyā*) of the true nature of things through ritual sacrifice and meditational insight. As we shall explore further in the next section, this very insistence that *karma*, through memories and accumulated dispositions, was a quality of the self inspired the Nyāya philosophers to make a provocative criticism of Sāṃkhya, namely, that the latter, by representing affections, attachments, and deeds as rooted in the subtle karmic body, were guilty of rendering that body itself conscious, a clear error in the ancient Brāhmiṇical world of philosophy.

Interestingly, however, writers going back to the origins of Brāhmiṇical logic were not averse to worrying aloud that people who were persuaded by Indian materialist ideas that only one physical life was in store for each being and no punishments or rewards awaited in successive lives would have precious little motivation to be moral. The *Nyāyasūtrabhāṣyam* attributed to Vātsyāyana argues that, if we believed we are reducible to our bodies, all kinds of morally unacceptable consequences would result. First, since the body itself as a physical phenomenon changes from one moment to the next, we could not punish the present body for sins committed by a past body that is no longer in existence. Furthermore, if virtuous people suffered unfortunate fates in a single lifetime, their virtuous deeds would be deprived of their meaning (*kṛta hāni*), and if the unrighteous found themselves happy in a single lifetime, they would experience gain even in the absence of meritorious deeds (*akṛitābhyāgama*).[24] It turns out then that classical Indian philosophers openly worried that the rejection of the belief in *karma* would entail a life divested of both moral meaning and deprived of moral incentive. Though Buddhist opponents of the Brāhmiṇical worldview would famously reject their theory of a permanent spiritual self, and even of a self that endured from one moment to the next, they also were deeply concerned about the moral nihilism that may easily ensue without a justifiable belief in moral retribution or reward. And so, they, too, would devote some considerable effort to salvaging the idea of *karma* and the consequences of present deeds in future lives, though they traced these consequences through causal heritages rather than injecting them into either karmic bodies or eternal souls.

Time, Identity, and the Abode of Memory

While, in principle, Sāṃkhya and Nyāya philosophers concurred that an eternal spiritual self was the truly conscious part of persons, while the body, on its own, was utterly unconscious, thus accounting for the experiential unity of our identity through time, they differed markedly over the relationship of consciousness to selfhood. This difference implicated correspondingly divergent views about the temporality of consciousness and what role the body, differently conceived, played in this temporality.

In the Sāṃkhya tradition, the primal and eternal support of matter (*pradhāna*) originally exists in various subtle (*sūkṣma*) states, like the *guṇa*-s and basic, persistent configurations (*tamātra*-s) such as elements. It undergoes transformations (*parimāṇa*) or modifications (*vṛtti*) of potentiality (*śākti*) and activity (*pravṛtti*) that results in specific, concrete (*sthūla*) phenomena passing from an unmanifest (*avyākta*) to a manifest (*vyākta*) mode of existence. These changes of state of potentiality to actuality in *prakṛti* themselves give rise to the temporal determinations of past, present, and future. Indeed, the ninth-century commentator on the *Sāṃkhyakākrikā*, the brilliant Vācaspati Miśra, takes this very notion of the real transformations that happen in subtle and concrete matter to be a direct refutation of what he believes to be the Vijñānavāda Buddhist position, to be examined in the next chapter, that temporality is only a process of cognitions and not attributable to real things.[25] It is these modifications, and the temporal determinations that emerge from them, that are the objects of the conscious, primordial person (*puruṣa*), which itself supposedly never changes. The experience of temporality then, in Sāṃkhya, involves the apprehension by spirit of various kinds of actual modifications of primal matter, which make invisible potentialities of energy into visible things.[26]

The Naiyāyikas noticed that there was something oddly peculiar about this depiction of temporal experience that, as far as they were concerned, did not ring true either to common sense or intelligible explanations of causality. The Sāṃkhya view represents spirit as seeing temporal change but never undergoing it or participating in it. The core of our being, according to the narrative of the "Enumeration" school, watches change happen to matter, but itself neither suffers change nor brings change to the world itself. Moreover, in causal terms, the Sāṃkhya view leads to the inevitable conclusion that, in a strictly causal sense, nothing really new ever happens in the world; there is no novel production, since all changes are simply modifications of the same basic stuff; and all dynamic interchanges of energy are nothing more than localized transfers of the same, underlying energy. This was not in any way a consequence that Sāṃkhya philosophers denied. On the contrary, they put on offer positive refutations of the Nyāya view that temporality involved decisive changes, including changes to the innermost self that was, while in essence eternal and all-pervasive, in terms of knowledge, qualities, and actions, always causally engaged with the world in both directions. We find these views expressed already in the *Kārika*, in the form of reasons that production of entirely novel effects is impossible.

> *asadakaraṇādūpādānagrahaṇāt sarvasaṃbhavābhāvāt /*
> *śāktasya śākyakaraṇāt karaṇābhāvāca sat kāryam //*

> From nonexistence's lack of efficacy, from depending on a material base, from the non-occurrence of the becoming of everything, from the efficacy to produce similar from similar, and from (the fact that) effects have an essence, the effect exists. (*Sāṃkhyakārika* 9)

To clarify these arguments is not difficult. First, if we are to suppose that something entirely new is produced, it must previously not exist. But, the passage points out, nonexistence cannot cause anything. Second, something that we could accurately characterize as pure novelty would lack any material existence whatsoever before being produced. But everyone acknowledges that effects must rely on an already existent material basis (*upādāna*) and are only modifications of that matter. Third, effects are not merely random but bear continuity with their attendant causes. Finally, the essence of an effect is to be the effect of the cause to which it is related, since cause and effect are not separated by a supposed forgoing nature of the cause on the one hand and a complete novelty of the effect on the other. Indeed, the philosophers of the Sāṃkhya lineage went further, intimating that the Nyāya-Vaiśeṣika metaphysics itself had in the end to admit of a primary state of being from which all effects proceeded, given the facts that their most pervasive and all-encompassing general (*samavāya*) category was existence (*satta*) itself.[27] The unavoidable conclusion for Sāṃkhya was that there had to be a primary configuration of matter from which all transformations arise. But because material existence cannot, as seen earlier, account for consciousness and consciousness was considered the utter opposite of matter, they also believed that temporality and the changes from which it actually arises itself are merely witnessed by a self that is timeless.

But, the Naiyāyikas objected, this characterization of things leads to an unacceptable conclusion. If the eternal spiritual self at the core of our consciousness really does see all transformations of primary matter, and further, if the direct objects of each individuated spirit are the fluctuations of the karmic body (*liṅgam*), where not only present deeds but past memories and future potentialities are contained, then there is no reason that the consciousness in each of us should not be fully aware, at every moment, of the past, present, and future of its accompanying karmic body. It would, in other words, not make just any two given cognitions simultaneous but would effectively make them all simultaneous.

> *na yūgapadagraharaṇāt* /
> *śrapratyabhijñāne ca vināśaprasaṇgaḥ* /
> *kramavṛtitvādayūgapad grahaṇam* / . . .
> *śralātacakradarśanavatadūpalabdhirāśūsacchārāt* /
>
> (Cognitions) are not from simultaneous apprehension. Furthermore, in the termination of recognition can also be found the lack of sense (in your position). The successive activity (of cognitions) exhibit a dependence on the procession of time. . . . Like seeing the circling of a firebrand, apprehension (of cognitions) arises from rapidly successive activity. (*Nyāyasūtra* 3:2:4–6, 62)

We are aware from our common, everyday experience that our attention shifts from one thing to the next, awareness of things arises and ceases, and even recollections come and go. This fact precludes, for the Naiyāyikas, the possibility that the inner sense can act like a container that holds on to the cognitions that it processes. For if it were, when the ever-and-limitlessly conscious self shines its light on that inner sense, none of its stored cognitions could hide from that illumination, and we would be aware of all of its fluctuations, past, present, and potential, all it once. The succession that we experience may sometimes be so rapid that it escapes our notice, since apprehension of sensations, too, is contingent and has specific causal factors, which just means at times we have sensations we don't notice. But we must not mistake this rapidity for simultaneity. The fact that our cognitions do occur in temporal succession, however, does prove several very important things for Nyāya thinkers. It proves first that the inner sense (*manas*) is unstructured (*nirākāra*); it does not have internal or functional divisions that contain cognitions but rather is partless, which is to say atomic. The succession we experience is accounted for by the fact that the inner sense moves around the body with incredible speed, making contact with the body's external and internal organs and being stimulated by each in their turn as it goes. The inner sense, however, because it is a physical organ, is not itself aware of these stimulations. By contrast, since the inner self (*ātman*) pervades the space of the entire body, it can become aware of the inner sense's mediation of contact. Indeed, both Vaiśeṣika and Nyāya philosophers held that cognitions (*jñāna*-s) can only occur when there is a tangible connection (*saṃyoga*) between the self, the inner sense, and a sense organ. When confronted with the question of how the *ātman* could undergo a connection with anything given the fact that it is supposedly not a physical phenomenon, or indeed how the *manas* could either given its purportedly atomic nature, the schools responded by asserting that, since connection can take place between substances so long as one of them is of limited size, and since, during life, the self and inner sense were housed in the physical body, connection between them and the body's sense organs was possible in an embodied environment.[28] In the embodied environment, therefore, spiritual selves could both be effected by and enter into the causal process. Selves, therefore, could acquire memories, affective dispositions, abiding desires, and cognitive states as well as initiate and suffer the consequences of action, all in the form of *guṇa*-s, so long as they were residents of physical bodies. In other words, for Nyāya, it was the concrete physical body, and not any subtle karmic body, that enabled the eternal self to live in time rather than just passively witness it.

Indeed, the Naiyāyikas went even further in their indictment of the Sāṃkhya position, particularly with regard to the vocabulary that the latter philosophers used to speak about the *buddhi*, the faculty of "awareness" that was one of the tripartite functions of the inner sense. In Sāṃkhya thought, this faculty of awareness, as seen earlier, possesses the capacity of objective discernment (*adhyavaśaya*), which is not only capable of sensuous awareness and powers of affective disposition but is also capable of discerning the difference between primal matter and spirit. Sāṃkhya writers themselves referred to these capacities of the *buddhi* as merely "semblances" of consciousness that were derived from the relative proximity (*aparatva*) of this part of the inner sense to spirit in circumstances where karmic attachment continued to obtain. Given the fact that spirit, in Sāṃkhya thought, was also considered non-active, the exertions of recollection must also be considered activities of the karmic body that called upon the powers of both awareness and *manas*, where the combination of ideas (*saṃkalpaka*) took place. The Naiyāyikas objected to this representation, suggesting that if the *buddhi* itself was capable of various kinds of discernments and if the *manas* in turn was capable of cognitive synthesis, then there would be every reason to consider the inner sense itself the agent (*kaṛtr*) of cognitions rather than just their instrument (*kāraṇa*), especially since spirit was thought to do nothing but, so to speak, light up the show of the process.[29] This would further effectively render the body itself conscious, an implication the Sāṃkhya philosophers overtly resisted, but, as far as the Naiyāyikas were concerned, they could not avoid. The inner sense might constitute a subtle body and not a gross body, to use the Sāṃkhya terminology, but since the subtle body was all the same a manifestation of *prakṛti*, the implication stood.[30]

In principle, the schools agreed that consciousness had to be either the essence or property of spirit, since one overarching shared quality of physical matter as such was supposedly its lack of consciousness. One of the crucial differences between them was how to articulate the relation between the temporality of physical events and the belief, shared by both schools, that spirit, the core of our personhood, was eternal. The Buddhists, as we shall see, took the implication that our experience was temporal with the utmost seriousness. They insisted that a philosophically earnest consideration of the fact that our experience was not only temporal but that consciousness was itself impermanent would eventually cost us the conviction that there was any such thing as an eternal self. One of the most fascinating peculiarities of the Nyāya position was that it did not hold the impermanence of the self to be a consequence of the temporality of consciousness. Yes, the Naiyāyikas admitted, consciousness could only occur in an impermanent body, but that would not necessarily imply that an eternal self did not exist; it only necessarily implied that the eternal self, once released from embodied existence, was eternally deprived of consciousness. All things considered, then, the Sāṃkhya and Nyāya-Vaiśeṣika conceptions of the self were, though they shared certain general features, not only different but almost radically so. Their respective convictions represent two quite divergent Brāhmiṇical models of spiritual selfhood.

Selves as Persons in Brāhmiṇical Thought

The very suggestion that the two major Brāhmiṇical conceptions of spiritual selfhood can be even thought of as the core of our personhood, as I repeatedly use the phrase here, may strike some as highly dubious. After all, as Sāṃkhya thought insists, *puruṣa* is utterly and completely distinct from the contingencies of both any individual body in which it might happen to mysteriously reside but also from the subtle karmic body that does survive the transition from one life to the next. Similarly, in Nyāya-Vaiśeṣika thought, while the self does serve as the possibility for conscious awareness during bodily existence and engages in worldly life rather directly while embodied life lasts, it also persists from one life to the next and, upon release from rebirth, is deprived of all associations from the lives of any of the persons it inhabited in its beginningless earthly journey. One could point to the fact that, for Sāṃkhya, the primary producer of individual identity, the *ahaṃkāra*, is a faculty of the inner sense and a constituent of the karmic body, and so personhood lies in this rather than the physically transcendent *puruṣa*. With regard to Nyāya, one could also argue that the notion of *ātman* formulated in this school represents only a very "thin" conception of identity that mostly serves the epistemological function of explaining self-consciousness and does not serve any personally narrative role.[31] But such conclusions, it will be shown, ought to be reassessed in light of several crucially important commitments each *darśana* makes with regard to the notion of the eternal, spiritual self. First, both schools agree that selves are individuated, such that the self abiding in the body of one being is not the same self abiding in the body of another. The belief in the idea that the same undifferentiated self was at the core of all beings was unique to the Advaita Vedāntins and so was distinctly a minority view among classical Brāhmiṇical philosophers. The individuality of each spiritual self was pivotal for both Sāṃkhya and Nyāya-Vaiśeṣika doctrines (*siddhānta*-s), as each self had its own unique history and karmic heritage. Furthermore, both schools, despite their pronounced differences on the nature of the self, held that it was the only possible basis for our experience of ourselves as persons. In Sāṃkhya, *puruṣa* is said to be not only the primary basis (*adhistāna*) upon which the experiences of pleasure and pain rest but also their enjoyer (*bhoktṛ*), and in the final analysis, its experience of the world and its apprehension of the karmic body entail that the entire play of natural existence is solely for the purpose (*artha*) of spirit. In Nyāya, as we have noted several times, feelings, habits, memories, cognitions, and actions along with their moral fruits are thought to be exclusively owned by the self while it was embodied. So, while the whole story of our personhood certainly cannot be told in the ancient Brāhmiṇical world without reference to the physical and karmic bodies and the temporal experiences of any and all of the latter, as we have rehearsed, it is just as much the case that we could not be persons without selves either. Selves do then play directly thematized constitutive roles in making us the persons we are.

The *Sāṃkhyakārika* wastes no time in asserting all these commitments in quick succession toward the opening of the text in the midst of declaring its basic definitions.

> *saṅghātaparārthatvātrigūṇadiviparyayādisthānāt /*
> *pūruṣo'sti bhoktṛbhāvāt kaivalyārtha pravṛteśca //*
> *janmamaraṇakāraṇanāṃ pratiniyamādayūgapatpravṛteśca /*
> *puruṣabahutvaṃ siddhaṃ trigūṇyaviparyayācaiva //*
> *tasmāccha viparyāsāt siddhaṃ sakṣitvamasya puruṣasya /*
> *kaivalyaṃ mādhyasthyaṃ draṣṭṛtvakarartṛbhāvaśca //*

> From the purpose of all compounded things for another, from its distinction from the three *guṇa*-s, and from the fact that it serves as a primary basis, (we know that) the primordial person is the essence of enjoyment, and its purpose is to be isolated. From birth, death, and the instruments (sense organs), from the distinctive causes of natural activities and from the distinct fluctuations brought about by the three *guṇa*-s, the multiplicity of primordial persons is certainly established. And from this distinction, the essence of being a seer and the essence of being a non-agent is therefore established with regard to the primordial person, which is of the nature of a witness, isolated and neutral. (*Sāṃkhyakārika* 17–19)

These positions with regard to the self are intimately bound up with one another. The notion of enjoyment (*bhokta*) is a common idiom in philosophical Sanskrit for the idea of "subjectivity," or being the experiencer of events. But in its own context, while the three *guṇa*-s are, as we have seen, energy strands that carry affect, and while the sense organs of the physical body and cognitive machinery of the karmic body are considered instruments (*kāraṇa*) that are used to process these affects and objective relations, neither are considered "enjoyers" of natural activities or objects because none of them are thought to be conscious. It is *puruṣa* that is said to be the basis (*adhistāna*) upon which enjoyment of experience rests, precisely because it is spirit that has the capacity to be a seer (*dṛṣṭṛ*) and a witness (*sakṣin*). The *buddhi* (awareness), *ahaṃkāra* (ego-generation), and *manas* (sense and deliberation) would not be able to perform their functions lest they were proximate enough to the light (*prakāśa*) of the primordial person to borrow it and reflect it onto their respective activities and objects. It is further claimed that there is a plurality, or manyness (*bahutva*), of primordial persons given the fact that different embodied persons meet different ends at different times and are impelled by unique circumstances and affects, which is taken to demonstrate that each karmic body attaches to individually distinct *puruṣa*-s. And because each primordial self is an enjoyer of its experiences, and since the karmic body and physical body are thought to be its instruments, it is therefore deduced that, ultimately, these bodies are devoted to the purpose (*artha*) for which the *puruṣa* employs them, that being the self's final isolation from natural existence. But it must always be kept in mind, in the Sāṃkhya framework, that, in a strict sense, the self is not considered to be ever really trapped by the play of nature and the journeys of the karmic body, for it is ever free and only watches the dance of matter in order to take notice of its own eternal distinctness. But, very importantly, when such notice is taken, it is not spirit that is freed, but the *buddhi* of the karmic body.

> tasmann badhyate'sau na mūcyate nāpi saṃsārati kaścit /
> saṃsārati badhyate mucyate ca nānāśrayā prakṛtiḥ //
> rūpaiḥ saptabireva tu badnātyātmānāmātmanā prakrṛtiḥ /
> saiva ca pūruṣārtha prati vimocayatyekarūpeṇa //
> evaṃ tatvābhyāsānnāsmi na me nāhamityapariśeṣam /
> aviparyayādviśuddhaṃ kevalamutpadyate jñānam //
> tena nivṛtaprasavārthavavātsmtarūpavinivṛtām /
> prakṛtiṃ paśyati puruṣaḥ prekṣakavadavasthitaḥ
> svacchaḥ //

> Therefore, he is not bound, nor released, nor wanders. It is matter, the non-basis, that wanders, is bound, and is released. Matter, by means of her seven forms, binds only herself, and only she, for the benefit of spirit's purpose, by means of one form, achieves final release.Thus, cultivating the essences, without any remainder, she says: "I am not, it is not mine, there is no I," and the cognition is produced that is uncontradicted, pure and isolated. With that, after the suppression of activity, and after spirit's purpose has been achieved of suppressing the seven transformations, the primordial person sees matter, and, having the essence of a spectator, rests, pure. (*Sāṃkhyakārika* 62–65)

The identity that the karmic body, in the forms of natural configuration she has taken up, denies is her own identity as a self-sustained ego (*ahaṃ*). The reason that identity is denied is not because, as in Buddhism, there is no self at all, but rather because the affective, desiring, acting, and attached self is a false one, for its source of awareness is rooted in the consciousness of the primordial person. The karmic body's journey ends when it is revealed in the full luminescence of spirit, and spirit beholds its own distinctness by beholding its other. It is therefore *puruṣa,* and not the bodies that foray through the world of nature and deeds, that is the real person in each of us.

In at least much of early Vaiśeṣika thought, individuation or particularity (*viśeṣa*) is the mark of all the substances (*dravya*) classified as permanent (*nitya*), including sound-space (*ākāśa*), physical space (*dik*), time, atoms, atomic mental organs (*manas*), and selves (*ātman*).[32] It seems to be necessary to single these out as featuring numerical particularity because, while such individuation appears an obvious feature of the composite objects we deal with in everyday life, the question of whether or not particularity obtained in invisible substances needed clarification. In early Nyāya texts, other arguments were manufactured to witness to the particularity of distinct selves residing in each individual body. The conviction was grounded, for example, in the fact that selves could only have awarenesses within a particular body as well as the need to account for different people experiencing different circumstances of fortune and misfortune based on the karmic inheritance of their spiritual selves and the moral character of their own deeds.[33] However, engaging debates that went more to the core of their paramount philosophical concerns, the Naiyāyikas also argued that the disparate awarenesses, memories, desires, and affects we experience, as well as the deeds we do, are experienced by us as belonging to a unitary self. The issues surrounding these arguments would involve trenchant contestations between the Naiyāyikas and various Buddhist schools for centuries on end. In order for us to consciously experience an awareness, for instance, as a memory, the different qualities of a thing, such as its sight and smell, must be recalled by a numerically identical self who was a perceptual witness (*śākṣin*) to the original experience. This must be so in order for the many heterogeneous objective qualities of form and odor of past experiences to be associated with one object, since individual sense organs cannot do this. In like manner, in a current recollection, that the "I" that experienced the initial occasion and the "I" that remembers it must be the same in order for me to identify an experience as a memory.[34] Under normal circumstances, it can be added, one self residing in one body cannot be the owner of the memories of a different person. There must therefore be a plurality of individual selves.

But, as has been attested several times, the self of the Naiyāyikas is more obviously and robustly the abode of our personhood than is the case with the *puruṣa* of the Sāṃkhya *darśana*. This is the case precisely because, in almost complete contrast with the latter framework, in Nyāya, the self is the direct possessor, as opposed to some subtle karmic body, of its experiences and deeds.

> icchādveṣaprayalasukhaduḥkhajñānāni śrātmano liṅgam /
>
> Desire, aversion, will, pleasure, pain, and cognitions are identifying marks of the self. (*Nyāyasūtra* 1:1:11)

The merely momentary contact of the sense organs, both outer and inner, with their objects that results in their sensation, combined with the body's supposed unconsciousness, preclude for Nyāya the possibility that affective states, dispositional states, memories, and knowledge can have the body as their basis, meaning that they must reside in the self. Similarly, while physical bodies may simply be impelled to move and interact with other bodies due to mechanical circumstances, a living person is often seen to interact with others through being impelled by acts of will and initiative, implying that actions, too, both belong to and in terms of moral responsibility accrue to the self.[35] In the Nyāya-Vaiśeṣika model, then, everything we are intuitively inclined to associate with our personhood, including our accumulated knowledge, experience, habits of character, past, present, and future are rooted in our spiritual selves, and remain so until the final release of the spiritual self from the karmic round of rebirth erases all those associations into eternal unconsciousness.

As we shall see in the following chapter, classical South Asian Buddhists engaged with Brāhmiṇical models of personhood in both a sharply critical and a deeply serious way. While the Buddhists found no reason to believe in an eternal, spiritual self that was both distinct during life and separable after death from the body, they did feel profound needs to maintain some fundamentally crucial themes from the inter-Brāhmiṇical debates on personhood. They believed, first, that, so long as the notion of an enduring *ātman* was extirpated from the theory, *karma* and its attendant conceptions of moral reward and moral dessert had to be maintained in order to make sense of our experience and society as well as safeguard against the dangers of the materialist's alleged sole commitments to pleasure (*kāma*) and wealth (*artha*).[36] Like the Naiyāyikas, the Buddhists would find it crucial to account both for the fundamental temporality of human experience, which included the harsh truth of human impermanence, as well as the fact that we do stand in possession of memories, awarenesses, and latent potentials to act that for long stretches of time could remain unconscious. And, like the Sāṃkhya philosophers, the Buddhists were profoundly committed to the conviction that human life held the potential to attain a final and lasting condition of peace that, while not the essence of a transcendent spiritual self, lies ever waiting in a boundlessly illuminating principle of consciousness. It is the latter belief that we now begin to trace as part of the Buddhist idea of personhood that would attain a transformed but far-reaching legacy in the Central Kingdom.

3

Eliminating Identity and the Luminous Mind in Yogācāra

Having examined some major pre-Buddhist Chinese conceptions of personhood as well as a few major alternative theories of personhood in its rival South Asian Brāhmiṇical traditions, we come to the Buddhist treatment of personhood as it is depicted in the Vijñānavāda or "Cognition Doctrine" school of Yogācāra. The most conspicuous feature of the Buddhist tradition from its inception has, of course, been the teaching of no-self (*anātman*), the denial that persons possess either eternal "souls" that are the core of their being or even that human beings possess a temporally stable identity during their individual worldly lives. The many different Theravāda and Mahāyāna schools of ancient South Asia articulated this teaching in a variety of ways depending on their respective scriptural corpuses and their respectively unique interpretations of the teaching of the tradition's founder and preceptors. But despite this great variety of approaches to Buddhism, they shared the same ultimate goal. In order to free people from their futile, obsessive attachments to the world, and indeed to liberate them from the pain that impermanence leaves them victims to, even the most residual germs of the notion of self, whether conceived as spiritual or worldly, had to be uprooted. Buddhist theory and practice were, to a significant degree, driven by the imperative of eliminating identity, an end as dramatic and provocative in classical Asia as it is for the world of today.

We shall focus in this third chapter on the Vijñānavāda school for several reasons most pertinent to this study. First, despite continuing uncertainty about the authorship of its founding philosophical treatises,[1] the originators of the "Cognition Doctrine" school were great heirs of the long-standing tradition of Abhidharma, the interpretive analyses of the Buddha's teachings as they are found in recorded discourses, but they modify the Abhidharma framework in order to address crucial problems that had since arisen in Buddhism. Early scriptural representations had argued that persons were nothing more than collections (*skandha*-s) of dynamically ever-changing matter, sensations, perceptions, dispositions, and accumulated attachments. In the face of this, questions arose from without and within Buddhism about how to account for the seemingly continuous identities we hold, that others impute to us, and that the moral agency that makes it possible to hold individuals responsible for acts appear to require. This worry became especially pressing when the other major school of Yogācāra, the Sautrāntikas, argued that the most consistent interpretation of the Buddhist notion of impermanence was that even one conscious moment (*kṣana*) literally did not survive into the next.[2] A school of Buddhists contesting this reductionist view arose, known as the Pudgalavādins or "personalists," arguing that, while the *skandha*-s out of which we are constituted do constantly change, the persons we are, though theoretically elusive, must have some real continuity lest the very intelligibility of our experience and praxis be lost. In response to these worries, the Vijñānavādins undertook to explain in detail how continuous constructed associations of identity could be manufactured even out of psychic processes that were constantly changing. But, with their dramatic alterations to the Abhidharma framework, the Vijṅānavādins also tried to solve another problem in a particularly compelling way, namely, how to account for both the possibility that unenlightened human beings can become enlightened, as well as to explain how consciousness, once enlightened, could maintain its new state despite, once again, its seemingly constant transformation. It is because the Yogācāra solutions to these problems, I would argue, dealt squarely with challenges to Buddhism's conception of personhood that it merits being featured in this study. In order to better understand these issues, we will, while incorporating other materials from the larger Buddhist tradition, focus primarily on two Yogācāra texts, the *Madhyānta Vibhāga* and the *Trimśatikā*, along with some of their accompanying commentarial materials, particularly those of Sthīramati and one of the most important early translators of Vijñānavāda texts into Chinese, Paramārtha. The other reason for highlighting the teachings of Yogācāra in this work is that, of all the Indian schools of thought to have great influence on the formation of Buddhist schools in China, including Huayen (華嚴) and Chan (禪), the doctrines of the Cognition school as mediated by Paramārtha and Xuanzang were most meaningful.

Much of the attention directed to Yogācāra philosophy, both in ancient times and in the last century, has been devoted to determining the kind and degree of metaphysical "idealism" it espouses. This chapter, by contrast, will concentrate on how the school's understanding of personhood under the condition of its attachment to identity, its ultimate goal to effectively transform that attachment, and its conception of enlightened consciousness are related. We will begin by demonstrating how the Vijñānavādins understand human awareness as distributed among the sensations of bodily organs, inner sense, ego-construction, and a basic store of psychic tendencies. Their term for discrete states of human awareness is *vijñāna,* which etymologically denotes discrete or condition-specific (*vi*) cognitions (*jñāna*). They do not, it is crucial to note, understand "consciousness" to be a mass noun identifying some unfaltering capacity of cognitive luminosity (*prakāśatva*) that is present in any and every state of awareness, as many of their Brāhmiṇical adversaries might. Instead, they understand cognitions to be determined both by the bodily or psychic organ that gives rise to them—as in visual cognitions, tactile cognitions, emotive cognitions, and even identity cognitions—as well as in terms of their specific content. For this part of their worldview, the Yogācārins rely on long-established Abhidharma precedent as well as amending and adding to it. But a review of these principles will be helpful in distinguishing South Asian Buddhist thought from what we have heretofore covered. For here, the body is not as a whole conscious or unconscious as such but can give rise to certain states of awareness that intermingle with other psychic and bodily states to produce the flow that is our experience.

We will next examine how Yogācārins believed our inner senses of continuous identity are produced. For them, personal identity was the result of the interactions of two distinct kinds of *vijñāna*, one featuring an inherited and accumulated kernel of dispositions that actuates some potentials in its encounter with the present while preserving others, and another cognition that observes the transformations of the first *vijñāna* and, identifying with it, says the word "I." This artifice self is the primary factor in our habituated proclivity to imagine that there is some ultimate distinction that can be made between the contents of our awarenesses and our psychological power to grasp those contents and make them our own. This compulsion to erect a stable identity permeates an otherwise ever-flowing onrush of experiences. Our sense of continuous identity, on this view, is itself a habit, an imaginary act, a mighty psychic clinging to our own objectifying ideations (*kalpanā*) and that magic word, "I," lest it be swept away in the torrential waters (*srotasangha*) of the ongoing transformations (*pariṇāma*) that are our experiences. In Yogācāra thought, self-making is an achievement of sheer imagination (*vijñāpti mātra*), an achievement that can alternatively be reinforced or undone.

Undoing the process of self-making is very much the work of enlightenment, for once the activity of the cognition that manufactures the word "I" has been suppressed, our obsessive afflictions (*kleśa*) and the moral impurities that they lead us to are thought likewise to cease. But how is this possible? How are we able to arrest this seemingly beginningless and psychologically powerful generation of ego and change our fundamentally operative motivations from passionate and uncomprehending (*avidyā*)[3] ones to enlightened and compassionate ones? The Vijñānavādins have a twofold response, and for this response, we will not only make reference to the earliest texts and commentaries of the school but also refer in particular to the mediation of the tradition into the philosophical world of China through Paramārtha. Some of the seeds (*bija*) of our basic store of mental capacities are, and have ever been, pure, and their potentials are activated and reinforced upon an encounter with morally effectual deeds or words of wisdom, and when the ego has been eliminated, their full potentialities become utterly unobscured and unhindered. Thus, while final awakening is certainly an achievement, the outcome of cultivation and practice, it is also, in most if not all beings, stored up within us, and this accounts for our capacity to become perfected. But the second element in the Yogācāra answer lies in their invocation of an idea already articulated in the Pāli Buddhist literature, namely, that of the "luminous mind" (*prabhāsvaraṃ cittaṃ*). As we will see, the sudden reliance on this idea at a crucial stage in the Cognition school's account of enlightenment has perplexed many commentators. It not only seems out of place and perhaps even superfluous to the rest of the emancipatory process being described in the system but seems to give a positive description of emptiness (*śūnyatā*), the source of all transformation, at the precise point where all other oppositional and differentiating attributes of emptiness are being denied of it. But the Vijñānavādins insist that such an ever-luminous mind lies at our core, and if it were not so, then everything that would happen to us, including enlightenment itself, would have to be explained away as mere contingency (*āgantuka*). This conviction that perfection already somehow resides whole and undiluted within us triggers an important reevaluation of human nature within the Buddhist tradition that, if not genealogically, at least thematically makes way for the transition to Chan and Zen in East Asia. And, as we will have the opportunity to see clearly in the following chapter, Huayen and Chan Buddhists were quite aware of this and employed it in their articulation of human authenticity.

Bodily-Cognitive Interdependence

For all the prevalent and understandable talk of Yogācāra "idealism," it often goes quite unnoticed that the arising and ceasing of cognitions in this system is represented in often irreducibly sensuous terms. And in this, it is continuous with and not disruptive of the foregoing Buddhist philosophical discourse. In some cognitions, the sense organs, given their constitution and interaction with the environment, are the decisive and not merely, as in Brāhmiṇical thought, the instrumental causes. However, in the construction of our ideations of things, while the organs may produce cognitions that arise from their interaction with the elemental character of things, these are almost always accompanied by cognitions that originate in our habits of objective differentiation and feeling. Sensory cognitions then do not, in most cases, occur independently from feeling and disposition cognitions. They are not the same cognition, and they are by no means reducible to one another, but in our experience, they almost always work in tandem.

> tritiyaḥ ṣadvidhasya ya /
> viṣayasya upalabdhiḥ sa kuśalākuśala adva ya //. . .
> paṅcānām mūlavijñāne yathā pratyayam udbhavaḥ /
> vijnānānām saha na vā taraṅgāṇām yathā jale //

> What is from the third (transformation of cognitions) is of the sixfold apprehension of objects; which could be pure, impure, or indifferent . . . There is arising of the five (sense cognitions) in the root cognition in accordance with causal conditions. There are cognitions either (occurring) together or not (together) in just the same way as waves (arise) in water. (*Triṃśatikā* 8, 15)
>
> abhūtaparikalpaśca citta caitas tridhātukāḥ /
> tatra artha dṛṣṭir vijñānam tad viśaṣe tu ciattasāḥ //
> ekam pratyata vijñānam dvitiyam aupabhogikam /
> upabhoga pariccheda prerakas tatra caittasāḥ //
>
> The imagination of nonphysical things is mind and mental activities, and is so in the constitution of (all) three realms. There (occurs) a cognition that is the seer of objects, but it is from mental activities wherein its particularity (is found). One is the primary basing cognition, the second is the enjoyment (cognition). The mental activities, then, are enjoyment, discrimination, and motivation. (*Madhyānta Vibhāga* 1:9–10)

We must clarify at the outset that what is being spoken of here as the "five sensory cognitions" and the "sixfold apprehension of objects" are drawn rather straightforwardly from the early Buddhist discourses as well as Abhidharma categories. In this framework, the five kinds of sensory cognitions are visual (*caksu*), auditory (*śrotra*), olfactory (*grāhṇa*), gustatory (*jihvā*), and tactile (*kāya*) with the inner sense (*manas*) serving, as in most classical South Asian models, as the sixth sense organ, and their corresponding organs are of course the eyes, ears, nose, tongue, skin, and internal sensory organ. In most interpretations of Abhidharma, the sensibilia that are visible, tangible, elemental qualities (*dharma*) of things are referred to as the "external spheres" (*bāhyāntana*-s) of cognition, whose elements are, as has become a familiar theme, made of the same stuff out of which the sense organs themselves are made. Even the earliest of canonical discourses affirmed over and over that cognitions did not occur at the behest of either the essence or agency of some abiding spiritual consciousness but only when the necessary contact (*sannipāte*) between the sense organs and their corresponding external elements produced them. In the preceding stanzas, there is no denial that cognitions that merely see, or perceive, their objects occur, nor that the arising of cognitions is dependent on the entire array of necessary causal conditions (*pratyaya*-s). However, in prototypical Vijñānavāda fashion, these cognitions arise, or are given their primary impetus and almost all of their ideational content, from other cognitions that are their primary cause or most proximate basis (*pratyata vijñāna*).

The activities of cognition (*caitta*-s) are enumerated as "enjoyment," "discrimination" (*pariccheda*), and "motivation" (*preraka*), and it is these that confer upon a mere undifferentiated object (*artha*) its particularity (*viśeṣa*). We will shortly delve a bit more into the most fundamental mechanics of how this particularity is rendered. But the result of these mental activities is the imagination or distinctive ideation (*parikalpa*) that, as it appears and feels to us, does not correspond to any physical thing (*abhūta*) but instead has only those physical characteristics (*bhautika*-s) that our basic or "root" cognitions themselves attribute to them. This near-complete autonomy of the root cognitions to construct our experiences of things has led both many classical Indian and Chinese commentators and no small number of modern ones to think of Vijñānavādins as some sort of "absolute idealists" or purveyors of the thesis that only consciousness is real. Such readings are not in the strict sense warranted given that the sense organs continue to play indispensable roles in the kinds of cognitions that are enumerated in the system. We shall also explore this further in greater detail later. We do not find in these texts a denial that physical things (*bhūta*-s) exist but merely an insistence that in whatever experiences we have that consist of ideational content, that content does not derive from physical qualities.[4] Indeed, the commentator Sthīramati in places asserts that cognitions that involve any of the sense organs as causal conditions depend on sense organs being in contact with their objects. This contrasts conspicuously with what we saw of the Nyāya position in the preceding chapter, as the Vijñānavādins, while arguing for sense organ and object contact, replace the conscious *ātman* of the Naiyāyikas with the occurrent cognitions themselves.

trayānām hi indriyaviṣayavijñāna sannipāte /
indriyasya sukhādivedanā utpatti /
anukūla yas triprakāra vikāras tatpariccheda sparśaḥ /

> Of the threefold (transformation of cognition), there occurs contact between the sense organ, object, and cognition. (Thereupon,) the pleasant sensation and so on of the sense organs arises. Touch (*sparśa*) is the modification that discriminates whatever multifarious kinds the threefold (transformation of cognition) take the form of. (*Madhyānta Vibhāga Kārika Bhāṣya Tikā* 1:11)

We notice here that there is a terminological distinction between "touch," which describes the imbuing of cognitions with affective feeling, and the "contact" that must exist between a sense organ (*indriya*), its object (*viṣāya*), and cognition (*vijñāna*) that is an independently identifiable part of the process of cognitive transformation. While affect-permeated sensations do not originate from the objects of the sense organs, sense organ contact with their objects must occur for a specific cognition to arise. Now, this hardly detracts from the fact that, in this framework, it is the "touch" of internally generated affect that provides for the proliferation of cognitive discrimination (*pariccheda*) with regard to the objects encountered. But without the object of sense organ contact, no full account could be given of cognitions in the first place. In classical Vijñānavāda, then, sensuous bodily experience is an indispensable part of the cognitive process, and this part of the account treads on long-established Abhidharma ground.

As was alluded to earlier, it is indeed quite significant that the Cognition school emphasizes the capacities of the sense organs themselves to facilitate cognitions that are specific (*vijñāna*-s) to them. In contrast to the Brāhmiṇical systems we examined in the previous chapter, which took the sense organs to be the instrumental cause (*kāraṇa*), and thus merely the unconscious machinery of the self, Sthīramati calls the same sense organs the "basing causal condition" (*ālambanapratyaya*). It is only in accordance with the arising of such cognitions that any sense of self can be acquired to begin with.

> yathā pratyayam udbhāvaḥ iti /
> yasya yasya yaḥ pratyayaḥ sannihitasṭasya tasya /
> niyamena udbhāvaḥ ātma lābhaḥ /
>
> (it is said that) "according to the arising of the causal condition," whatever causal condition delivers an impression

> of anything, it is by such means that there is arising of self-apprehension. (*Triṃśatikā Bhāṣya* 1:15)

Sense consciousness, that is, serves as a precondition for the arising of a sense of self-awareness, not the other way round as the Brāhmiṇical philosophers would have it. Furthermore, as we shall see in a subsequent section, sensory cognitions continue to operate via the living body of the enlightened person even after any residual sense of self is supposedly eliminated entirely. It turns out then that sensory cognitions may and do operate quite apart from a grounding in self-consciousness. No preexisting or enduring conscious self uses the sense organs as its tools to become aware of the outside world of things and the inside world of feeling, but instead, the sense organs themselves produce these awarenesses. To that degree, then, the living body in Cognition school thought can be considered a conscious organism that is in contact with a world.

However, it is at the same time crucial to emphasize that the degree of awareness the sense organs can account for leaves a very great deal of what we ordinarily take to be our conscious lives yet to be explained. After all, the sense organs in Vijñānavāda do not themselves distinguish between their various sensory spheres, they do not account for how we take our experiences to be our own, nor do they serve as the wellsprings of our habits, memories, inclinations, or potentials. The body then provides for some of our awareness but decidedly not all of it. Our orientation in the world and our sense of identity are produced by quite distinctive transformations of mind.

"Self" as a Reification of Habits

The notion of psychic seeds (*bija*) is surely not a Vijñānavāda invention. In the construals of Abhidharma exegesis, the idea of a psychic seed was introduced to explicate how, in an impermanent world, memories, potentialities, and habits could be retained from one moment to the next and one lifetime to the next. More specifically, in foregoing Sautrāntika commentarial literature, a seed was said to be a "power" (*śakti*) for perpetuating obsessive attachments through the process of rebirth and redeath.[5] However, the "theory of momentariness" (*kṣanikavāda*) that began to prevail among the

Sautrāntikas, which stipulated that no feature of one moment of awareness survived into the next, naturally gave rise to the question of how it was possible for psychic seeds to transfer their powers and inherited obsessions to successive moments, not merely between lifetimes but even within one lifetime, if none of their features survived the one moment they exist. Indeed, as centuries passed, the Yogācāra Sautrāntika view of momentariness seemed to grow only more radical. For example, while the compiler of the *Abhidharmakośabhāṣya* tries to reconcile the theory of momentariness with memory by claiming that memories are not "owned" by a self but by the initial experience that facilitated the memory, the eleventh-century logician Ratnakīrti rejects the very idea that the remembered impression is identical in any way with the initially experienced object.[6] For the Yogācāra Sautrāntikas then, defending the Buddhist doctrine of impermanence implied an outright denial of any real continuity or even any viable sense of continuous identity. This problem led our Vijñānavāda Yogācārins to postulate that a psychic seed resided in a basis (*āśraya*), which they famously dubbed the "abode cognition," better-known as the "storehouse consciousness" (*ālayavijñāna*).[7] The transformations of this repository of cognitions make possible the maintaining and perpetuation of our psychological tendencies through time. These habits impel us to both cognitively and affectively discriminate between different objects of our experience and, when this process is itself objectified, serve as the basis for our ego identity.

In simplest terms, the seeds of the "storehouse consciousness" or "abode cognitions" are habituated tendencies that have been built up through a heritage of causally connected lifetimes. These include what we might term perceptual habits, our tendency to see things and people in our environment in accordance with our own accreted experience, attitudinal habits—including attractions, repulsions, and indifference—and behavioral habits, tendencies to act in paradigmatic ways in various situations. These habits can be characterized either by particularized obsessive attachment that brings upon us various kinds of affliction (*kleśa*) either in the presence or nonpossession of something or the absence of such attachment and affliction. All of these habits can either lie dormant or be activated depending upon the specific experiences we are having at any moment. On its own, however, so long as it is not influenced by persisting attachments, the constant, onrushing transformations of the "storehouse consciousness" are "indifferent" (*upekṣa*), even while its connections to sensation, cognitions, and volitions persist.

> tatra ālayākhya vijñānam vipākaḥ sarvabijākam /
> asaṃviditakopādisthānavijñāptikam ca tat //
> sadā sparśamanaskāravitsaṅjñācetanā anvitam /
> upekṣavedanā tatra anvṛtā avyakṛtam ca tat //
> tathā sparśa ādayastacca vartate srotasaugavat /
> tasya vyakṛtis arhattve //

> There, in what is called storehouse consciousness, is the fruition that is the nature of all the seeds. And that is what makes up the ideations of these collective cognitions, remembrances, intimations, and situations. There is a persistent connection with touch, mental construction, knowledge, sensation, and volition. It is, furthermore, there indifferent to feelings, unconcealed, and not to be articulated. It is thus unreceptive to touch and its action and has the nature of onrushing water. In the perfected renouncer, there is disassociation from it. (*Triṃśātika* 2–4)

The abode cognition, or "storehouse consciousness," maintains during life a persisting connection (*anvita*) with sensations, mental activity, and even the "touch" (*sparśa*) with which feelings (*vedanā*) imbue our awareness. However, even in the midst of this abiding connection, and despite the torrential river of our ever-flowing experiences, so long as it is not covered (*avṛta*) with attachments, the abode cognitions that are the maturing seeds maintain a state of indifference (*upekṣa*). It is not, therefore, the fact that we have sensations, feelings, or even mental constructions (*manaskāra*), ideations, or imaginations (*vijñāpti*) that presents a problem for human existence. What most fundamentally differentiates an "afflicted" seed from a "non-afflicted" seed is whether or not the cognitive, attitudinal, or behavioral habit it embodies is motivated by a tendency to distinguish between what is called the "grasper" (*grāhaka*) of the habit and the things toward which the grasping activity is directed (*grāhya*). In the ongoing process of cognitions, absent the imagination of the difference between grasped and grasper (*grāhya grāhaka vikalpa*), there is, insofar as any given awareness must be a cognition, a unity of the grasped content that is mediated by the external or internal sense organs and the attributions of objectivity that the abode cognitions make to them.[8] It is the introduction of the imagined distinction between grasper and grasped that lights the spark that sets aflame the fuel of desire and attachment, for it creates the basic separation in psychological life between self (*ātman*) and thing (*dharma*). This imagined separation in its own turn creates the distance between them that desire attempts to eliminate through pursuit and acquisition, which, in time, is always frustrated.

So then, how is this distinction between self and thing first imagined into existence in the life of awareness in the Vijñānavāda view? On the "grasped" side of the equation, as we have seen, seeds that have accreted the habits from foregoing experiences of imagining physical characteristics (*bhautika*-s), such as color, texture, qualities of taste and smell, and so on, and attributing them to things that do not possess them (*abhūta parikalpa*) create though these attributions the panoply of our "graspable" objects. A visible thing, for example, while it does have a form of some sort, is not itself "really" red or orange; nor is a touchable thing, though it does have a physical surface, "really" rough or smooth; nor is something that can be tasted, though it does contain different ingredients, "really" bitter or sweet. It is our own habituated imaginations that associate these characteristics with things that we sense. Once again, this process of imagination that imbues things with cognitive and affective qualities does not of itself present a problem. After all, even in the perfect renouncer (*arhat*), while there is a psychological disassociation (*vyakṛti*) from these projections, they do continue to occur right up until the point when all the seeds of the abode cognitions have exhausted their capacity (*samārthya*) to transmit their habits to another embodied being, and at that point the termination of the life process occurs. It is the imagination of the self as grasper, which in part arises from these objectifying habits, that provides the key element in the desire-fueling process.

It is a particular, and quite contingent, kind of cognition that imagines a self into existence through an act of observation, and that cognition is dubbed the "deliberatively naming cognition" (*manonāmavijñāna*). The "deliberate name" it uniquely assigns is the name "self."

> tad āśritya pravartate /
> tad ālamban manonāmavijñānam mananātmakam //
> kleśais caturbhiḥ sahita nivṛta avyakṛtai sadā /
> ātma dṛṣṭi ātma moha ātma māna ātma sneha saṅjṅitai //
> yatrajas tanmayair anyaiḥ sparśa ādyaiśca arhatp na tat /
> na nirodha sannāpatau mārge lokottare na ca //
> dvittyaḥ pariṇāmo'yam /
>
> Its activity being based in and apprehending that (the abode cognitions), it is the deliberatively naming cognition, and its nature is deliberation. It is associated with four afflictions and is always concealed and unarticulated; the view of self, pride of self, thought of self, love of self. (It is also associated) with other (things) like touch, and the rest, that are constituted of that which is found where there is birth. It does not exist with the perfect renouncer, nor in the state of suppression, nor on the path that is marked by stillness and transcends the world. This is the second transformation. (*Triṃśātika* 5–7)

The cognition that says the word "I" does so by internally sensing the abode cognitions, taking them as its "objective support" (*ālambana*) just as the sense organs take external things and internal feelings as their objective supports, and then deliberating (*manana*). Its deliberation results in the notion of self (*ātman*) and the subsequent attachment to it that results in pride and other emotive valuations. It must be keenly noticed that the vocabulary used here is intentionally meant to distinguish this Buddhist concept of self-formation from the ego formation that is spoken of in Brāhmiṇical thought. In the latter, the ego is a false objectification of the mere body as the self, whereas the actual self is spiritual. Here, in Vijñānavāda thought, the notion of "I" is not a false objectification of the body but instead a false objectification of the accreted habits, inclinations, and potentialities of the abode cognitions, and out of that objectification arises the fabrication, the mere imagination, of a self (*ātman*) where there "really" is none, where all that really is there is a constantly changing accretion of collective habits that are housed in one psychophysical store. It is also most conspicuous here that, after enlightenment occurs to the perfect renouncer, the Vijñānavāda texts assert that, while the objectifying powers of the seeds persist until death, the notion of self has been entirely eliminated. The real power behind the imagined distinction between grasper and grasped then lies in the fabricated imagination of the grasper; it is the decisive source of all our afflictions.

Just how far the Vijñānavādins went in insisting that the notion of self was nothing more than the sheer imagination created by the "deliberatively naming cognition" can be gleaned from provocative statements they make about such topics as intersubjectivity and murder. These arguments are found in the *Viṃśātika*, but we must touch on them here, as opponents of Vijñānavāda believed the following examples were tantamount to the denial that real, distinct individuals exist.

> deśa ādi niyamaḥ siddaḥ svapnavat pretavat punaḥ /
> santāna aniyamaḥ sarvaiḥ pūyanadī ādi darśane //
>
> Establishing the determination of location and all else is already possessed in sleep and by ghosts; there is no determination of continuity in the visual perception of the river of pus and all else (in hell) by all of them. (*Viṃśātika* 3)
>
> anyonya adhipatitvena vijñāpti niyama mithaḥ /
> middhena upahatam cittam svapna tena asamam phalam //
> maranam paravijñāpti viśeṣād vikriyā yathā /
> smṛti lopādikā anyeṣām piśācādi manovaśāt //
> katham vā daṇdakārasya śūnyatvam ṛṣīkopataḥ /
> mano daṇdo mahāvadyaḥ katham vā tena sidyati //
>
> The mutual determination of mental acts is the means by which (beings) mentally influence one another. By sloth, the mind is overpowered in sleep, and the fruits (acquired) by that (sleep) are unequal. Just as, from particular mental activities, there is the change of death, the interruptions of memory are brought about by demons' and other beings' minds. How, otherwise, could the Daṇdaka forest have been rendered into naught by the sages' anger? How, otherwise, could mental injury be widely spoken of as a commission of indolence by them? (*Viṃśātika* 17–19)

Such passages have made it sound to many commentators as if Vijñānavāda proffers the view that other beings are merely illusory, since they supposedly posit that there is no difference between intersubjectivity in waking and dream life and that bringing about death is nothing more than a mental act instead of a physical act. What is, however, being denied in the first passage is that the experience of continuity (*santāna*) is anything more than a mental construction, as it can be experienced in sleep as well as in waking life. The second passage defends the notion that the mind of one being can not only influence the minds of others (*anyonya*) but can bring about things like the destruction of real forests. Indeed, in the text's most proximate commentary, also attributed to Vasubandhu, the elaboration of the final verse explicitly makes the point that, when one being's mind brings about the death of another being, the harm that results in that death occurs to the victim's bodily "vital organs" (*jivita indriya*). It is not, then, the plurality of individuals that is being refuted here, but instead something is being forcefully affirmed, namely, the powers of the mind, powers that, when they become destructive, can often bring great harm upon others.

More than any other Buddhist philosophers in South Asia, the Vijñānavādins went to great efforts to explain our experience of continuous identity in analytical detail. Other Buddhist thinkers, from the inception of the tradition, were so furiously focused on the insistence that nothing in our experience justifies the belief in a stable, unchanging identity, despite the Brāhmiṇical philosophers' convictions, that even many internal attempts to account for the fact that we have a sense of identity, however logically problematic this sense may be, were quashed for fear of giving countenance to some mutated conception of selfhood. The Cognition school attempted to explain both our sense of continuous identity as well as its artificial and manufactured status with their elaborate model of human cognition. The cost of constructing this detailed model was that they had to court some potentially dangerous metaphysical problems and misunderstandings.

One of these problems was the notion that the psychic seeds that carried our habits and dispositions were posited to have a psychic abode as their basis (*āśraya*). The notion that ever-changing phenomena could never simply wander about in empty space, as it were, but had to be attached in some way to a locus was a very familiar presupposition of Brāhmiṇical metaphysics, and we have seen examples of it in both Sāṃkhya's argument that the karmic body's basis was in the web of natural causes and in Nyāya's axiom that cognitions had their basis in a spiritual self.

To suggest that the *ālayavijñāna* was the *āśraya* of the karmic seed tendencies ran the risk of reifying the former into a metaphysical substrate (*dharmin*) of its own kind. The Vijñānavādins made this philosophical move, however, to buttress their account of our experienced sense of continuity, both in that the "abode cognition" served as a place wherein presently inactive seeds could be stored up or housed and in that the "deliberatively naming cognition" could behold something as its basis (*ālambana*) and reify it as a persistent self. Indeed, Vijñānavāda commentators refer to the *ālayavijñāna* as the causal condition that always precedes (*samantatara pratyaya*) the occurrence of any other cognition and thus can be considered the root (*mūla*) of all cognitions. Brāhmiṇical Naiyāyikas and Buddhist Mādhyamikas alike believed that, in representing things in this way, the Cognition school philosophers had basically made *ālayavijñāna* into their own version of a self.[9] And, at the very least, in the larger context of the meditative traditions, the "abode cognition" does seem to bear some general resemblance to the Sāṃkhya notion of the karmic body or *liṅgam*. The Vijñānavāda texts try to dull such charges with their repeated remonstrance that the "abode cognition" is itself only a distinct set of transformations (*pariṇāma*) that is exhausted at the death of a perfect renunciant and is not survived by anything like an enduring self.[10] At any rate, the thinkers of the Cognition school were adamant that, despite the fact that the notion of an enduring inner self is both a fabrication and the worst culprit in our suffering, the experience that intimated of such a self, the experience of continuous identity, required nothing less than a thorough philosophical explanation.

Given that other contemporary Indian theories of human existence tended to invest the most authentic sense of personhood in the eternal, spiritual self, it may be tempting to see the Buddhists, who reject the entire notion of selfhood as in some way anti-personalist, or, at the very least, committed to a project that has a kind of depersonalization as its ultimate aim. While it is, of course, the case that, with their conception of final *nirvāṇa* or "extinguishing," the Buddhists envision a termination of a certain karmically connected heritage of persons, it would be misleading to think of an enlightened being, as conceived by Vijñānavādins, as no longer a person. While the *arhat* in Vijñānavāda has presumably eliminated all vestiges of the false notion of selfhood as well as disassociated herself from obsessive attachments to everything in her environment, that in no way entails that, before death, the enlightened practitioner no longer has experiences, feelings, or even habituated inclinations. We will discuss the latter more fully in the next section. But, for the moment, it is important to emphasize that the Buddhist conception of enlightenment not only leaves body, senses, perceptions, feelings, and interactions with others functioning, but, if anything, it incredibly enhances each of these through the removal of their previous domination by egocentric habits, biases, and "self"-enclosing limitations. Arhatship is the pinnacle, the ideal, of human existence, an ideal for which human existence is uniquely and solely suited, and decidedly not, at least not before death, its terminus. The modes of enlightened existence and compassionate bodhisattvahood represent the most provocative archetypes of human achievement in Buddhism, for they embody the possibility of living a human life that is not fundamentally driven by obsessive compulsion, the possibility that persons can not only survive and thrive without desire and ego but can reach perfection without them.

But since the hypostatized self, for the Buddhists, did indeed lie at the foundation of all our delusions, futile aspirations, and pain, it required not just a detailed explanation but also a solution, or, more accurately, a dissolution. But how, given the incredible and powerful store of accreted egoistic habits, is such a dissolution possible? As it turns out, the habits that are stored up in our inherited seeds of inclination and action are not all shot through with affliction. On the contrary, some of them, according to the Cognition school, are pure, perfect, and luminous. Our very awakenings, before their potentialities are fully released through practice, are stored up within us.

Stored-Up Awakening and the Luminous Mind

We recall at the outset of this section that the abode cognitions, when they merely operate on the basis of their maturation from foregoing seeds, have the basic disposition of indifference, "overlooking" or "ignoring" (*upekṣa*) whatever impulsions of feeling or habit that past experiences compel upon the unenlightened person. In like manner, the potentialities of the third transformation of cognition, those of the bodily sense organs themselves, may not only be afflicted and attachment producing, but also merit-making. That is to say, cognitions, whether they originate from seeds or from active sensation and inner sense, can be either good or bad depending on their co-occurrent conditions.

> sarvatra gair viniyotaiḥ kuśalaiś cetasair asau /
> samprayakta tatha kleśair upakleśais trivedanā //
> ādyāḥ sparśadayat chanda adhimokṣa smṛtayaḥ saha /
> samādhi dhibhyām niyataḥ śraddhā atha hrīr apatrapā //
> alobhā ādi trayam viryam praśrabdhiḥ sa apramādikā /
> ahiṃsā kuṣalāḥ kleśa rāga pratigha mūḍhayaḥ //
>
> It proceeds together with all of the mental activities that are distinct, good, and general, as well is with afflictions of the primary type, secondary afflictions, and the three feelings. The general are touch and the rest, together with allure, concentration on release, and memory, meditation, illumination, restraint, faith, as well as shame and embarrassment. Non-covetousness and the rest, valor, tranquility, inerrancy, non-harm, are the third, the good, while passion, enmity and acting out of foolishness are the afflictions. (*Triṃśātika* 9–11)

The experiences that emerge from sensory cognitions are termed by the Vijñānavādins forms of enjoyment (*upabhoga*), in contrast to the mere indifference of the abode cognitions. But, merely because a sensory cognition may partake in enjoyment is not in itself censorable; on the contrary, there are forms of enjoyment cognition that are positively good (*kuśala*), such as concentration on release, faith, shame, and so on, which can all be conducive to meritorious practice. Indeed, the only one of the three transformations of cognition that is never associated with merit is the second, the cognition responsible for the manufacture of the "self." If, that is, Buddhist praxis and the approach to ultimate awakening can be experienced with satisfaction, freedom, and joy, it is because the active forms of enjoyment cognition make it so, and there is nothing to derogate in this.

However, to reiterate the question asked at the end of the last section, how precisely is the dissolution of our afflictions, rooted as they are in the postulation of a false self, brought about? It cannot simply be haphazard or uncaused, for that would militate against the entire South Asian Buddhist conviction that, just as suffering is a contingency of life tied to identifiable causes, so release from suffering can be achieved through the effects of praxis. In the Vijñānavāda texts attributed directly to Vasubandhu, the argument is proffered that, once the features projected onto things by our own consciousness are recognized as such, and once the activity of the "deliberatively naming cognition" that reifies the abode cognition into a self has been halted, the resulting awareness itself brings about enlightenment. The elimination of the imagined difference between the merely cognitively produced, and not independently real, "grasper" (*grāhya*) and the "grasped" content we falsely take to characterize things (*grāhaka*) allows for the arising of what these root texts call alternatively "world transcending knowledge" (*jñānam lokotaram*) and "apprehension of the limitedness of things as only seeming" (*syād vibhūtva upalambhatā*).[11] Consistent with foregoing Buddhist teachings, this accomplishment would presumably be the outcome of practice. However, as the Cognition school developed, its thinkers delved further into the problem of how psychological habituations of objectification and self-making that had been so strongly reinforced through incalculable lifetimes could be uprooted. The tradition's philosophers ultimately tended toward the view that the causal support of complete psychological transformation and final liberation could not be the same as the causal support for the afflictions and ignorance that keep us tied to our obsessions and the world of rebirth.

It is here, where Vijñānavāda makes its transition from classical South Asian to Chinese thought, where one of the key steps in our narrative is taken, and we find it taken in the translations and commentaries of Paramārtha.[12] Adopting a term used only once in the *Abhidharmakośabhāṣya* to describe enlightened realization as producing no karmic effects of its own, Paramārtha labels another kind of cognition, entirely distinct from the "abode cognition" and which serves as the basis of enlightenment, the "untainted cognition" (*amalavijñāna*, 阿摩羅識). In other words, in Paramārtha's line of Vijñānavāda thought, a very specific moment of realization that fundamentally transforms the character of all successive cognitions is talked of as a continuing (*nitya*) basis of purity from which experienced enlightenment can emerge.

> All that is included under the head of defilements (煩惱 *kleśa*) in the category of karmic conditioning (i.e. "volition," *saṃskāra, skandha,* 行) is gathered together in the fundamental consciousness (*ālayavijñāna*) [thus, when,] because of repeated cultivation (*āsevita-bhāvita*) on the part of wisdom that takes Thusness as its objective support (*tathatā-alambanavijñāna*), the fundamental consciousness is abandoned, which is to say that a revolutionary transformation (*parāvṛtti*) is brought about in the nature of the ordinary worldling (凡夫性 *pṛthagjanatva*), such that all the qualities of the ordinary worldling (凡夫法, *pṛthagjanadharmāḥ*) are discarded, then the fundamental consciousness is extinguished.
>
> Because this consciousness is extinguished, all defilements are extinguished, and by means of [the] counteragent(s) (對治 *pratipakṣa*) to the fundamental consciousness, the *amalavijñāna* is realized. . . . The fundamental consciousness is the basis 根本 for all the defilements but does not act 作 as a basis 根本 for the noble path (聖道, *ārya mārga*). *Alamanavjñāna,* on the other hand, is not the basis for the defilements but only 但 acts as a basis for the noble path and the attainment of the path. The *amalavijñāna* acts as a cause for the predurance (*pratiṣṭhā-hetu*) but does not act as a cause for the generation (*janma-hetu*) of it.
>
> *Jueding zang lun* 1025c26–35a17 (Radich 2008, 52–53, 54)[13]

Very shortly after this passage, in a gloss of other Vijñānavāda commentaries that explicitly deal with the locus of purified seeds after enlightenment continuing to be located in the "abode," Paramārtha very conspicuously locates the possibility for the world-transcending *dharma*-s noted previously in the "untainted cognition."

> In the perspective of the established exposition of the fundamental consciousness, we would rather say: "All worldly *dharma*-s take the fundamental consciousness as their basis, whereas all transcendent *dharma*-s (一历周法出世間者, *sarvadharmāḥ lokottarāḥ*) and *dharma*-s of the path not

> to be abandoned have *amalavijñāna* as their basis. (*Jueding zang lun* 1022a15–17 [Radich 2008, 60])

Paramārtha goes to great lengths in his works to emphasize, even in contrast to what the root texts of his own school overtly claim, that the "untainted cognition" not only has nothing in common with the "abode cognitions," since the latter contain only afflicted seeds and the former only pure ones, but also that the *ālayavijñāna* actually dissipates and ceases to exist upon enlightenment. At that point, the *amalavijñāna* takes over the life span of the physical body until the final death of both.

In tandem with the notion of the "untainted cognition" as explaining the possibility for enlightenment and the complete transformation of consciousness, Paramārtha's writings also align it with some elusive but still pivotal references in the root texts of the tradition to the "luminous mind." In the *Madhyānta Vibhāga*, at the conclusion of a discussion about how the transformations of cognition, since they contain seeds of both afflicted and nonattached habituations and thus exhibit the potentialities for both continued suffering and liberation, a scriptural reference to the "luminous mind" is invoked.

> saṅkliṣṭaced bhaven na asau muktās tyuḥ sarva dehinaḥ /
> viśuddhāced bhaven na asau vyānāna niṣphala bhavet //
> na kliṣṭā na api vā akliṣṭā śuddhā aśuddhā na ca eva sā /
> katham na kliṣṭā na api ca aśuddha prakṛtyā eva //
> prabhāsvaratvāc cittasya /
> kleśasya āgantukatvataḥ //

> If it were not continuously afflicted, then all embodied beings would be ever released; If it were not purified, then (even) breathing in would be without any fruit. It is not afflicted nor is it nonafflicted; it is not pure, nor indeed is it impure. How can it be neither afflicted nor again impure? This is owing to its primordial nature (*prakṛtyā*). Its nature is the luminosity of the mind, its possession of affliction is contingent. (*Madhyānta Vibhāga* 22–23)

The contingency of an unenlightened state of mind was a standing feature of Buddhism since its inception, as we have noted. The bedrock doctrine of *pratitya-samutpāda* or "(causally) conditioned co-arising" articulated in the earliest of the Buddha's discourses stipulated that present desires arose out of past circumstances and could be removed through practice. The present stanzas reemphasize that idea by arguing that, if consciousness were essentially afflicted, liberation would be impossible, whereas if consciousness were essentially pure, practice would be fruitless. But then, at the conclusion of the text, both the afflicted and pure states of consciousness are said to be grounded in the mind's luminosity (*prabhāsvara*). This final verse has appeared to many to be simply out of place, given the furious efforts of the text up to that point to stress that the mind is, in itself, nothing more than a streamlike series of transformations (*pariṇāma*) and that its emptiness (*śūnyatā*) consists in both the unreality of its projection of the self-object distinction and the capacity of consciousness to both posit and then negate that distinction. Suddenly, we have a stanza that says of the mind (*citta*) as a whole that its possession of luminosity, or alternatively "splendor" or "clarity," accounts for the contingency of its imperfections. Recent scholars have suspected that the stray reference may be a scriptural quotation, since the Pāli lexical equivalent of *prabhāsvaraṃ cittaṃ* is alluded to in the Nikāyas.[14] However, the early Buddhist scriptures appear to associate this terminology of the "luminous mind" with constant practice. Specifically, keeping the mind luminous required both the techniques of disciplining it to concentrate on fleeting (*javana*) states like compassion and kindness as well as on prolonged and methodically preserved meditative states of tranquility (*bhavaṅga*) that are also described as luminous.[15] Sthīramati attempts to resolve this conundrum with the assertion that the locution "luminous mind" in this instance should be understood as meaning nothing more than the basic nature (*dharmatā*) of mind, which is supposedly equated with the mind's emptiness by Vasubandhu anyway.[16] For his own part, Paramārtha, following closely upon his earlier connection between the possibility of enlightenment and "untainted cognition," links the notion of the "luminous mind" with *alamavijñāna*.[17] He argues, in an addendum to his commentary on the *Madhyānta Vibhāga* verses cited immediately before, that impurity is a contingent defilement of the "untainted cognition" itself.

> If we say that the principle 理 (*li*) of emptiness is absolutely impure, then all efforts would be inefficacious 無果報, because the essential nature (自性, *svabhāva*) of the element

> of emptiness (空接, *śūnyatādhātu*) itself would be impure; and therefore, even when the path had arisen 生道, one would remain incorrigibly worldly/profane 俗不可除, so that the path would be useless. Because it is not thus 無此義故, we know that emptiness is not impure by nature.
>
> Question: If this is the case, then given that there is no impurity by essential nature 自性净, how can it be ascertained 分判 that the *dharma* realm (法接 *dharmadhātu*) is neither pure nor impure?
>
> Answer: *Amalavijñāna* is the aboriginally pure (Skt. "luminous") mind (自性清净心, *prakṛtiprabhāsvaracitta*). It is only because it is tainted 污 by adventitious dirt 客塵 that we speak of it as "impure"; because of adventitious dirt, [that is,] we establish that it is also impure. (*Shiba kong lun* 863b06–21 Radich [2008, 74–75])

In a separate but related commentarial context, Paramārtha identifies "untainted cognition" with what remains of consciousness, which is to say its real and enduring principle, after both cognitions that are implicated in imaginary projection and the "abode cognition" have been quite literally eliminated by the experience of awakening. He indeed reiterates in many late commentarial passages equivalent assertions that the "taintless cognition," being one with "thusness" or ultimate reality, may be considered the only thing, in the strictest sense, actually existent. This also solidifies him as one of the first thinkers of the Cognition school to assert the theme of so-called absolute idealism as the hallmark of Yogācāra thought.

> In the perspective/stage of perfect insight (正觀, *abhisamaya*), we dispose of 遗荡 both the deluded consciousness and mind of *saṃsāra*, and of its object, [such that] both are completely purified, and there is only the taintless (阿摩羅, *amala*), pure, luminous mind (清净心, *prabhāsvara-citta*). (*Shiba kong lun* 864a25–28 [Radich 2008, 78])

We see in the making here the distinctive step taken toward the promulgation of a doctrine of a pure, luminous mind that underlies the more common mind of sensations, emotions, and volitions. For many reasons, this step was to be a seminal one in the history of Buddhist thought. It seems certainly to be so in the case of Vijñānavāda, for commentators both classical and modern have tended to view the root texts and earliest works in the school to ultimately treat the differentiations among *vijñāna*, starting from the sensory cognitions and including the "abode cognitions" themselves as functional and even metaphorical in nature. Since, in the strictest terms, this representation runs, all early philosophers of the school speak of are transformations of cognition that causally belong to a stream, any talk of discretely separate "kinds" or "levels" or "bases" of cognition is only an analytical manner of speaking that helps, ideally, to facilitate insight into the sources of our fixations. In addition, as has been outlined, early Vijñānavāda thought seems to place, within this very stream of cognitive flow between the six sense cognitions, the identity-manufacturing cognition, and the abode cognitions, tendencies that both can tie one more firmly to world attachment or enable one to take delight in and cultivate Buddhist praxis.[18] Of course, as we have also seen, these philosophical commitments courted certain risks of metaphysical misunderstanding by both Brāhmiṇical adversaries and contesting Buddhist schools. But they did seem to stick close enough to Abhidharma precedent, despite important and unique developments, so as to give a new albeit faithful articulation of long-standing Buddhist principles of belief and practice. As Yogācāra continues to develop, and conspicuously as it enters the Chinese world, the idea that the possibility of thoroughly transformative wisdom had to reside in some core of the mind that remained ever clear and pure (清净心 *qing jing xin*) begins to take root. And those roots flourished into the centuries upon centuries of reflection and debate that were to give East Asian Buddhist thought its characteristic themes and controversies. These controversies extended from Xuanzang's reflections on whether or not all human beings possessed the potential for awakening to the debates between the Japanese transmitters Saichō and Tokuitsu over the same issue to the Buddha-nature theorists to modern-day discussions initiated by the "Critical Buddhism" scholarship speculating about how authentically Buddhist the latter lines of thought may be. We shall, in the following chapter, take a close look at where these strands of thought, at least philosophically initiated by Paramārtha, led in Chinese Huayen and Chan.

In the greater perspective of the second half of this study, we shall have occasion to reflect fully on how early Chinese thought, in its encounter with Buddhism, comes to entertain a broad-ranging and profound dialogue of mind with the Buddhist tradition as it was appropriated from the Indian subcontinent. As we have seen and will explore a bit further in coming chapters, the idea of an ever clear and pure mind was hardly unknown to the foregoing sediments of Chinese speculation, for such vocabulary had been employed to diverging but related ends in the slowly concretizing lineages of Confucian and Daoist thought in the context of both moral and mystico-social writings. But what emerged from this great, centuries-long philosophical encounter between the South and East Asian traditions was to become a provocative new source of inspiration to the reflections particularly of the latter cultural sphere. In thinking about human existence, about what it means to be a person in all spheres from the individual and meditative to the social and political, are there compelling reasons to believe that there is a luminous aspect to our consciousness that not only stands as an inalienable principle of our nature but also represents an ideal for our growth and our individual and shared aims? Philosophers, psychologists, and scientists of our own era, in their dedication to understanding the physical workings of the mind, as well as all the trauma and human frailty and evil of the last several centuries of human civilization, have perhaps given up on this conviction, compelled by the fragmentation, disunity, limitedness, and often hidden and dark motives that seem to have prevailed in our experience. With just as much energy and commitment, however, Chinese philosophers of the early and late Middle Ages tried to articulate a vision of the possibility of human perfection and map out the avenues for its realization, despite the fact that their own historical world was also horribly rent with disruption and chaotic violence. It ought to be remembered that Buddhist philosophers hardly deserve to be accused of underestimating human frailty and limitedness, with their long catalogues of deleterious emotions, their condemnation of identity as driven by hidden compulsions of acquisition, and their overarching tendency to see life as ultimately something that ought to be renounced. All the same, Buddhism in China persisted in seeing within human nature, not merely coexisting with these frailties but underlying and even supervening them, an unsullied core, its purity impenetrable, that gave, in the end, everyone without exception the potential for conquering not only their own delusions and limitations but for helping those around them to make these conquests also. This broadened and deepened conception of the heart and mind gave to Chinese Buddhism not merely a new metaphysical vocabulary but a new access to an ennobling vision of what it means, in the most profound senses, to be a person. The great legacy of the cross-cultural philosophical dialogue between South and East Asia promises still to hold something of enduring value for us, as we attempt better to understand it.

4

Mind, Nature and Conduct

Two Approaches of Chinese Buddhism

Chinese philosophical conceptions of personhood had, up till and through the arrival and flourishing of Buddhism, always been linked, sometimes vaguely but always closely, with the notion of 性 (*xing*). Commonly translated as "nature," 性 *xing*, in its most stringently literal senses, points alternatively to what leads to the "generation" or "birth" (生 *sheng*) of a being and what features or behaviors most immediately attend its phenomenal existence, such as a person's gender or most basic, life-preserving instincts or moods. In the first chapter, we dealt, though hardly comprehensively, with some of the resonances of pre-Buddhist Chinese philosophical speculations surrounding *xing*, in particular how it was invoked in moral arguments about the original dispositional endowments and capacities of the heart (心 *xin*).

Of course, the philosophical debates over the relationship between the activities of the heart and one's nature did not simply remain inert between early Chinese movements and the flourishing of the Buddhist tradition. Quite the contrary. These debates flourished and became more and more pertinent as the centuries passed and in ways that made the intellectual and spiritual ground, as it were, quite fertile for Buddhist contributions. Specifically, from the third to the fifth centuries CE, during the Wei-Jin period, trenchant discussions ensued between thinkers of the hermeneutically diverse "Dark Learning" (*xuanxue*) Daoists precisely about these issues. Alan K. L. Chan surmises that these issues arose from what he refers to as "two lines of argument in response to the problem of desire" that can already be found in the *Zhuangzi* as well as other early Confucian and proto-"Daoist" texts.[1] The problem that arose in this period had to do with how, though it was natural for the human heart to respond to things and events in the world with desires and judgments, it was also considered the consummation of "nature" for the true sage to transcend such desires and judgments, either by stilling them or eliminating them entirely. Wrapped up with these difficulties was the attendant problem of how the sage could possibly gain this capability, either through an usual endowment of inborn virtue not found in others or through a gradual and hard-won perfection in cultivation. Representing alternative "sides" on this latter question were He Yan and Zhong Hui, who maintained that sagehood must be a unique inborn disposition of "vital energy" or *qi*, and Wang Bi and Guo Xiang, who, believing that *dao* provided the ground for the formation of all things, insisted that all people in principle could draw from this inner basis in perfecting themselves. But perhaps most relevant to our present considerations is the vocabulary that Wang Bi began to employ in thematizing the ideal state of human existence and conduct. The perfected person could exhibit an attained degree of "spiritual luminosity" (神明 *shen ming*).[2] The sage is able, upon the acquisition of such "luminosity," to restore the emotions and desires of the heart, and thus one's nature, to a presumed "original" state of equanimity, balance, or stillness, and in so doing, restore one's present humanity to a state that, in concert with the *Zhuangzi*, both Wang and Guo label "genuineness" (真 *zhen*).[3] We see then that in native Chinese philosophical reflection, the possibility that the heart could be possessed of an imperturbable clarity, and even that such clarity could be inborn, was a living one by the time Vijńānavāda Buddhist texts were rendered into the intellectual environment. However, the Buddhists would effect this environment in deeply meaningful ways, for their framework pushed both the categories of the heart-mind and the original condition of nature to new levels of both abstraction and universality.

When Chinese Buddhist translators and thinkers employ the vocabulary of 心 *xin*, they tend to somewhat divest it of senses of feeling or emotion and align it with other terms such as "thought" (念 *nian*) and "knowledge" or "awareness" (知 *zhi*), showing a clear proclivity for understanding it as the Chinese equivalent for the Sanskrit term *citta*. But, given the enlightenment-enabling status granted to the concept of *citta* by the Vijñānavādins, Chinese Buddhists persisted in locating the most salient aspects of the nature of personhood in this recast idea of 心 *xin*. This inclination to locate the vital core of human nature in the "mind" would become unalterably defining as the centuries progressed, not merely for Chinese Buddhists but for the Neo-Confucian tradition as well.

The initial steps in this fateful conceptual connection were largely made by the Chinese rendition of the Vijñānavāda school known as 唯識 *Wei Shi* or "Consciousness Only" in the texts of its earliest major translators and commentators Xuanzang and Paramārtha. We examined in the final section of the previous chapter how this identification of alternatively pure seeds in the "abode cognition" and a separate pure, "untainted cognition" developed in Vijñānavāda thought. Perhaps contemporaneous with Xuan Zang and Paramārtha, a text claimed to have been translated from Sanskrit but probably a Chinese original known as the *Awakening of Faith in the Mahāyāna* (大乘起信論) cemented this connection. In the *Awakening*, "original enlightenment" (本覺 *ben jue*) is said to be a pregiven state of mind free from thoughts as well as objectifications of things and self. The fundamental existence of this root form of awakening makes the experience of enlightenment upon the culmination of practice possible. Despite the many varieties of doctrine and practice that arose and flourished in the Chinese tradition, most of which were disseminated to Korea and Japan, we can observe two basic ways in which this notion of an originally pure mind was employed by Chinese Buddhist thinkers. The first was, as noted, to identify this pure mind with the basis of our nature (性 *xing*) and thereby see in this natural grounding of personhood an explanation not merely for how we can transform from an unenlightened to an enlightened state but also for how we are born into the world as persons in the first place. The second approach attempted to show how our possession of this originally luminous mind, if we only have "trust" of "faith" (信 *xin*) in it, can help us in our conduct to illuminate the world and our relationships, and enable us, in vocabulary reminiscent of the ancient classic *Zhuangzi*, to become "genuine persons" (真人 *zhen ren*). In the present chapter, we will focus on these two applications of the identification of the luminous mind as our nature by examining the texts *Discussion of the Origin of Persons* (*Yuan Ren Lun*), attributed to the ninth-century

Chan and Huayen synthesizer Guifeng Zongmi, and the *Linji Yu Lu,* a late collection of teachings associated with the iconoclastic ninth-century Chan master Linji Yixuan.

We will begin by taking a detailed look at the *Yuan Ren Lun*'s argument for the superiority of Buddhist teachings to those of the pre-Buddhist but coexisting Chinese traditions of Confucianism and Daoism in explaining human existence. Chinese Buddhists like Guifeng Zongmi do profess admiration and respect for the moral commitments of Confucianism and the emphasis placed on understanding cosmic origin in Daoism. Nonetheless, the *Discussion of the Origin of Persons* argues that Buddhist teachings can complete their respective aspirations by offering a more cogent explanation of human beginnings (源 *yuan*). In the final analysis, it is proffered, neither the Confucian belief that people are simply endowed with their bodily and moral apportionments by heaven (天 *tian*) nor the Daoist conviction that all beings are grounded in "nothingness" (無 *wu*) could provide credible accounts of how people, in contrast to other things, could come to possess awareness, of people's varying moral qualities and potentialities, or could establish a "basis" (基 *ji*) for recommending one path of normative conduct over another. This lack of grounding explanations is adjudged to be a serious philosophical deficiency of Confucianism and Daoism. In the preferred Chinese idiom, the "branches" or "extremities" (末 *mo*) cannot be understood without reference to their "root" (本 *ben*), and in like manner, the actions and characteristics of persons cannot be assessed or guided without a fundamental understanding of their nature. Buddhism, in the argument of the *Discussion*, gives us just such a grounding by allowing us to see the physical and conscious aspects of human beings as emerging in the causal processes associated with foregoing actions and intentions (*karma*).

Once, however, the notion of *karma* has been accepted as an explanatory framework for the origin and development of persons, the *Discussion* turns to establishing the supremacy, within Buddhist thought, of the idea that an originally pure mind should be considered the basis of our existence. Were we to assume, on the one hand, that only sheer emptiness (*śūnyatā,* 空 *kong*), apart from any associations with consciousness, is what constitutes the causal process, or if we take merely the transformations of the cognitive processes in the "abode cognition" to themselves explain our nature, then we will end up with an insufficient account of both our origins and potential. What remedies these examples of single-faceted explanation is supposedly recourse to the Buddhist notion of the pure mind, for it reveals how, first, there is something that is transmitted from one birth to the next besides *karma* itself, namely, the "conscious spirit" (心神 *xin shen*), and second, given the pure mind's fundamentally enlightened character, how it makes experiential awakening possible. To understand, in this view, the pure and intrinsically enlightened mind is to understand our origins and thus our nature as persons. Zongmi, the attributed author of the *Discourse*, makes a robust case that this view can provide a foundation for all traditions of praxis, which in the end are complementary and not contradictory. At the same time, he insists, a fully metaphysical account of the mind avoids the perils of what he sees in some strands of Chan Buddhist thought as a provocative and dangerous rejection of any natural basis for conviction and practice.

The Hongzhou lineage of Chan was what Zongmi was most worried about, a lineage that passed from Mazu Daoyi to Linji Yixuan, since it often seemed to flaunt the rarified purity of the heart and all the metaphysical doctrines that propped it up. Everything from the former's slogan that "the everyday mind is *dao*," eschewing the need for cultivation, to the latter's seeming equation of even the most common bodily movements with enlightenment only added fuel to such worries after the Hongzhou teachings received official valorization by the eleventh-century Song court. And yet, what we see in the records of Linji's teaching, when understood on its own terms, is a translation of the notion of mind from theoretical speculations about human nature into the realms of human conduct. We shall, in turning to the *Lunji Yu Lu*, first examine the Hongzhou Chan insistence that a mind unencumbered by artificial deliberation and anxiety over the ego, a "mind unified" (一心 *yi xin*) with immediate bodily activities, manifests a "singular bright essence" (一精明 *yi jing ming*) that could illuminate a person's interaction with everyone and everything in their environment. Such a mind, the *Linji Yu Lu* argues, represents the most authentic core of personhood that, though it "dwells upon" the body and its *skandha*-s, can make use of that body and manifest human authenticity even in the most common activities such as putting on clothes, walking, or eating. The need to conceptualize practice as the attainment of something one does not possess, as something beyond what one already is and thus needing to be sought out and acquired, is, it turns out, utterly inconsistent with the assumption that we already have a mind that is, as the scholastic traditions claim, already and ever pure. Mysterious metaphysical formulas and abstract technical jargon can entirely give way to concrete action and colloquial communication, for what is paramount about awakening is its realization and its manifestation in our lives, not its definition and supposed doctrinal superiority.

We will then see how this sidelining of theory in favor of practice also brings down the assumed barriers of "position" or "rank" (位 *wei*), both within the Buddhist monastic community and in social relations more generally. All relationships, in their specific and unique situations of communication between persons, become occasions for enlightening interaction. In the dynamic method of teaching developed in the Hongzhou lineage, instead of giving long hermeneutic sermons on Buddhist *sūtra*-s, teachers would, with unexpected turns of phrase, shouts, strikes, and other provocations, attempt to shock students out of their habituated mindsets and prompt them to react, not according to a preprogrammed pattern of conduct but spontaneously and unhesitatingly in a way that teased out genuine responses. Very often, in such interchanges, students could also confound teachers, and the enlightening result of the confrontation, dramatically called "*dharma* battle," could travel in an unforeseen direction that represented a switching of roles. Such illuminating dialogue allows one to relate to others, in addition to the long-standing ideal of the *Zhuangzi*, as a "genuine person of no rank" (無位真人 *wu wei zhen ren*). In its relationships with others, the mind of an awakened person is not beclouded by doubt or confusion and does not merely inertly react to the interpersonal environment. It is instead at every turn able to use that interpersonal environment, just as it uses the body in which it lives, to enlightening ends. In the Chan view, we always have this mind, and even in the midst of the direst forms of afflicted attachment on the one hand and the most protocol-driven ritual expectations on the other, we are able to make it present.

Origin, Nature, and Causality

The *Yuan Ren Lun*, attributed to the early ninth-century scholastic master Guifeng Zongmi, begins by stating that, while all "three teachings" of Confucianism, Daoism, and Buddhism ought to be practiced in the interests of bringing about moral conduct and social order, only the Buddhist teachings are complete. This is, as he sees it, because they allow us to understand the structure or "causal principles" (理 *li*) of things and thus fully realize our nature (性 *xing*) and "arrive at the ultimate root of one's origins" (至於本源 *zhe yu ben yuan*).[4] Confucians and Daoists, according to the *Discussion*, share a basic cosmological framework according to which vital vapor (氣 *qi*) provides people with their physical bodies and vitality. *Qi* itself is thought to originate, alternatively in the two theoretical frameworks, from either "heaven" (天 *tian*) or "nothingness" (無 *wu*). This presents a problem, however, for ultimately, all good fortune and misfortune, and even one's individual capacity to carry out virtuous or vile actions, must be attributed to natural forces that, beyond the point of simply invoking them, are not themselves explicable. We shall deal with how the *Discussion* critiques these alternative conceptions in turn, even though, as will be evident in the passages that follow, characterizations of the Confucian and Daoist positions and their implications are often fused with one another.

With regard to Daoism, the *Discussion* charges that, in the final analysis, the emergence of nature as a whole is thought to have come about "just so," or in a manifestation of "spontaneity" (自然 *zi ran*). The first major problem with this model is that it allows for the spontaneous generation of anything and everything and so cannot account for the causal regularity that we daily observe in natural processes.

> 又言萬物皆是自然生化非因緣者, 則一切無因緣處悉應生化, 謂石應生草, 草或生人, 人生畜等. 又應生無前後, 起無早晚, 神仙不藉丹藥, 太平不藉賢良, 仁義不藉教習, 老莊周孔何用立教為軌則乎?

> Again, their claim that the myriad things are all spontaneously engendered and that it is not a matter of causes and conditions (因緣 *yin yuan*) means that everything should be engendered and transformed (even) where there are no causes and conditions. That is to say, stones might engender

> grass, grass might engender humans, humans engender animals and so forth. Further, since they might engender without regard to temporal sequence and arise without regard to due season, the immortal would not depend on an elixir, the great peace would not depend on the sage and the virtuous, and benevolence and righteousness, would not depend on learning and practice. For what use, then, did Lao-tzu, Chuang-tzu, Duke of Chou and Confucius establish their teachings as invariable norms? (*Yuan Ren Lun*, 708b9–13 [Gregory 1995, 90])

Remaining true to the basic Buddhist commitment to the governance of phenomena by causes, the Daoist tradition is critiqued not for its principles or practices, but because these laudable principles and practices have an entirely inadequate theoretical basis. If the process of "engendering" or "generation" (生 *sheng*) is believed to be causally capricious, then regular generation of like kinds within species and the causal dependence of practical results upon practical causes will have no natural grounding. Systems of practice that lay claim to the establishment of moral ideals must link their intended results with a recommended set of practices that bring them about, and without them, they lack normative force. Therefore, moral systems need causal theories. To reject causality in their explications of the origins of nature, as the *Yuan Ren Lun* accuses Daoism of doing, therefore leaves emergent nature with no governing causal principles and by extension deprives us of any reason for supposing certain results will be realized if certain actions are taken. In the Buddhist view being articulated here, cosmology and ethics, or if one prefers, naturalism and morality, cannot be delinked. One cannot simply opt out of this dilemma, in the Buddhist perspective, by the mere invocation of culture or custom (俗 *su*) either. For such a bare invocation would posit that there is a space of human activity that, as aforementioned, should somehow be exempt from the rule that our activities are governed by causes. Culture lies on the continuum of nature and human conduct but not outside of it. As the *Discussion* at one point puts the matter, there are different ritual practices and their specific rules of propriety in different cultures, from China to India (天竺 *tian zhu*) to Tibet (吐番 *tu fan*), but the virtues that bring about moral behavior, which in turn prompt respect, in each of these cultures should not, just because of the variety of their ritual protocols, be assumed different.[5] A system of practice worthy of being recommended, therefore, must be propped upon a coherent cosmology.

In addition to this, the *Discussion* argues that, without a causal theory that explains the distinct origins of distinct beings, we will be left with no explanation for why some of those beings possess awareness (知 *zhi*) while others do not. There is an interesting, though not completely overlapping, consonance between Buddhist and pre-Buddhist Chinese thought being brought onto the table here. As we saw in our opening chapter, pre-Buddhist Chinese philosophical discourse seems to have been largely characterized by the assumption that not merely the heart but the bodily organs had their own likes and dislikes, attractions and revulsions, and all of this was considered to be the body's "knowledge" or "awareness" (知 *zhi*). In the Buddhist model of experience, of course, cognitions (*vijñāna*-s) were associated, in the case of the senses, with bodily organs as well, and one's karmic heritage infused into us various kinds of preferences regarding our sensations. The *Yuan Ren Lun* brings these resonant assumptions to bear on the criticism of Daoist thought as too theoretically simplistic to account even for why certain beings and not others should be born with such conscious preferences, not to mention the distinctions of these between different beings.

> 又言皆從元氣而生成者, 則欻生之神未曾習慮, 豈得嬰孩便能愛惡驕恣焉? 若言欻有自然便能隨念愛惡等者, 則五德六藝悉能隨念而解, 何待因緣 學習而成?
>
> Again, since their claim that [the myriad things] are engendered and formed from the primal pneuma (氣 *qi*) means that a spirit (神 *shen*), which is suddenly born out of nowhere, has not yet learned and deliberated, then how, upon gaining [the body of] an infant, does it like, dislike and act willfully? If they were to say that one suddenly comes into existence out of nowhere and is thereupon able to like, dislike and so forth in accordance with one's thoughts, then it would mean that the five virtues and six arts can all be understood . . . in accordance with one's thoughts. Why then, depending on causes and conditions, do we study to gain proficiency? (*Yuan Ren Lun* 708b13–17 [Gregory 1995, 96])

And here we can see the beginning of the Buddhist position that the *Discussion* will formulate regarding why a causal account of human origins must be conceived in connection with foregoing acts and intentions, which is to say, with the process of *karma* and rebirth.[6] The fact that people are born with observable likes and dislikes requires, on this argument, that these be determinately constituted in foregoing causal conditions rather than merely pawned off to a mysterious unfolding of *qi* that would, in the end, explain nothing of what and who individuated persons are.

Moving to the Confucian tradition, the situation is no better, and more than likely worse, in the view of the *Yuan Ren Lun*, if we replace the notion of vital vapor with that of "heaven's endowment" or "the mandate of heaven" (天命 *tian ming*) in explaining human origins. In the case of originally impersonal *qi* and the decidedly impersonal "nothingness" out of which it evolved, the Daoists can at least deny that the iniquitous capacities and fortunes among people were the result of some purposeful divine intention. That is to say, in the case of Daoist cosmology, that while causality might be capricious, at least to a certain degree, the Daoists are consistent to the extent that they call all social norms into question. But in the end, their narrative falls apart anyway insofar as it recommends certain practices that may lead to long life, spiritual advancement, and even the attainment of immortality over others. But, in the case of the Confucian's persistently anthropomorphic notion of heaven and concomitant idea of heaven's intentions and desires for human society, it is impossible to avoid the conclusion that heaven is responsible for the very evil results and conduct that often prevail in human experience. There results from Confucian teaching, that is, the curious theoretical admixture of an inadequate narrative of human origins and an overdetermination of destiny. If, after all, all specific causal capacities are traced back to the agency of heaven, then heaven is ultimately the author of all outcomes.

又言貧富貴賤賢愚善惡吉凶禍福皆由天命者, 則天之賦命奚有貧多富少, 賤多貴少, 乃至禍多福少? 苟多少之分在天, 天何不平乎? 況有無行而貴, 守行而賤, 無德而富, 有德而貧, 逆吉義凶, 仁夭暴壽, 乃至有道者喪, 無道者興? 既皆由天, 天乃興不道而喪道? 何有福善益謙之賞, 禍淫害盈之罰焉? 又既禍亂反逆皆由天命, 則聖人設教, 責人不責天, 罪物不罪命, 是不當也! 然則. 刺亂政, 讚王道, 稱安上, 號移風, 豈是奉上天之意, 順造化之心乎? 是知專此教者, 未能原人.

Again, as for their claim that poverty and wealth, high and low station, sageliness and stupidity, good and evil, good and bad fortune, disaster and bounty all proceed from the mandate of heaven, then, in heaven's endowment of destiny, why are the impoverished many and the wealthy few, those of low station many and those of high station few, and so on to those suffering disaster many and those enjoying bounty few? If the apportionment of many and few lies in heaven, why is heaven not fair? How much more unjust is it in cases of those who lack moral conduct and yet are honored, those who maintain moral conduct and yet remain debased, those who lack virtue and yet enjoy wealth, those who are virtuous and yet suffer poverty, or the refractory enjoying good fortune, the righteous suffering misfortune, the humane dying young, the cruel living to an old age, and so on to the moral being brought down and the immoral being raised to eminence. Since all these proceed from heaven, heaven thus makes the immoral prosper while bringing the moral to grief. How can there be the reward of blessing the good and augmenting the humble, and the punishment of bringing disaster down upon the wicked and affliction upon the full? Furthermore, since disaster, disorder, rebellion and mutiny all proceed from heaven's mandate, the teachings established by the sages are not right in holding human beings and not heaven responsible and in blaming people and not destiny. Nevertheless, the [*Classic of*] *Poetry* censures chaotic rule, the [*Classic of*] *History* extols the kingly way, the [*Book of*] *Rites* praises making superiors secure, and the [*Classic of*] *Music* proclaims changing [the people's] manners. How could that be upholding the intention of heaven above and conforming to the mind of creation? (*Yuan Ren Lun* 708b28–708c10 [Gregory 1995, 103–104])[7]

In a restricted sense, some early Confucian texts and passages actually embrace the problem being focused on by the *Discussion* here. It is part of the tragic archetype of the Confucian sage that, should the time be decreed by heaven not ripe for the reception of the sage's teachings, the sage can do little about it other than to retreat into seclusion and perhaps continue to instruct disciples privately, as Confucius himself is said to have done. But, according to the *Yuan Ren Lun,* this is not good enough, for the notion of "heaven's endowment" is presumably an explanation of the capacities and ends of all people, not just sages. So, if heaven really does dictate that virtuous people suffer sad fates and contemptible people enjoy happy lives, then heaven cannot but be implicated, and there is very little indeed to recommend the moral superiority of the Confucian program of self-cultivation. This all is implied, the *Discussion* concludes, by the defunct explication of human origins bound up with the notion of the "mandate of heaven."

A word might be said, before we move on the intra-Buddhist debates taken up by the *Yuan Ren Lun,* about whether or not the portrayal of Confucian and Daoist cosmological theory in the aforementioned polemics is entirely accurate. After all, Han dynasty philosophical and political texts were quite rich in cosmological theory, particularly with the so-called correlative cosmology of the *yin-yang* and "five phases" variety, and how these natural forces and their dynamic interaction could shed light on everything from the passing of the seasons to the evolution of dynastic empires, from the various states of health and illness of the body to the phases of war and peace in a kingdom, from the evolution of natural phenomena to the gender and gender roles of persons. Though notions resembling causality in these cosmological models were certainly not focused on changes of the capacities of phenomena in connected temporal states, as the Buddhists were, it seems difficult to fairly maintain that the Han dynasty *yin-yang* and "five phases" cosmologies that Confucians, Daoists, and advocates of other philosophical and political perspectives all partook of simply overlooked the issue of causality as it pertains to theory and practice entirely. This question might even become more pertinent if we assume the author of the *Discussion* to indeed be Guifeng Zongmi, as he is attested to have been thoroughly trained and accomplished in classical learning in his youth. But, in a more philosophical vein, why should a Buddhist text critique other traditions' conceptions of ultimate origins instead of their ideas of more proximal causes in the project of understanding the particularities of human existence? This is especially relevant when Buddhism in general itself rejects entirely any theory of an ultimate origin precisely for the purpose of focusing on more proximate causes in its analysis of human experience. Without feigning to adjudicate the justification for this focus here, two answers suggest themselves, one interpretive and the other more straightforwardly theoretical.

As is well known, by the time of the composition of the *Discussion* in the early ninth century, Buddhism in China had historically evolved from a fledgling immigrant tradition trying to accommodate the concerns of prevailing philosophical assumptions to one more robustly asserting its superiority to other practices. Their conception of "superiority" was, however, unique, and the literary genre in which it was expressed was the special Chinese Buddhist style of "discerning the teachings" (判教 *ban jiao*), which began to flourish in the sixth century as a form of intra-Buddhist debate but which was by the ninth century, in both China and Japan, extended to other philosophical persuasions. The idea was that different philosophical systems could be ranked from the one that accounted for the least in nature and human experience to the one that explicated the most, with the latter being thought the most "round" or "encircling" (圓 *yuan*), which is to say, the most all-encompassing. This approach to other philosophical systems does not judge them to be utterly false but tries to concede whatever sorts of theoretical or practical truth exist in them, qualified by their supposed degree of understanding and their comprehensiveness. Thus, as a historical matter of what then stood for Buddhist textual hermeneutics, the previous criticisms of Confucianism and Daoism are attempts to "put them in their place," as it were, making allowances for the praiseworthiness of their practices but attempting to show why these very practices don't receive sufficient justification. As we have seen, sometimes the *Discussion* and many other apologetic or polemical texts like it try to demonstrate this insufficiency by citing a tradition's own texts against it, for instance, when the Confucian classics are referred to as demanding ritual propriety and just rulership at the expense of the notion of the "mandate of heaven," which would supposedly make such demands nonsensical.

Turning to the philosophical justification for this focus on origins, it might be argued that what the *Discussion* is talking about in the previous selections is not just the primordial and ultimate origin of nature but precisely the proximal origin of the person, particularly in its reiteration of the problem of "generation" (生 *sheng*). After all, *qi* in Daoist thought and heaven in Confucian depictions did not merely exist "in the beginning" and, after the early evolution of natural phenomena, cease to produce things. Rather, *qi* and heaven are continuously involved in the ongoing generation of nonconscious and conscious beings, and so play roles in the proximate origin of each specific phenomenon and creature. As such, they should, one has a right to suppose, contribute something causally to the specificity of each thing or person, and that contribution should likewise lend itself to detailed explanation. The *Discussion* however makes the case that Daoist representations of *qi* and "nothingness" lead to underdetermined accounts of origin, for they allow for causal randomness and so greatly blur the distinctions between beings with no awareness and those with it as to make the specific nature (性 *xing*) of a person disconnected from his or her generation (生 *sheng*), and thus his or her origin (源 *yuan*). In Confucianism, on the other hand, the singular agency of heaven, giving each individual their apportionment of physical, psychological, and moral qualities, overdetermines the character and destiny of each person to such an extent as to actually divest the latter's projects, and very existence, of their own achievement and meaning. These deficiencies do not require that the teachings and aims of Confucianism and Daoism be discarded by any means; they merely require rootedness in a causal story that ties together what we are with what we may become.

Making Our Nature Our Aim

In the working out of the *Yuan Ren Lun*, the Buddhist conviction that we ought to become fully enlightened beings must entail that we are capable of this end. This capability must include both our ability to carry out the practices recommended by Buddhism to their perfection and our motivation to attain their intended ideal. As is well attested, early Buddhism primarily sought the origins of that motivation in a discovery that living a life pursuing desires can never leave us with lasting contentment in an impermanent existence in which we are inexorably bound to lose everything. The Chinese appropriation of

Vijñānavāda, however, marked a crucial step in the transformation of Buddhist thought, for the positing of an ever-pure, "untainted" mind that, though obscured by intervening desires and deeds, was uncorrupted by them ultimately made the motivation to attain enlightenment not a discovery but a recovery, an appreciation not of what is not yet understood but of what we already and irreducibly are. In the carrying out of the 判教 *ban jiao* discourse through what the *Discussion* represents as the evolution of Buddhist doctrine, Buddhism reaches the truth of our irreducible nature in a series of stages. The series begins with the insight that our present bodies are constituted out of past deeds and intentions and culminates in a conception of mind that both enables and apprehends the realization of awakening.

This evolution begins with the problem of trying to identify the mechanism that can transmit past deeds and intentions from one bodily life to the next. Persons do not, as seen earlier, simply arise out of nothing or spontaneously but instead are produced as effects of foregoing causes. That mechanism cannot simply be the body, the physical organ of the heart, or the energizing emotions, because feelings are transitory and the bodily substance, once it dies, cannot transmit any further effects.[8] Therefore, the earliest Buddhist teachings, designed as they were for "beginners" according to the *Discussion* in a by-then-familiar Mahāyāna caricature, maintained that desire, greed, and clinging, all based on a false notion of selfhood, were the most fundamental mechanisms that created, preserved, and transmitted *karma* (業 *ye*).[9] The idea that the body is the product of foregoing mental dispositions and visible matter was designed to convince novitiates that neither the changing dispositions nor the body should be thought of as a self.[10] However, the *Discussion* argues, this early framework still does not explain, given the nonpermanence of matter and the many different kinds of interruption of cognition, how the process of rebirth can continue in the uninterrupted manner that it does. This unfulfilled demand that continuity between lives be explained therefore led to the idea of the "abode cognition" (*ālayavijñāna*).

As articulated in the works of Xuan Zang, the *Discussion* reports, the *ālayavijñāna* explains a very great deal about our experience, ranging from how we construct false ideas of the self and the objects it pursues to how psychic seeds created by past conduct can be preserved and inherited from one lifetime to the next. Most importantly, however, the correct understanding of the *ālayavijñāna* helps one realize that "consciousness constitutes the root of bodily existence" (識為身本 *shi wei shen ben*).[11] It is important to take a moment to understand the precise meaning and philosophical nature of this proposition as it is laid out in the *Yuan Ren Lun*. At this stage in the development of Buddhist teaching as it is depicted here, the notion that bodily existence owes its origin to consciousness (識 *shi*) arises primarily from the need to explain rebirth. Besides being material stuff, the body and its sense organs don't just carry out tasks proscribed by their physiology but are imbued with psychological dispositions, attractions, repulsions, behaviors that are habituated from birth and so on. These dispositions are, in Buddhist terminology, the *skandha*-s that are distinguished from mere material form, and simply assuming these dispositions can be accounted for by matter itself is rejected because matter, in the case of the body as "flesh" (肉 *rou*), doesn't produce them when dead. And since these dispositions are just that, dispositions or continuous states of inclination and feeling, they beg to be classified as forms of consciousness that, though they are, of course, amenable to both passive change and conscious cultivation, persist. The fact then that we find our eyes are attracted to certain forms and our tongue is repulsed by certain tastes, for example, demonstrates that those organs receive individually particularized dispositions not because of their fleshly structure alone but because of consciousness. The notion of the *ālayavijñāna* therefore gets us closer to the root (本 *ben*) of our personhood and thus closer to understanding our true nature.

And yet, the *Discussion* continues, we must not be tempted to stop there and assume the *ālayavijñāna* explains our nature fully. Referring to Vijñānavāda passages that liken the objective determinations of waking awareness to dream awareness, the *Discussion* asserts that such texts demonstrate that none of the eight kinds of cognition can be thought to have a real nature of their own (無自性 *wu zi xing*).[12] Lacking a unique nature is, of course, the very definition of the Buddhist notion of emptiness (*śūnyatā*).[13] But, if it is the case that bodily existence is rooted in consciousness and consciousness is emptiness, then our bodily existence itself is rooted in emptiness (空 *kong*).[14] The Mādhyamika Buddhist might be satisfied with such a result, since it establishes the emptiness of all things. All we have in the end, on this view, would be the interdependent causality that both brings about events in the natural world and, in human experience, is what holds out hope for unenlightened consciousness to be transformed by causes that can contribute to its awakening. But the *Yuan Ren Lun* maintains that, if we are searching for the innermost core of our nature, our real origin, then pervasive emptiness that renders both the body and consciousness themselves illusions leaves us with no one at all who can apprehend the truth of emptiness and be awakened by it.

> 若心境皆無, 知無者誰? 又若都無實法, 依何現諸虛妄? 且現見世間虛妄之物, 未有不依實法而能起者.
>
> If the mind and its objects are both non-existent, then who is it that knows that they do not exist? Again, if there are no real things whatsoever, then on the basis of what are the illusions made to appear? Moreover, there has never been a case of the illusory things in the world before us being able to arise without being based on something real. (*Yuan Ren Lun* 709c26–29 [Gregory 1995, 173–174])

Once again we are confronted with the question of the basis, for supposedly illusory things and modes of consciousness cannot just spontaneously arise without relying (依 *yi*) on something for their appearance. Now, where the Mādhyamika might want to retort that the reliance in question is based on the entire process of dynamic causation, the *Discussion* insists that even illusions or dreams must appear to someone who fantasizes them. Emptiness in its entirety does not answer to the question of "who." No attempt to account for origins, not merely in the abstract but specifically for our origin as persons, simply responds to the question of "who" with silence. Truth is not truth to no one, after all, but is truth only if it is manifested, and such manifestation cannot occur but to and for someone. The exact same thing can be said of illusion, for illusion is always illusion that deceives someone, and so illusions also require manifestation. What is needed to explain our origin as persons therefore is a conception of consciousness in which both illusion, which tempts us to cling to the world, and truth, which compels us that illusions are indeed only illusions, can appear. Since "emptiness" on its own gives us no answer to the question of manifestation, and since the *ālayavijñāna* presumably only gives us illusions, we must seek our ultimate basis in a kind of mind that apprehends both.

The *Discussion* proceeds to first give a description of this kind of mind, which is the ultimate basis of our nature, and then elaborates on how that mind is obscured by causes and conditions that precipitate the formation of an *ālayavijñāna*, which, in its turn, constitutes physical bodies.

> 五一乘顯性教者, 說一切有情皆有本覺真心, 無始以來常住清淨, 昭昭不昧了了常知, 亦名佛性, 亦名如來藏. 從無始際, 妄相翳之不自覺知, 但認凡質故, 耽著結業受生死苦.
>
> The Teaching of the One Vehicle that Reveals the Nature holds that all sentient beings without exception have the intrinsically enlightened, true mind. From [time] without beginning, it is permanently abiding and immaculate. It is shining, unobscured, clear and bright ever-present awareness. It is called both the Buddha-nature and the *tathāgatagharba*. From time without beginning, deluded thoughts cover it, and sentient beings by themselves are not aware of it. Because they only recognize their inferior qualities, they become indulgently attached, enmeshed in *karma*, and experience the suffering of birth and death. (*Yuan Ren Lun* 710a11–15 [Gregory 1995, 178])

While all of the familiar vocabulary of Paramārtha's description of the "untainted" consciousness is employed here to describe the most fundamental level of continuous enlightenment, we must be keen in observing important differences in the *Discussion*. The abiding enlightened consciousness is referred to as the "originally awakened genuine mind" (本覺真心 *ben jue zhen xin*) and described as "illustrious" (昭昭 *zhao zhao*), "unconcealed" (不昧 *bu mei*), "completely comprehending" (了了 *liao liao*) "constant awareness" (常知 *cheng zhi*). This presumably ever-present awareness is, though never extinguished, "not attended to by conscious beings" (不自覺知 *bu zi jue zhe*) because "states of uncomprehending actively conspire to conceal one another" (妄相翳 *nei xiang yi*). On the face of it, this obscuration of originally all-illuminating awareness seems to be quite a mysterious occurrence indeed, for why it should come to be so concealed by a host of other obfuscating awarenesses is not by any means immediately clear. But much of this mystery can be clarified when we realize that we are not dealing here with two completely distinct kinds of mind, two separate 心 *xin*, one pure and the other impure, and trying to work out a formula for how the two enter into a certain kind of relation. Instead, we are dealing with two kinds of activity (為 *wei*) of one and the same 心 *xin*, one of which we are already familiar with from everyday experience, the activity of self-other distinction, discursive thought and desire, and the other of which apprehends these first activities without performing any of them. In ordinary waking life, the merely apprehending or, as the description obtains here, illuminating activity of the mind becomes obscured and hidden by the projecting activities. The cultivation of Buddhist practices, the work of enlightenment that requires our effort, involves disciplinary and meditative techniques that facilitate the insight that these projections are just and only that, projections of the mind that arise to the degree that it is governed by causal activity. But the techniques that cultivation employs can only work in the first place precisely because the merely manifesting activity of mind, though ordinarily hidden from view, does indeed always function. In Buddhist praxis, that is, we are working toward the recovery of the fundamental nature of mind, and we can succeed in this recovery precisely because of the mind's nature. Unenlightened experience proceeds from the ways in which the illuminating and projecting activities interrelate in the 心 *xin* that we all already possess. And so comprehending this interrelation enables us to understand our nature, our origin, how we came to be persons, and everything that being a person entails.

In the end, discerning the relationship between our mind and our bodily form has to do with seeing the mind and body as two degrees of activity that lie on a spectrum, as it were, that emerge in ordinarily imperceptible "rarified" (細 *xi*) activity and become visible in its evolved "coarseness" (麤 *cu*). In the culminating passages of the *Discussion*, this spectrum actually unities the South Asian philosophical categories that describe the constitution of conscious experience and the East Asian categories that erect a cosmology of nature. Both the primordial origins of human beings and the origin of each individual human being begin with the surprisingly asserted oneness of mind and vital vapor (*qi*), and from this union emerges the *ālayavijñāna*, objectification, desire, the Buddhist *skandha*-s, and then the material elements of both the aforementioned *yin-yang* and five-phases Han dynasty cosmologies.

> 然所稟之氣, 展轉推本, 即混一之元氣也: 所起之心, 展轉窮源, 即真一之靈心也. 究實言之, 心外的無別法. 元氣亦從心之所變, 屬前轉識所現之境, 是阿賴耶相 分所攝, 從初一念業相, 分為心境之二, 心既從細至麤, 展轉妄計乃至造業 (如前敘列); 境亦從微至著, 展轉變起乃至天地 (即彼始自太易, 五重運轉乃至太極, 太極生兩儀. 彼說自然太道, 如此說真性, 其實但是一念能變見分. 彼云, 元氣如此一念初動. 其實但是境界之相). 業既成熟, 即從父母稟受二氣, 與業識和合成就人身. 據此則心識所變之境, 乃成二分. 一分即與心識和合成人, 一分不與心識和, 即成天地山河國邑. 三才中唯人靈者, 由與心神合也.

> Nevertheless, the vital force (氣 *qi*) with which we are endowed, when it is traced all the way back to its origin, is the primal pneuma (元氣 *yuan qi*) of the undifferentiated oneness, and the mind that arises, when it is thoroughly investigated all the way back to its source, is the numinous mind of the absolute (即真一之靈心 *ji zhen yi zhi ling xin*, perhaps better rendered as "enlightened mind of completely genuine unity"). In ultimate terms, there is nothing outside of mind. The primal pneuma also comes from the evolution of mind, belongs to the category of objects that were manifested by the previously evolved consciousness (識 *shi*), and is included within the objective aspect of the *ālayavijñāna*. From the phenomenal appearance of the activation of the very first thought (念 *nian*), the *ālayavijñāna* divides into the dichotomy of mind and objects. The mind, having developed from the subtle to the course, continues to evolve from false speculation into the generation of *karma* (as previously set forth). Objects likewise develop from the fine to the crude, continuing to evolve from the transformation (of the *ālayavijñāna*) into heaven and earth (天地 *tian di*). (The beginning for them starts with the grand interchangeability (太易 *tai yi*) and evolves in five phases to the great ultimate (太極 *tai ji*). The great ultimate (then) produces the two elementary forms. Even though they speak of spontaneity (自然 *zi ran*) and the great way (太道 *tai dao*) as we here speak of the true nature (真性 *zhen xing*), they are

> actually nothing but the subjective aspect of the *ālayavijñāna* in a single moment of thought (一念能變見分 *yi nian neng bian jian fen*); even though they talk of the primal pneuma (元氣 *yuan qi*) as we here speak of the initial movement in a single moment of thought (一念初動 *yi nian chu dong*), it is actually nothing but the phenomenal appearance of the objective world) (境界之相 *jing jie zhi xiang*, lit., the "mutuality of the extent and boundary [of the world]"). When *karma* has ripened, then one receives one's endowment of the two vital forces (二氣 *er qi*, the common designation for *yang* and *yin*) from one's father and mother, and when it has interfused with activated consciousness (業識 *ye shi*, which technically refers to the active sense cognitions but literally means "karmic consciousness"), the human body (人身 *ren shen*) is completely formed. According to this, the objects that are transformed from consciousness immediately form two divisions: one division is that which interfuses with consciousness to form human beings, while the other division does not interfuse with consciousness and is that which forms heaven and earth, mountains and rivers, and states and towns. The fact that only humans among the three powers (of heaven, earth, and humans) are spiritual (靈 *ling*, lit., "conscious spirits") is due to their being fused with spirit (心神 *xin shen*, lit., a "minded spirit"). (*Yuan Ren Lun* 710c8–20 [Gregory 1995, 205–206])

What the *Discussion* does here with the conceptual inventories of pre-Buddhist Chinese thought and South Asian Buddhist philosophy is quite extraordinary. What stands as the ultimate foundation of the world is mind (心 *xin*), and the very first act of mind is to manifest a single thought (念 *nian*). As soon as this act occurs, the primordial mind becomes consciousness (識 *shi*), and the objective form that this first thought takes is that of the naturally primordial vital vapor (元氣 *yuan qi*). Every successive act of consciousness, and here "act" is overtly understood as a karmic act of imagination, produces incrementally more concrete energies and realms, beginning with *yin* and *yang* and culminating in the natural world of heaven, earth, and persons, including, in the latter's case, their social and political creations. And, providing the necessary account of individual origins that was at first found lacking in Confucian and Daoist thought, the

Yuan Ren Lun posits that preexisting acts and intentions in the now fully emerged web of causes and conditions give rise to a particular person's share of *yin* and *yang*, and from this share is constituted one's body and its apportionment of physical qualities, virtues, vices, fortunes, and sufferings. And because our bodily acts are always intermingled with consciousness, the death of an individual passes on their karmic inheritance to a newborn in the next generation in the form of a conscious or minded spirit or vitality (心神 *xin shen*). The world, in its concrete, material reality, though it did emerge in part from vital vapor, its two basic patterns of *yin* and *yang* and the elements as these were understood by classical Chinese cosmologists, existed from the beginning as a world manifested, and such manifestation implies that consciousness, the ever-luminous mind, was the basis of it all. The world, that is to say, is both concretely real, as Chinese naturalism insists, and also an act of imagination. It follows then that a person, while indubitably a body constituted out of vital energies and the physical elements, is not conscious because the vital energy and bodily matter are themselves conscious but because our original nature (性 *xing*) is conscious spirit, and indeed the body we possess is itself derived from the heritage of imaginative acts of that conscious spirit.

The legacy of philosophical thought found in the *Discussion* then simply could not have existed were it not for the entire intellectual legacy of Buddhism itself. For, regardless of how one may assess the legitimacy of the *Yuan Ren Lun*'s particular ranking of levels of truth offered by Confucian, Daoist, and Buddhist thought, the underlying convictions that it adheres to arise out of all of the encounters of mind that accreted through the South Asian and East Asian history of the traditions it attempts to synthesize. To a significant degree, in its South Asian contexts, Buddhist thinkers responded to a Brāhmiṇical depiction of the intermingling of conscious spirit and an unconscious body in the constitution of persons with their own models that represented cognition and matter as interdependently co-constitutive. It is this basic conception of the relation between mind and body, though it had been mediated by a complex history of intra-Buddhist scholastic debate, that the *Yuan Ren Lun* brings to an elucidation of the relationship between unenlightened and enlightened consciousness. In the Buddhist *Discussion*, remarkably, the notion of spirit is retained and not discarded, but an attempt is made to explain its relationship to the body in causal terms. In its East Asian contexts, on the other hand, the *Discussion* tries to engage with what was by then centuries of strongly naturalistic thought, for which the heart is a bodily organ that can make us into moral and sagely beings, and then recontextualizes how we should think of the heart as the source of our personal nature and the only sure font of a genuineness that is always available to us. The legacy of this Buddhist synthesis of South and East Asian philosophical conceptions of mind would go on, in the case of both Daoist and Confucian thought, not merely to appropriate traditional concepts of the latter but to change the way those traditions thematized their own worldviews as well. In the next chapter, we will see how this process played out among the most important Confucian thinkers of the Song and Ming Dynasties. The event of cross-cultural philosophical creativity that was precipitated by the extended reception of Buddhism in China was, it turns out, as profound as it was far-reaching. In the *Yuan Ren Lun*, we see how Tang Buddhist philosophers grounded their recommended practices in the fusion of a Buddhist conception of mind with classical Chinese depictions of bodily existence, all in an attempt to demonstrate how the end we ought to seek, enlightenment, is attainable because it lies at the very roots of our own nature.

Lumps of Flesh with Bright Minds

The legendary ninth-century Hongzhou Chan master Linji Yixuan is reported never to have minced words when it came to his disdain for the feats of metaphysical speculation like those of Zongmi's *Discussion*.

> 學人信不及. 便向名句上生解. 年登半百. 秖管傍家負死屍行. 檐卻檐子天下走. 索草鞋錢有日在.
>
> Because your faith in yourselves is insufficient, you students turn to words and phrases and base your understanding upon them. Until you've reached the half-century mark you continue dragging [your] dead bodies up blind alleys

> and run about the world bearing your heavy load. The day will come when you will have to pay for the straw sandals you've worn out. (*Linji Yu Lu* 501a20–21 [Sasaki and Kirchner 2009, 248])

The *Linji Yu Lu* (臨濟語錄), or *Recorded Sayings of Linji*, reached its present, standard form over a two-centuries-long period of compilation in which teachings in two literary genres congealed around Master Linji, who was elevated to orthodox status with the endorsement of his Chan lineage in the Song court.[15] These two genres were the so-called Separate Records (瞥錄 *bielu*), which are composed of "encounter dialogues" (機緣問答 *jiyuan wenda*), and the Extensive Records (広錄 *guanglu*), which are comprised of sermons. Both of these genres grew out of the highly personalized pedagogical practice of Chan, for which the traditional form of learning Buddhism through scriptures and philosophical treatises was overtaken by treating the words and deeds of teachers and students in their conversational interaction as exemplary models of enlightened behavior, recording these, and passing them on within a monastic lineage.[16] That is to say, in Chan, as Peter Hershock has pointed out, that "enlightenment is characteristically realized in (the) unprecedented conduct . . . of student and master."[17] It may be all too easy to dismiss the otherwise vibrant rhetoric of the *Linji Yu Lu* as a wildly romantic idealization of human "spontaneity" that, after all, was canonized in the strictly ritually regulated and practiced hierarchical circumstances of Tang and Song monastic institutions. However, even the great modern critic of Chan, Bernard Faure, is willing to admit that Chan rituals provided "a sacralization of everyday life."[18] It is through their focus on the colloquial, the everyday dialogical encounter, the intentional and shocking breakup of habits and conventional expectations, ironically practiced and formalized though they were, that the combined genres of the *Linji Yu Lu* work. They magnify how the luminous mind that is our original nature manifests in our most simple bodily activities and in the interactions we have with one another where our genuineness breaks forth, helping people realize enlightenment together.

The *Recorded Sayings* makes common references to the identification of human genuineness with the mind that illuminates the world, and that mind, in turn, is said to "use" the body, even as it rests "upon" the body.

> 上堂云. 赤肉團上有一無位真人. 常從汝等諸人面門出入. 未證據者看看. 時有僧出問. 如何是無位真人. 師下禪床把住云. 道道. 其僧擬議. 師托開云. 無位真人是什麼乾屎橛. 便歸方丈.
>
> The master, taking the high seat in the hall, said: "On your lump of red flesh is a true man without rank who is always going in and out of the face of every one of you. Those who have not yet confirmed this, look, look!" A monk came forward and asked: "What about the true man without rank?" The master got down from his seat, seized the monk, and cried: "Speak, speak!" The monk faltered. Shoving him away, the master said: "The true man without rank—what kind of dried piece of shit is he?" Then he returned to his quarters. (*Linji Yu Lu* 0496c10–14 [Sasaki and Kirchner 2009, 129, 131])

Here, the unexpected dynamics of "encounter dialogue," what was classically called "*dharma* battle" between master and student, is on full display. We will explore these dynamics in the following section. For the moment, it is asserted in the previous quotation that a "person" (人 *ren*) is said to dwell "upon the lump of red flesh" (赤肉團上 *chi rou duan shang*), but that very person passes constantly out and in through the gates of the face (常從汝等諸人面門出入 *chang cong ru deng zhu ren mian men chu ru*). As the translator Ruth Sasaki points out, the vivid phrase "lump of red flesh" (赤肉團*chi rou duan*) was a colorful rendition of the earliest revision of this very dialogue recorded in the *Zutangji* (祖堂集), where the more technical Buddhist phrase "five *skandha*-s" (五蘊*wu yun*) is used to describe the body upon which the genuine person lives but at the same time travels in and out of, presumably in communication and interaction with others. It seems then that the person being referred to here cannot be identified as belonging to or as itself produced by the *skandha*-s. Indeed, in the "Extensive Records" chapter of the *Recorded Sayings*, this relationship between the genuine person and the body is further articulated.

> 道流. 爾秖今聽法者. 不是爾四大能用爾四大. 若能如是見得. 便乃去住自由. 約山僧見處. 勿嫌底法. 爾若愛聖. 聖者聖之名.
>
> Followers of the Way, the you who is right now listening to my discourse is not the four elements; this you makes

> use of the four elements. If you can fully understand this, you are free to go or to stay [as you please]. From my point of view, there is not a thing to be disliked. If you love the "sacred," what is sacred is no more than the name "sacred." (*Linji Yu Lu* 0498c23–26 [Sasaki and Kirchner 2009, 202])

We see here a bit of the antinormativity of the Hongzhou tradition of Chan that so vexed the author of the *Yuan Ren Lun*. The rejection of the "sacred" in this passage is actually the rejection of the "sage" (聖 *shen*), which emphasizes the description of the "genuine person" in the *Linji Yu Lu* as having "no rank" (無位 *wu wei*) in comparison to others. Such rank is denied precisely because the genuineness of each person is indistinct from the genuineness of anyone else. Uncovering this genuineness in oneself is a matter of mere recognition and immediacy of activity. But, to return to the problem of the immediately apparent dualism between person and body being presented in the preceding passages, the person being spoken to is said to be distinct from the "four elements" of earth, air, fire, and water out of which the body is constituted but instead puts that body to use (用 *yong*). This "use" of the body is perfected by a person who simply acts free from doubt, and this freedom from doubt is itself identified by the *Recorded Sayings* with awakening.

> 大德. 爾且識取弄光影底人. 是諸佛之本源. 一切處是道流歸舍處. 是爾四大色身不解說法聽法. 脾胃肝膽不解說法聽法. 虛空不解說法聽法. 是什麼解說法聽法. 是爾目前歷歷底. 勿一箇形段孤明. 是這箇解說法聽法. 若如是見得. 便與祖佛不別. 但一切時中更莫間斷. 觸目皆是. 秖為情生智 隔想變體殊. 所以輪回三界受種種苦. 若約山僧見處. 無不甚深無不解脫. 道流. 心法無形通貫十方. 在眼曰見. 在耳曰聞. 在鼻嗅香. 在口談論. 在手執捉。在足運奔. 本是一精明. 分為六和合. 一心既無. 隨處解脫.

> Virtuous monks, you must recognize the one who manipulates these reflections. "He is the primal source (本源 *ben yuan*) of all the buddhas," and the place to which every follower of the Way returns. This physical body of yours, composed of the four great elements, can neither expound the *dharma* nor listen to it; your spleen and stomach, liver and gallbladder, can neither expound the *dharma* nor listen

> to it; the empty sky can neither expound the *dharma* nor listen to it. Then what can expound the *dharma* and listen to it? This very you standing distinctly before me without any form, shining alone—just this can expound the *dharma* and listen to it! Understand it this way and you are not different from the patriarch-buddha. Just never allow interruptions, and all that meets your eyes will be right. But because "when feeling arises, *prajña* is barred, and when thinking changes, the substance varies," people transmigrate through the three realms and undergo all kinds of suffering. As I see it, there are none who are not of the utmost profundity, none who aren't emancipated. Followers of the Way, mind is without form and pervades the ten directions. In the eye it is called seeing, in the ear it is called hearing. In the nose, it smells odors, in the mouth it holds converse. In the hands it grasps and seizes, in the feet it runs and carries. Fundamentally it is one pure radiance; divided it becomes the six harmoniously divided spheres of sense. If the mind is void, wherever you are, you are emancipated. (*Linji Yu Lu* 0497b24–c07 [Sasaki and Kirchner 2009, 162, 165])

Given everything else we have covered about both pre-Buddhist Chinese thought and the philosophical traditions of Buddhism, there is much in these passages that deserves careful attention. The person within who hears, understands, communicates, and acts is said to "shine," or in other words is "clear" and "luminous" (明 *ming*), and this formless person is equated with the formless mind (心 *xin*). When the mind inhabits the position of, or is located "at" (在 *zai*), one of the sense organs, we sense in the corresponding fashion, and when it is located in one of the organs of activity, we can grasp and move accordingly. Despite the fact, that is, that the mind on its own can be considered a "singular essence of brightness" or, perhaps better, a "singular, pure luminosity" (一精明 *yi jing ming*), it "distinctly acts" (分為 *fen wei*) as the "six awarenesses" (六和 *liu zhi*). The vocabulary being used here, until the end of the quotation, might tempt the reader to think that a kind of dualism is being described, particularly with regard to how the bodily organs are claimed not themselves to be able to sense but instead are only amenable to sensation when they are being alternatively used by the indwelling person or inhabited by the mind. This appears to stand in stark contrast both to the early Confucian, Daoist, and Mohist notions that would represent the organs themselves as being their own distinct "offices" of sensory awareness, as well as the general Buddhist idea that the organs produced, in interdependent operation with the karmically inherited dispositions and sometimes with the *ālayavijñāna*, their own sensory "cognitions." All consciousness, in the preceding passage, seems to be invested in the mind alone. Two important details, however, mitigate this otherwise seemingly apparent dualist reading. First, this luminous mind or person is said several times to be without form (無形 *wu xing*), and, second, it is said in the final analysis to perform the activity (為 *wei*) of the senses when it inhabits them. Mind, therefore, is not a "thing," its singularity is not one of substance but instead one of activity, and, when functioning properly, it inhabits one activity at a time, fully uses one sense or motion at a time. In one's own activity, therefore, one is advised not to interrupt "a single moment of time in the midst of its change" (一切時中更 *yi qie shi zhong geng*), where such interruption can only be done by becoming attached to a particular feeling or thought. That is to say, what we have here is not so much a description of what the mind is as a description of what the mind does. Or, perhaps even more appropriate to the context of the pedagogical priorities of Hongzhou Chan, we are being told what to do with the mind, how to make it fully attentive only to its present experience rather than to self-limiting patterns of desire and fixation on preconceived ends. To be sure, pointing this focus on the activity of the mind, on its functional priority with regard to the bodily organs, is not meant to deny that the relationship between 心 *xin* and body here is in definite ways different from the relationship being described in pre-Buddhist Chinese and foregoing Buddhist thought that became most influential in China. For the former, as we have discussed at length in the opening chapter, the heart was generally thought to have been only one of the sensing organs, sometimes enjoying moral and cognitive priorities over the other organs—though sometimes not, but certainly not the sole locus of awareness. For the latter, as we have detailed in the previous chapter and the first half of this one, awareness is functionally differentiated among the various sense organs, inner sense, and a level of consciousness that stores foregoing afflicted and pure inclinations, and sometimes the last of these functions is invested in a "pure mind" that in some texts even has cosmological functions. It is hardly denied by the *Linji Lu* that the kinds of awareness we have through our sense organs is specific to those organs, and the foregoing Buddhist framework of the *skandha*-s is assumed as an accurate constitutive model of human psychology throughout. What is really unique in the assertions about mind in the *Recorded Sayings* is how the mind seems to be singularly responsible for bringing awareness to our sensations and activities and the way in which the mind is identified with the "genuine person." As we also recall from the first chapter, the *Zhuangzi* made extensive use of the concept of the "genuine person," and that vocabulary appears to be appropriated here. But in the former work, the genuineness of the person is more often identified with "spirit," whereas here it is identified with the rightly functioning mind.

The kinds of activity that ideally focus awareness in the *Recorded Sayings* are not lofty states of meditation, rarified forms of awareness that are maximally disassociated from the body or developed sedimentations of theoretical learning, but instead are the most simple and ordinary kinds of conduct. No action that is motivated by preconceived desires enables us to be fully attentive, to make the mind fully present, in our circumstances as they are, not even actions motivated by the desire to attain enlightenment. The mind's luminosity only fully engages every present circumstance if it is not distracted by things sought.

> 但能隨緣消舊業. 任運著衣裳. 要行即行. 要坐即坐. 無一念心希求佛果. 緣何如此. 古人云. 若欲作業求佛. 佛是生死大兆.
>
> Conforming with circumstances as they are exhausts his past *karma*; accepting circumstances as they are he puts on his clothes, when he wants to walk he walks, when he wants to sit he sits; he never has a single thought of seeking buddhahood. Why is this so? A man of old said: "If you seek buddha through *karma*-creating activities, buddha becomes the great portent of birth-and-death." (*Linji Yu Lu* 0497c13–16 [Sasaki and Kirchner 2009, 171])
>
> 向爾道。無佛無法無修無證. 秖與麼傍家擬求什麼物. 瞎漢頭上安頭. 是爾欠少什麼. 道流. 是爾目前用底. 與祖佛不別. 秖麼不信便向外求. 莫錯向外無法. 內亦不可得. 爾取山僧口裏語. 不如休歇無事去.

> I say to you there is no buddha, no *dharma,* nothing to practice, nothing to enlighten to. Just what are you seeking in the highways and byways? Blind men! You're putting a head on top of the one you already have. What do you yourselves lack? Followers of the Way, your own present activities do not differ from those of the patriarch-buddhas. You just don't believe this and keep on seeking outside. Make no mistake! Outside, there is no *dharma*: inside, there is nothing to be obtained. Better than grasp at the words from my mouth, take it easy and do nothing. (*Linji Yu Lu* 500c04–08 [Sasaki and Kirchner 2009, 238])

One is not, that is, to undertake new tasks (事 *shi*) in addition to functions that are already before oneself (前用 *qian yong*) in the immediate circumstances, without serving the artificial ends of desires or goals.[19]

Since the mind need not be found or obtained but is already present and available to each person, and since that mind, when not interfered with, "illuminates" everything around it, the work of enlightenment, in the *Recorded Sayings,* is bringing that luminosity to bear on one's interactions and relationships, such that every instance of communication can become one of learning and teaching. It was certainly no novelty in Buddhism for Chan to have promulgated the idea that people strive for and attain awakening in community, for the *saṅgha* had been one of the "three jewels" of the tradition since its inception. What is provocative about Hongzhou Chan is its insistence that enlightening communication be "unprecedented," not grounded in scriptures and sermons and formulae. Of course, as noted earlier, there is great irony in this overt embrace of the "unprecedented" moment of communication in Chan, since, for instance, by the time the *Linji Yu Lu* itself had become a more or less unified canonical work, the "encounter dialogues" found within it and similar texts were quite formulaically and ritually enacted in monastic contexts, contexts in which, on top of these regular reenactments, were piled very strict daily routines of tasks and comportment.[20] But even these monastic reinforcements can easily be understood as attempts to ingrain the pedagogical approach to human communication being advocated. Communication is where the mind disseminates and shares its brightness.

道流. 即今目前孤明歷歷地聽者. 此人處處不滯. 通貫十方. 三界自在. 入一切境差別不能回換. 一刹那間透入法界. 逢佛說佛. 逢祖說祖. 逢羅漢說羅漢. 逢餓鬼說餓鬼. 向一切處游履國土教化眾生. 未曾離一念. 隨處清淨光透十方. 萬法一如.

Followers of the Way, the one who at this very moment shines alone before my eyes and is clearly listening to my discourse—this man tarries nowhere; he traverses the ten directions and is freely himself in all three realms. Though he enters all types of situations with their various differentiations, none can confuse him. In an instant of time, he penetrates the *dharma* realms, on meeting a buddha, he teaches the buddha, on meeting a patriarch, he teaches the patriarch, on meeting an *arhat*, he teaches the *arhat*, on meeting a hungry ghost, he teaches the hungry ghost. He travels throughout all lands bringing enlightenment to sentient beings, yet is never separate from his present mind. Everywhere is pure, light illuminates the ten directions, and "all *dharma*-s are a single suchness." (*Linji Yu Lu* 0498b08–13 [Sasaki and Kirchner 2009, 192])

Guests, Hosts, and Trust in Oneself

One of the most striking features of the *Linji Yu Lu*, particularly given Buddhist monastic norms and the larger Chinese social context, is the ever-present rejection of investment in social authority. Once again, as we may recall from our opening chapter, a good deal of moral normativity was assumed to attach to various sorts of social status in pre-Buddhist Chinese thought, not to mention in prevailing Chinese institutions. But this recurrent theme in the text also militates against the assumed superiority of the enlightened master of the Buddhist monastery. In its discursive pursuit of human genuineness, even the literary genre of the *Recorded Sayings* and the pedagogical methods it endorses are especially dedicated to embracing the ideal that human authenticity has nothing to do with "position" or "rank."

The practitioner who may serve as a model, in the *Recorded Sayings*, in all "environments" (境 *jing*), plays the role of the "host" (主 *zhu*). These two intertwined concepts are especially crucial in bringing into relief the significance of the interpersonal in the Chan conception of personhood being considered here. The "encounter dialogues" (機緣問答 *jiyuan wenda*) that make up so much of Chan literature, featured in three *Linji Yu Lu* sections and described in some detail in the sermons section, portray dialogical interchanges between a "host" (主 *zhu*) and a "guest" (賓 *bin*). The phrase "encounter dialogues" originates from the work of Yanagida Seizan, and it describes a typical, usually brief, interchange between a questioner or "guest," who may be a student, layperson, or official patron, and a teacher, whose responses make him the default "host." These brief interchanges slowly evolved from earlier sermon literature that included question-and-answer sessions as well as longer dialogical interchanges between masters and students. Guests often approached with questions not about Buddhist doctrine or scriptures but about enlightenment, and hosts' responses, whether they came by way of words, shouts, or blows, exposed the faultiness of the assumptions underlying the questions. However, at times "hosts" and "guests" would reverse roles, with the latter getting the better of the former and thereby undermining even preconceived expectations regarding who was and was not enlightened.[21] So intense are the encounters that they are routinely described as instances of "*dharma* battle" (法戰 *fa zhan*).

The *Linji Yu Lu* contains an overt pedagogy regarding how hosts and guests interact, and how such interactions manifest different "environments" for the participants, with their respective responses to the environment determining the outcome of the interchange. When a student "sets a trap" for a teacher that the latter does not recognize but responds to by lecturing or presenting doctrine, the latter is said to have a sickness "below the diaphragm and above the heart." In this case, the former wins, and the guest is said to "see through" the host (客看主 *bin kan zhu*). Alternatively, when the guest has a misplaced question undermined but refuses to let go of the obsession behind the question, the host "sees through" the guest (主看客*zhu kan bin*).[22] There are occasions when host and guest are equal to one another, with the student responding to a teacher with a "clean, pure environment" (清淨境 *qing jing jing*); the teacher reprimands him playfully and the student bows, and such cases are dubbed "host seeing host" (主看主 *zhu kan zhu*).[23] Finally, a student may come with a question that binds him to ignorance, and the teacher, failing to know how to address the problem, binds him further, and since the interlocutors have failed one another, the encounter is called "guest seeing guest" (客看客 *bin kan bin*).[24] Linji observes that students succeed in encounters when they "exert all their strength and pass through without a breath" (著力處不通風 *zhao li chu bu tong feng*) but tend to fail when they "bat an eye and feign a move," in which case the "experience of the exchange immediately fails" (即沒交涉*ji mo jiao she*).[25] It is not merely then the response that is at stake but its immediate fit with the circumstances of the interchange, and whether either enables or disables both is the environment that is brought to the encounter. None of this can be assessed before the actual encounter takes place.

Earlier in the sermons section, when asked about what he means by the "four kinds of environment without characteristics" (四種無相境 *si zhong wu xiang jing*), Linji identifies circumstances under which the "heart-mind" (心 *xin*) may be beset by doubt (疑 *yi*), love (愛 *ai*), anger (嗔 *chen*), and joy (喜 *xi*) but set free through the realization that each of these states of inordinate attachment are brought about by dreamlike illusions (夢 *meng*).[26] One who is not tossed about (轉 *zhuan*) by these environments but who can put them to use (處處用 *chu chu yong*) effectively may manifest genuine personhood in their interactions. Such passages emphasizing the capacity of the practitioner not to react to feelings but employ them are significant, particularly given the by then centuries' long association between the idea of mind and mere awareness in Chinese Buddhist texts. No longer is it a question of Buddhist praxis in this Chan framework to eliminate all traces of feeling but rather to master feelings in such a way as to exhibit a responsiveness that may transform human relationships into occasions of an unmasking of humanity that is unsullied by social artifice and the false relations of power that it creates.

The obvious capacity of any person, regardless of their foregoing preparation or status, to access their genuine mind and enlighten another person prompts Linji in the text to repeatedly warn against placing any trust or faith in "robes," or the colors of robes, which indicates the rank and presumed state of accomplishment of any would-be sage. He simultaneously praises and demeans his followers in calling them Buddhas and patriarchs, for these are at times compared to "filth in the latrine" (廁穢 *si hui*), while the enlightenment and *nirvāṇa* that they seek are referred to as "hitching posts for asses" (繫驢橛 *xi lu jue*).[27] Conceptions of rank and status between human beings, such as those between "sages" (聖 *sheng*) and "dull, worldly mortals" (凡*fan*) are mere "names" or labels (名 *ming*) that ultimately "hinder" (礙 *ai*) practice. The *Linji Yu Lu* often seems a bit at odds with itself over this counsel, for it is also said that genuine persons, who are specifically identified as monks who have "left the household" (真出家 *chen chu jia*), must be able to tell the difference between sages and common mortals, lest these very practitioners themselves be considered only "genuine worldly folks" (真俗家人 *zhen su jia ren*).[28] The emphasis seems to be on eliminating esteem for the social cache of the designations of these spheres of life. For while the practitioner is to extract their human genuineness from their experience like a *haṃsa* extracts milk from water, to "love sages and hate common mortals" (愛聖憎凡 *ai sheng zeng fan*) is what is denounced.[29]

In the midst of all these pedagogical reflections and their performance, a phrase in the *Recorded Sayings* is constantly and conspicuously reiterated. That phrase is the imperative for the student or practitioner to have "trust" or "faith" in him- or herself (自信 *zi xin*). That is to say, even with everything being said and shown in the text regarding how people may enlighten one another through dramatic and mutually challenging conversational interaction, the accompanying admonishment that awakening is not to be found somewhere outside oneself, but within one's own ever-present luminous mind, means that "trust" or "faith" must be turned reflexively toward one's own capacities for illumination and enlightening conduct. This theme, too, represents a rather unique use of the notion of "trust" or "faith" and its reflexive exercise. Once again, as we remember from our opening chapter on pre-Buddhist Chinese thought, the notion of 信 *xin* was predominantly considered by philosophers a relational category, both in terms of knowledge and action. The heart (心 *xin*) in a variety of these early texts was thought to have the ability to "tally," which covered everything from integrating perceptual content from the sense organs in the determination of what kind of a thing something is to determining whether a person's deeds matched his or her words. The persons most worthy of trust in this early framework were those whose actions were consistent with their pledges or stated principles, and the most trustworthy of persons were those who managed affairs beneficently and only then articulated what principles of beneficence they espoused. In the foregoing Chinese Buddhist tradition, beginning with the construals of Vijñānavāda thought that coincided with the dissemination of the widely read *Awakening of Faith in the Mahāyāna*, faith in the possibility of human awakening could be informed by the conviction that every person's nature was grounded in a level of karmically pure mind. In the *Linji Lu*, however, faith is to be placed very concretely in oneself, meaning one's own person and actions. This is one reason why the equation of the genuine person with one's own luminous mind is so crucial to the text's stance. Human authenticity, it is argued, should not be sought in foregoing preparation, study, doctrinal refinement, or especially rank, whether that rank belongs to oneself or others, for the shared assumption of investing any of these with decisive value is precisely that enlightenment is an end of some cultivational or social process. It is this very assumption that the Hongzhou Chan school of Buddhism at least thematically commits itself to uproot at every turn. The real person in each of us lies in the immediate and full engagement of awareness with present circumstances. The sole reason such a formulation seems to be so vague and empty is precisely because it demands to be carried out in the particularities of one's practical and personal "environment," where active and not merely reactive responsiveness is key. If what is to be avoided in identification and conduct is artifice, then, it is argued, it is precisely the unique demands of the present that make precedential artifice irrelevant. What is left in guiding one to deal with the unprecedented is one's own capacity to comprehend and creatively respond to it. The mind in its brightness and the person in her conduct then, in the views expressed by the *Recorded Sayings*, are what Buddhism is all about.

As we shall see in our next chapter, this conception of 心 *xin* as both the causal basis (理 *li*) of the natural and human orders and the ever-present guide to conduct that emerged from the Chinese Buddhist tradition were themselves to have profound effects on other Chinese philosophical movements, even when these overly rejected Buddhism. Both traditional Chinese and much contemporary English-language scholarship has assumed that the influence that Buddhist thought in China worked upon the Neo-Confucian strands of reflection during the Song and Ming dynasties operated on the level of metaphysical theory and to a certain degree thereby made later Confucianism at least partially an unrecognizable descendant of its ancient Warring States and Han dynasty ancestors. However, as we shall shortly see, the influence of Buddhism on Confucianism was more vital than that, having as it did striking implications for how Confucians thought about the ultimate source of moral norms in personal reflection and therefore the very meaning of their own tradition. This reworked conception of mind, in the hands of Song and Ming dynasty Confucians, provided a space for individual moral reflection that, when hermeneutically read into the tradition's history, was, even more than the written legacies of the classic books, seen as the key to Confucius's own sagehood.

5

A Space for Moral Reflection

The Confucian Rapprochement

In the last chapter, we saw how various major traditions of Chinese Buddhism, strongly influenced by South Asian Vijñānavāda thought, transformed the notion of 心 *xin*. For ancient Chinese philosophers, the heart was almost uniformly considered to be only one of the body's physical organs. While its natural abilities to verbally classify the objects of the other senses, to learn, to plan, and in some cases to give rise to uniquely moral feelings made it a distinctive feature of being a person, it was never thought to be the only locus of consciousness in the body. Furthermore, its malleability made it susceptible to error, distraction, misdirection, and even complete obfuscation by other desires. In the hands of Buddhist thinkers and practitioners, who equated the term 心 *xin* with a more rarified, and ultimately awareness-oriented, Sanskrit conception of *citta*, the "mind" could still be identified as the core of our humanity. But its most basic capacity of being able to illuminate (明 *ming*) the world was both what enabled the other bodily organs to sense and rendered its most fundamental condition of perfection and purity inalienable. Chinese Buddhists claimed that 心 *xin* was the most primordial cause of sentience in physical creatures, that it is the sole locus of awareness that, when it fully inhabits the respective sense organs, enables them to perform their functions. They also held that its most fundamental illuminative character made it possible for us to attain the highest human ideals of knowledge and conduct. As Buddhism received ever-widening patronage from imperial courts during the Tang (seventh to tenth centuries) and Song (tenth to thirteenth centuries) eras, other schools of thought that competed for state influence and support, most notably for our study Confucianism, fully engaged this transformed construal of 心 *xin*. They hardly did so in exclusively critical ways but far more often by applying this revised representation of mind to their own programs of learning and praxis.

Confucian philosophers of the Song and Ming periods, as we shall see, were themselves diffident about Buddhism. They decried what appeared to them to be the antisocial and antimoral tendencies in that tradition, but such complaints seem to be only reformulated laments that Confucians had expressed about Buddhism at least as early as the fourth century. Nonetheless, the leading figures who composed and disseminated these later texts could usually admit their admiration for the degree of understanding Buddhists demonstrated of the "highest" truths of the natural order and mind despite their supposed laxity in applying these insights to social norms and the polity. Intellectual histories of Song, Ming, and later forms of Confucianism have, therefore, often been solely devoted to apportioning Buddhist influences on Confucian thought in comparison to what those studies would variously enumerate as native Confucian insights. Some contemporary academic treatments that are quite philosophically invested in the supposed naturalism or social-construction interpretations of early Chinese philosophy have been downright critical of Confucian appropriations of Buddhist ideas, for these have supposedly made abstruse metaphysics and even "western" epistemology out of what were originally concrete psychological observation and pragmatic moral theorizing.[1] Recently, however, a much more compelling historical approach to understanding why Song and Ming Confucian philosophers were so enthusiastic about adopting these new conceptions of mind has been employed by Peter Bol.[2] He points out that the largely southern contingent of Song thinkers who built the foundations for so-called Neo-Confucian thought found themselves in opposition to the eleventh-century imperial court's economic and educational centralization policies. This put them in the position of not only criticizing their rulers, whose inheritance claims to the throne they didn't deny, but also objecting to the ways they tried to standardize the Confucian civil service examination system so as to produce scholarly elites who would lend their policy decisions orthodox legitimacy. This stance carried the implications, of course, that Confucian scholars, in at least some contrast to their most ancient counterparts, were not disposed to automatically call for imperial recentralization of a fragmenting empire just because of deference to the pedigree of rulership. Nor were they content to attribute moral authority to literati who had only mastered ancient texts, their commentaries, and ritual protocols, and invoked tradition as their primary justification. For this new group of Confucian thinkers, while understanding the classics was still essential and ritual protocols remained embodiments of normative social relations, what made the ancient sages into masters themselves, and what facilitates individual moral cultivation still, is learning. Their conception of learning not only related to mastering texts and ritual practices but also to understanding nature, and through it, the nature of human relationships and human feelings. By means of a thorough and personal reflection on these, one could realize and achieve human ideals. Confucian thinkers of the period therefore referred to their own approach as one that engaged in a "discussion of learning" (講學 *jiang xue*), since whether any individual practitioner is able to become a sage or not will depend on their acquired ability to "learn how to learn."[3] In this regard, it became philosophically quite important to determine what precise role the human 心 *xin* plays in the process of learning, how its nature makes moral reflection possible, and how far it can take us in realizing our individual goals of cultivation and social aims of community. To be sure, the Buddhist vocabulary that located in the mind the "principles" or "coherence" (理 *li*) not only of nature at large but of comprehending nature, and attributed to the mind the power of illuminating the world, were great sources of inspiration for the Song and Ming Confucian thinkers we will cover in this chapter. But the Confucians did not uncritically appropriate these associations without revision. Instead, they creatively incorporated them into a distinctly Confucian program in which both the person could become a moral agent in society and societies of individuals could, as the idiom went, act as one body in a grand unity with the natural order.

In most treatments of the writings of Zhu Xi (c. 1130–1200) and Wang Yangming (1472–1529), emphasis is placed on how their contrasting treatments of theory and praxis help to define the opposition between the two paradigmatic "wings" of medieval Confucian thought that they are believed to represent, namely, the 理學 *li xue* (Learning of Coherence) and 心學 *xin xue* (Learning of the Heart) traditions. While the present chapter will certainly pass through some of these thematic contrasts, we will largely adopt the approach that has been laid out in the previous chapters. In their own way echoing the efforts of Huayen Buddhists to make sense of the relationship between mind and the physical body in terms of "coherence" (理 *li*) and "vital vapor" (氣 *qi*), medieval Confucian philosophers tended in varying degrees to side with their own most ancient texts in asserting that 心 *xin* is indeed a physical organ, while at the same time emphasizing that it either possesses or acts in accordance with 理 *li*. That is to say, to the degree that 理 *li* is considered to be the ordered regularity that governs the natural relations between things, as well as between people and things and people with one another, the mind, like all things in nature, possesses this ordered "coherence" in its undiminished entirety. But unlike other natural phenomena, the mind, because of its constitution of the most rarified configurations of 氣 *qi*, can both manifest and apprehend this coherence to the utmost extent.[4] For Zhu Xi, who espoused the "possession" model of the physical mind's relation to 理 *li*, questions arose as to how priority could be assigned between the mind's embodiment of the world's patterned coherence and its physicality. Wang Yangming, for his part, dealt with this issue with the formulation that the mind's very acting, in the immediate illumination of the environing circumstances, is itself 理 *li*. Despite these differences, medieval Confucians came in the broadest sense to understand the mind as the most refined and thus the clearest and most transparent formation of physical matter. And this very refinement made it capable of being the most illuminating conduit and expression of the way the world should be understood and acted in.

However, this admission that the human 心 *xin* was in all cases a physical organ and that it alone, in contrast to the early strands of the Chinese thought that we covered in the first chapter, was the home of all psychological states posed a threat to this theoretical commitment. After all, among the entire collection of possible psychological states, desire (欲 *yu*) is undoubtedly one of the most prevalent among people. Confucians concurred with Buddhists in a general sense that obsessive desirous attachments posed the greatest danger to learning and normativity. Desires not only ensure that one will remain too much mired in one's own biases and wishes but also cause the most internal physiological and mental turbulence and so prevent the tranquil contemplation that study, reflection, and correct action demand. But, and very significantly, Confucian philosophers across the ages have shared the view that not only concepts and thought but also feelings and sentiments are legitimately morally informative and motivating, that feelings such as sympathy and outrage could be utterly vital to correct action and so must be at the disposal of both the person engaged in self-cultivation and the consummate sage. These twin theoretical and practical requirements that desire be rooted out and yet other sentiments were morally invaluable prompted Neo-Confucians to make fundamental distinctions between desire (欲 *yu*) and feeling (情 *qing*).[5] This distinction did not amount to the same thing in the two early alternative "wings" of the tradition, however. For Zhu Xi, certain basic "patterns" of virtue, themselves components of the mind's 理 *li*, such as the classical notion of "benevolence" or "co-humanity" (仁 *ren*), manifested themselves in feeling, in the present case as the emotion of "care" or "love" (爱 *ai*). Their ultimate origin in the human mind's inherent order enabled such feelings to be generated from static tranquility, and so even in their passionate psychological manifestations, they, unlike desires, would not obscure truth or goodness in the reflection or conduct of the person. In characteristic fashion, Wang Yangming rejected the vocabulary of mediate manifestation when it came to seeing an abstract pattern of "co-humanity" in the feeling of love, since for him the feeling itself, arising in the relational context of the circumstances, was the moral order directly experienced. Despite these differences, the inalienably moral nature of feelings compelled these "creative transmitters" of the late Confucian tradition to incorporate human feeling into their picture of not only the way the natural human order is but the way it ought to be.

Finally, and in line with the perspective adopted in this chapter outlined earlier, we will return to the relationship the medieval Confucians envisioned between their idealized notion of "coherence," the mind, and the process of learning (學 *xue*). The ideal person in their view, once again with an eye on the pervasive corruption both of the state's exploitation of the Confucian curriculum and the superficially common careerism of students, ideal persons in their deepest reflective capabilities and in their unyielding pursuits should be learners. While it is true, in this theoretical framework, that the human mind not only possesses the ordered coherence of the world but also is physically made in such a way as to be able to manifest that coherence better than any other creature, whether individuals contingently do so depends on their practice and experience of learning. To represent the spectrum of positions in this chapter once again, we will speak of some contrasts. For Zhu Xi, the learning process consists not just in the mastery of a certain body of texts but also in a certain approach to reading, not only in an abstract regard for the natural order but in intimate observation of natural relationships, not only in familiarity with history but with sensitivity to what its moral lessons demand of us now. For him, learning roots us indelibly in our world, a world in which, at the end of our studies, we will find a seamless continuity between natural phenomena and creatures, our human heritage and our social arrangements. In the thought of Wang Yangming, no thorough encyclopedic knowledge needs to be acquired as a result of a rigorous and premeditated process of study. Instead, persons find themselves in an already coherent and harmonious order, and they need only fully experientially immerse themselves in the apprehension of what it feels like and what it means to be part of that order to realize the already-consummate sagehood that resides in a natural heart. For Wang, the heart whose responses to the world are practiced and rehearsed to play out their expected roles in an inauthentic plan, and whose premeditated actions are dictated by externals, is not a heart that knows of and for itself what goodness is. To learn for Wang Yangming, then, is to learn one's own mind. Despite these differences, this Neo-Confucian conception of persons as fundamentally and inexorably learners and not just mimickers helps us to understand the full legacy of a reworked idea of 心 *xin* that resulted from the prolonged South and East Asian philosophical encounters of mind.

Mind as Matter and Sense

It is not difficult to discern a slow but conspicuous transformation in the development of Song dynasty Confucian philosophical texts with regard to the relationship between the mind and "vital vapor" (氣 *qi*). Early Song thinkers and commentators such as Zhou Dunyi and Zhang Zai do not take great departures from ancient Confucian thought, even with their increased efforts toward diagrammed systematization, in asserting that the mind is a physical organ whose most fundamental constituent is 氣 *qi*. They claimed that whether or not the mind is clear or obscure, tranquil or turbulent depends on the character of its 氣 *qi* and the degree to which an individual can master bodily cultivation so as to control it. But Zhu Xi, following his immediate intellectual predecessors, the Cheng brothers, fastens onto the notion of "coherence" because physical phenomena made of the two types of 氣 *qi*, namely, *yin* and *yang*, do not simply interact randomly but follow ordered patterns of "coalescence" (錯綜不失條緒 *cuo zong bu shi tiao xu*). This demonstrates that there must be "coherence" or regular causal principles (理 *li*) that govern the constitution of things and thus the possibilities of their interaction with other things.[6] In other places in Zhu's discourses, the relationship between coherence and matter is compared to the plans according to which one builds a structure and the structure itself. It is also sometimes mapped onto the by then age-old distinction between "substance" (體 *ti*) and "function" (用 *yong*), where, for example, the capacity of the eyes to see represents their "substance" or their underlying "principle," while using them to look at things represents their material activity or use.[7] This application of the distinction between *li* and *qi* to the issue of awareness as articulated in the latter example so far seems to echo rather precisely the conventional Chinese Buddhist characterization of the *li* or causal basis of awareness as the singular and luminous source of the consciousness in sentient creatures. However, in a fascinating hermeneutic and analytical maneuver that wraps this new formula into classical Confucian terms, Zhu Xi claims that the degree of awareness in any given creature is practically entirely dependent on the capacity of the creature's 氣 *qi* to serve as the conduit of the principles that make awareness possible.

> 性如水, 流於清渠則清, 流入汙渠則濁. 氣質之清者, 正者, 得之則全, 人是也: 氣質之濁者, 偏者, 得之則昧, 禽獸是也. 氣有清濁, 人則得其清者, 禽獸則得 其濁者. 人大體本清, 故異於禽獸: 亦有濁者, 則去禽獸不遠矣. 節. 有是理而後有是氣, 有是氣則必有是理. 但稟氣之清者, 為聖為賢, 如寶珠在 清冷水中: 稟氣之濁者, 為愚為不肖, 如珠在濁水中. 所謂 "明明德" 者是 就濁水中揩拭此 珠也.
>
> Nature (性 *xing*) is similar to water. If it flows through a clear channel, it remains clear; if it flows through a filthy

> channel, it becomes turbid. [Nature] that acquires clear and balanced psychophysical stuff (氣 *qi*) will remain whole—this is what happens to man. [Nature] that acquires turbid and unbalanced psychophysical stuff will become obscured. This is what happens to beasts. Psychophysical stuff is both clear (清 *qing*) and turbid (濁 *zhuo*). Men acquire the clear stuff, beasts acquire the turbid stuff. Men, for the most part, are fundamentally clear and thus different from beasts. But there are also those who are turbid and thus not so very different from beasts.
>
> Once there exists this principle (理 *li*), there exists this psychophysical stuff. Once there exists this psychophysical stuff, there is certain to exist this principle. It's simply that he who received clear psychophysical stuff is a sage or worthy—he is like a precious pearl lying in crystal clear water. And he who receives turbid psychophysical stuff is an idiot or degenerate—he is like a pearl lying in turbid water. What is called "keeping the inborn luminous Virtue (明明德 *ming ming de*) unobscured" is the process of reaching into the turbid water and wiping clean this pearl. (Zhu Xi, *Conversations*, 73:1–5 [Gardner 1990, 98])

In this representation, it is the always clear and whole coherence of things that is called luminous (明 *ming*), but the material bodies in which it exists may be configured by vital vapor (*qi*) that is in varying densities clear (清 *qing*) or obscuring, and these varying degrees determine whether a creature is a "bird or beast" (禽獸 *qin shou*) or a person (人 *ren*). And the variable character of *qi* in persons will determine whether they are sages or fools. As we shall see, it is entirely possible for the vast majority of persons who are not afflicted with severely impaired physical bodies to actively alter the quality of their *qi* in practice, which is precisely what makes ritual discipline, mental tranquility, and learning so important to the Confucian program. What we focus on for the moment though is that, in the thought of Zhu Xi, there is no thing or living being in the world that lacks the entirety and perfection of the "luminosity" of natural "coherence," from rocks and rivers to animals and persons. Indeed, it was Cheng Yi and Zhu Xi who insisted that the term "coherence" (理 *li*) was precisely what the ancient Confucian texts identified as "nature" (性 *xing*).[8] However, as formulated in Zhu's school, this "luminous virtue" of coherence in all things is not, considered on its own, a basic form of awareness, for it has no shape and is inclusive of things that possess no awareness at all. Instead, "luminosity" in this sense merely refers to the complete and imperturbable perfection of *li* as it is found in all natural things. It is, as noted, the "pearl" that can be found in all material things, regardless of whether that material is contingently dense or refined, "turbid" or "clear."

Awareness, therefore, is not a feature of *li*, even though its ultimate possibility and the conditions under which it can exist in different forms and levels of perfection are implicate in natural coherence. As far as its individuated existence and experience is concerned, it is instead a feature of 氣 *qi*. In this general commitment, Neo-Confucian philosophers remain faithful to the roots of their tradition in an important way, for awareness can really only be found in physical bodies and its qualities depend on the specific circumstances of those bodies. This leads Zhu Xi himself to occasionally make some quite remarkable claims about the capacity of certain kinds of animal species, such as tigers, wolves, bees, ants, and especially apes, which according to him are entirely similar to humans in form but lack only the ability to speak, for distinctively moral behavior in cases where their *qi* permits natural coherence to manifest in their own social behaviors. However, Zhu Xi is rarely as specific, even in his commentary on the *Mengzi*, as classical Confucian philosophers had been about the degree to which awareness could be uniquely located in the other sense organs like the eyes, ears, and so forth. He does aver, at any rate, that the eyes' "capacity" (才 *cai*) to see is derived from the "coherence" that is embodied in the material configuration of that particular organ. Zhu Xi is much more focused on the mind, which he sometimes refers to as "the one mind" (一心 *yi xin*).[9] The mind, like all other things in nature, is also constituted of *qi*, and it, too, has its own specific coherence that can be found in its particularized configurations. When it operates in a heightened state of "clarity" and "brightness" (炯 *jiong*), and thus is able to more clearly reflect and mediate coherence, it can control the bodily inclinations and activities well enough to enable people to achieve optimized individual and social ends without being compelled by external rules. Such imposed social norms exist only because people's minds easily become "scattered and slothful" (散緩 *san huan*).[10] As we shall see, the project of personal cultivation and study must therefore incorporate practices that render the mind's *qi* tranquil and unperturbed rather than tossed about in distraction and desirous pursuits. However, in his commentary on the Han Confucian text the *Zhong Yong*, Zhu Xi, in elaborating on the distinction between a mind in a state of clear calm and a mind buffeted about by excitation and distraction, articulates the possibilities and experiences of these two alternative states with the vocabulary of the "mind of the way" (道心 *dao xin*) and the "(merely) human mind" (人心 *ren xin*).

> 心之虛靈知覺, 一而已矣, 而以爲有人心, 道心之異者, 則以 其或生于形氣之私, 或原于性命之正, 而所以爲知覺者不同, 是以 或危殆而不安, 或微妙而難見耳.然人莫不有是形, 故雖上智不能 無人心, 亦莫不有是性, 故雖下愚不能無道心.二者雜于方寸之間, 而不知所以治之, 則危者愈危, 微者愈微, 而天理之公卒無以 勝夫人欲之私矣.精則察夫二者之間而不雜也, 一則守其本心之正 而不離也.從事于斯, 無少閑斷, 必使道心常爲一身之主, 而人心 每聽命焉, 則危者安, 微者著, 而動靜雲爲自無過不及之差矣.
>
> The mind, unprejudiced, spiritual and conscious (虛靈知 *xu ling zhi*, "empty, intelligent and aware")—is one. But that there is a distinction between the "human mind" (人心 *ren xin*) and the "ontological mind" (道心 *dao xin*, "the mind of the way") is because of this: the mind sometimes arises in the self-centeredness of the psychophysical stuff (氣 *qi*) and at times originates in the perfect impartiality of the moral nature decreed by heaven, so the resulting consciousnesses (知 *zhe*) are different. Hence the mind can be precarious and unsettled, or abstruse and almost imperceptible. Yet all men have a psychophysical form (形 *xiang*), so even the very wisest will also have a human mind, and all men have a moral nature, so even the very stupidest will always have an ontological mind. If the human mind and the ontological mind become mixed in the heart and one does not know how to control them, the precarious will become even more precarious, the imperceptible will become even more imperceptible, and the impartiality of the heavenly principle (天理 *tian li*, "natural coherence") will in the end be unable to overcome the selfishness of

> human desires (人欲 *ren yu*). "Be discriminating" means to distinguish between the human and ontological minds so that they do not become mixed. "Be undivided" means to protect the perfect impartiality of the original mind (本心 *ben xin*) so that it does not take leave of one. Should one devote oneself without interruption to these matters, making certain that the ontological mind always acts as master of the body (身之主 *shen zhi zhu*) and the human mind always obeys its orders, the precarious will become subtle and the almost imperceptible will become manifest. And in activity and tranquility, in words and actions, one will not err in going either too far or not far enough. (Zhu Xi, *Zhong Yong Jun Ju Xu* 12:7 [Gardner 1990, 144–145])

It is apparent that in this and similar passages, Zhu Xi is not suggesting that there are two entirely different minds within each person but instead rather one mind that is constituted of *qi* that can be either tranquil and thus clear; aware and impartial, and so reflective of the coherence both within and outside of itself; or beset with desires that obscure the way the self and the world actually are. This mind will only be able to have complete mastery over the words and actions of the 身 *shen* body if it can maintain its original (本 *ben*) state of tranquility, which is transparent to natural coherence. We shall return to why Zhu Xi, once again in the context of his commentary on the *Zhong Yong*, believes that the mind's original state is tranquil and even. We are here dealing with two possible general states of the physical mind's awareness and their alternative consequences in human conduct. The mind's capacity to clearly refract the luminosity of inner and outer coherence in its own nature and the natural order of the world depends on how its own *qi* is managed in intentional and purposeful conduct.

But stating things in the way Zhu Xi did involved some real philosophical perils. Even in the records of his own conversations, he is represented as being importuned by questions about whether the coherence of nature exists in a temporally or logically prior state to physical phenomena, and in responding he often struggles to articulate the precise relationship between *li* and *qi*. To the philosophical preceptor of the other major wing of Neo-Confucian thought, the Ming dynasty general and polymath Wang Yangming, Zhu's terminological distinction between the "mind of the way" (道心 *dao xin*) and the "(merely) human mind" (人心 *ren xin*) made it sound too much like there was supposed to be some fundamental metaphysical difference between the two. In our actual experience, Wang insisted, no such fundamental distinction is ever encountered. Instead, as is dramatized in his conversations with Xu Ai, Wang thought the confusion could be rectified by emphasizing that the distinction between the mind of the way and the merely human mind should be explicitly defined as pertaining to different and contingent temporal states of our awareness and experience.

> 愛問, "'道心常為一身之主, 而人心每聽命.' 以先生 精一之訓推之, 此語似有弊." 先生曰, "然. 心一也. 未雜於人謂之道心. 雜以人偽謂之人心 人心之得其正者即道心. 道心之矢其正者即人心. 初非有 三心也. 程子謂人心即人欲, 道心即天理. 語若分析, 而意實得之. 今曰 '道心為生, 而人心聽命, ' 是三心也. 天理人欲不並立. 安有天理為主, 人欲又從 而聽命者?"

> I asked: "[Zhu Xi said that] 'the heart-mind of the Way is always the governor of the self (身 *shen*, or the "*shen* body" or "person") and the human heart-mind always obeys it.' Seen in the light of your teachings regarding being wholly refined and wholly focused, this claim seems flawed."
>
> The master said: "That is correct. The heart-mind is one. Before it is mixed with what is human, it is called the heart-mind of the Way. After being mixed with human artifice, it is called the human heart-mind. When the human heart-mind attains its correct state (得其正 *de qi zheng*), it is called the heart-mind of the Way. When the heart-mind loses its correct state, it is the human heart-mind. From the very start, there are not two heart-minds. Cheng Yi said: 'The human heart-mind is human desire; the heart-mind of the Way is Heavenly principle (天理 *tian li*, again, probably best "natural coherence").' While this way of putting it seems to divide the heart-mind into two things, it succeeds in conveying the basic idea. Now to say that the heart-mind of the Way is the governor and the human heart-mind obeys its commands, this is to posit the existence of two heart-minds.[11] Heavenly principle and human desires

> cannot be at play at the same time (不並立 *bu bing li*, "do not simultaneously obtain"), and so, how could one have Heavenly principle as the governor and human desires subsequently (又 *you*) obeying its commands?" (Wang, *Quanxilu*, 1:10 [Ivanhoe 2009, 148–149])

This clarification might seem overly fastidious at first glance. But as we shall see in more detail later, Wang had additional concerns to this one that Zhu's system artificially externalizes natural coherence from the heart in his account of how people gain knowledge. It is important to note however that both Zhu and Wang concur that the mind ideally should be the "lord" or "master" (主 *zhu*) of the *shen* body (身) or person. But whether the mind does indeed act as the body's master depends on whether it is informed by its apprehension of coherence or is pulled in different directions by desire. Wang is emphatic here that the mind cannot manifest natural coherence and at the same instant be led to wayward conduct or that the mind can be inundated by desires and act as the true master of the body. So, whether it is described as a mind in accord with the true course (道 *dao*) of things or is, to wit, "all-too-human" (人 *ren*) depends not on whether it is in possession of coherence (天理 *tian li*), for the Song and Ming Confucians all confidently proclaim that mind, just like everything else, can never be deprived of coherence but instead hangs on what state the mind's *qi* is in. And, apart from cases of severe physical or psychological disability, the mind's *qi* can be cultivated sufficiently through practice and learning to enable any person to become ultimately wise and just. This is the renewed fashion in which ancient Confucians had expressed the optimistic view that any person in the street could become a perfected sage. The mind possessed its own coherence, and, because of the unique constitution of the human body, the mind was made of *qi* that was materially rarified enough to manifest the natural coherence of both the environing world and of ideal human conduct. The special manner, in the person, in which the mind existed as both matter and sense put the greatest goods in life within human grasp.

We seem, nonetheless, to so far have an insufficient account, for the desire and perfected awareness that have been dichotomized in these passages as two unrelated states of mind are just that, only two possible conditions of our experience. Furthermore, it could easily be argued, since the coherence of the mind simply means all the ways the mind can operate given its constitution, that at least logically nothing really falls out or is excludable from the *li* of the mind. This could have damning consequences for any sense of normativity one might wish to obtain from this theoretical framework. Indeed, the Song and Ming Confucians accused the Buddhists, given the latter's supposed fixation on *li* as the causal basis of sentience in nature, of excluding not merely moral distinctions from their idea of mind but also of laying by the wayside all those relational feelings and disciplines of study that combine to make us socially engaged creatures. But lest these moral sentiments and historical consciousness, long honored in the Confucian tradition, were themselves to be ultimately placed within the classification of distracting and obscuring human desires themselves, their tether to the mind's supposedly originary state of tranquility and pure awareness had to be found somewhere. How could other feelings and mental states associated with learning be distinguished from desires, especially with regard to the mind's supposedly "original" state of tranquility?

Coherence and Unity in Feeling

In the reorganization of the study curriculum worked out by southern Song Confucians, Zhu most prominently, a number of often formerly neglected Warring States and Han dynasty texts gained priority over the more ancient Zhou classics. One of these texts was the *Zhong Yong* (中庸), a work prized by the medieval scholars because of its focus on the inner development of feelings and their training in conduct and application in rulership. The first section of this work posits that all human emotions or feelings (情 *qing*) originate from a condition of psychological equilibrium (中 *zhong*), but once they have arisen, the proper aim of praxis is to maintain a constant state (庸 *yong*) of harmony between them in everyday conduct.

> 天命之謂性, 率性之謂道, 修道之謂教. 道也者, 不可須臾離也, 可離非道也. 是故君子戒慎乎其所不睹, 恐懼乎其所不聞. 莫見乎隱, 莫顯乎微. 故君子 慎其獨也. 喜怒哀樂之未發, 謂之中, 發而皆中節, 謂之和; 中也者, 天下之大本也; 和也者, 天下之達道也. 致中和, 天地位焉, 萬物育焉.

> What heaven decrees is called "the nature (性 *xing*)"; to follow the nature is called "the Way"; to cultivate the Way is called "instruction." The Way: it must not be abandoned for even a moment. What can be abandoned is not the Way. Consequently, the superior man treats with extreme care even that not visible to him, and treats with apprehension even that beyond the reach of his hearing. Before pleasure, anger, sorrow, and joy have arisen—this we call perfect balance (中 *zhong*). And after they have arisen and attained their proportion (中節 *zhong jie*, their "balanced portion")—this we call harmony (和 *he*). Perfect balance is the great foundation (本 *ben*, "root" or "origin") of the universe; harmony is the way that unfolds throughout the universe. Let perfect balance and harmony be realized and heaven and earth will find their proper places (位 *wei*, their "ranks") therein, and the ten thousand creatures will be nourished therein. (*Zhong Yong* 1 [Gardner 2007, 110–111])

This passage, cryptic on its own, leaves its explicators the challenge of elaborating on what sense can be made of saying that balance (中 *zhong*) is the origin of the natural world, and that maintaining balance among the arisen feelings will establish the proper order or rank (位 *wei*) among things in the world. In this context, it is crucial to remember that Zhu understands the first term defined in the passage, 性 *xing* or "nature," to itself denote coherence (理 *li*). For Zhu, then, this passage represents some crucially pivotal first principles that help us to both fundamentally understand the nature of human feelings as well as the varieties of their expression.

From these first principles, Zhu extrapolates the view that the coherence of the mind is all-inclusive, which is to say that the mind, whether in a state of originary tranquility and balance or active desirous pursuits, whether cultivated or uncultivated, always operates within the parameters of its own coherence. Of course, not all possibilities of the mind's activity are, by mere virtue of that fact, normative ideals. There is still a meaningful distinction to be made between the broadest range of what the mind can do and what the mind should do in order to optimize its capacities for knowledge and virtuous conduct. So, even while acknowledging that all of the mind's possible states, desires, feelings, and ideas are enveloped within the whole set of possibilities inherent in its physical constitution, it is crucial we not mistake that entire set of its potentials for its ideals.

> 心, 主宰之謂也. 動靜皆主宰, 非是靜時無 所用, 及至動時方有主宰也. 言主宰, 則混 然體統自在其中. 心統攝性情, 非儱侗與性情為一物 而不分別也.
>
> The mind is a term for the ruler. In both activity and stillness, it is the ruler. It is not that when one is still, it has no function or that there is really only a ruler when one is active. The ruler is the inclusive systematizing inside oneself (*hunran titong zi zai qi zhong*). The mind unites the emotions and the nature, [but] it does not form some crude entity together with nature and emotion that cannot be distinguished from them. (Zhu Xi, *Conversations*, 94:5 [Bol 2008, 178])

The phrase Bol translates here as "inclusive systematizing within oneself" 混然體統自在其中 (*hunran titong zi zai qi zhong*), describes the heart as "the substantial unity of the existing mixture within itself"; it is the totality of all its feelings, ideas, and states. However, while we can say that the mind collects into a unity (統攝 *tong shi*) both feelings (情 *qing*) and nature (性 *xing*), where the former is understood as active movements (動 *dong*) of the mind and the latter as its tranquil or stable (靜 *jing*) dispositions, it does not simply "constitute a single thing that is a crude and confused collection of nature and feeling" (儱侗與性情為一物 *long tong yu xing qing wei yi wu*). We can, in reflecting on the different activities of mind and the results they produce in conduct, not only identify feelings and ideas that are more conducive to its ability to possess genuine goodness and truth, but we can also discover what is at the core of its nature.

> "'天理人欲分數有多少? 天理本多, 人欲 便也是天理裹面做出來. 雖是人欲, 人欲 中自有天理.' 問: "莫是本來全是天理否?' 曰: '人生都是天理, 人欲郝是後來沒巴鼻生底.'"
>
> What are the percentages of heavenly principle (天理 *tian li*, once again, "natural coherence") and human desire? Heavenly principle is originally large. Human desire, then, operates from within the heavenly principle. And

> even though it is human desire, human desire naturally contains heavenly principle. Someone asked: Isn't it that originally it was all heavenly principle? Chu replied: At birth a person's all heavenly principle; human desire is produced later, without cause. (Zhu Xi, *Conversations*, 224:2 [Gardner 1990, 181])

The last two words of this translation, "without cause," are an unfortunate rendition, if only because they do not call sufficient attention to the surprising invocation of Buddhist vocabulary the sentence makes. The phrase 沒巴鼻生底 *mei ba bi sheng de* at the end of the passage, describing the arrival of desires in the mind, means that such desires "are not an acquisition from birth." The word for "acquisition," 巴鼻 *ba bi*, appears to be a Chinese transliteration of the Sanskrit term *prāpti*, which in Abhidharma Buddhist discourse refers precisely to the karmic "acquisition" of dispositions and fruits from previous lives in one's present birth. Thus, Zhu Xi is here at least partly taking a swipe at Buddhism by denying that we are born with desires and using the Buddhists' own terminology to do it. More pertinent to our present discussion, however, is the argument that, while the natural coherence of the human mind does allow for the possibility of the formation of desires, we are not born (生 *sheng*) with them, and so we can infer that desires are not an essential constituent of our nature (性 *xing*) but are instead an acquired state of mind. It is important to remember, of course, that in both the Buddhist discourse he is rejecting and in his own thinking, Zhu does not believe human desires (人欲 *ren yu*) refer to our physiological needs, such as our needs to breathe, drink, or eat, but rather that specifically human desires are obsessions with acquisitions of various artificial sorts. So, what Zhu Xi intends to emphasize here is that we are not born with our specific obsessions, but we pick them up as time goes on in our experience, and to whatever degree they cause psychological turbulence and upset and prompt us to chase after the possession of things that will ultimately be to our moral detriment, they inhibit and obscure the understanding of our true nature more than they reveal it. We become truly transparent to our own coherence when the mind's perturbations have been calmed and quieted.

And yet, we have many more mental states than simply those associated with the obsession to possess or attain things, which manifest themselves as feelings. We experience grief at loss, joy in community, sorrow in disappointment, outrage at unfairness, and love in intimacy. These feelings are, as we all know, very active emotional states, they cause physiological changes in the *qi* of the body's other systems and indeed often prompt us to move our bodies in active response. It is also entirely possible that all these emotional states and more may be experienced in pursuits that are not particularly virtuous. And yet, once again in agreement with a long-standing Confucian heritage, Zhu Xi firmly believed that these feelings could in specific circumstances be entirely morally appropriate and could serve as our primary motivations to undertake morally necessary actions. And there is yet another relevant difference between desire and other feelings in their respective capacities to help us actually know the world. Desires, on the one hand, may be thought of as merely acquisitive motives; they prompt us to pursue, achieve, and maintain things in a fixed state that suits our preferences for as long as possible. But such motives, powerful as they are, may do much less in revealing the nature of things as well as demanding certain kinds of moral response from us than feelings do. Love, for example, may be the only emotion we have that adequately captures the great uniqueness of an individual, or the great beauty of a place. Revulsion or anger may be the only thing that can fitfully reveal the degree of evil bound up with a certain act of destruction and can thus prompt us to sacrifice, rather than acquire, anything to correct it. Joy can be more than merely the acknowledgment of a bond between people but the particular happiness that is realized from the unique relationships they bear to one another. Grief may be the only response that can adequately reflect the meaning of what a lost loved one has contributed to the lives of those around them. These feelings, the Confucian might object to the Buddhist, are not just reducible to one form or another of desirous attachment, for they are not in every case manifestations of acquisitive motives, though they sometimes can be turned to that purpose, but can often be the only way some things and people in the world may be fully known. And so, Confucian philosophers through the ages have been compelled to defend the moral standing of emotions, despite the fact that doing so forced them to deal with a number of thorny theoretical challenges. The challenge that this commitment brought on Neo-Confucian thinkers had specifically to do with the novel theories of mind that they were developing.

The theoretical problem that arises, though, is that if we associate greater degrees of awareness of natural coherence with tranquil states of mind and yet admit that certain feelings that result in psychological and bodily activity involve mental excitations of various kinds, then a way must be found to root moral feelings in tranquil states of 心 *xin*. And it is here where we come upon one of the most important reasons that Zhu Xi is so committed to the notion of natural coherence to begin with. In his commentary on the famous passage from the *Mengzi* we dwelt upon in the first chapter that speaks of the spontaneous feeling of compassion people have when seeing a child about to fall into a well, Zhu Xi finds great significance in the distinction between the feeling (心 *xin*) of compassion and the virtue of benevolence or co-humanity (仁 *ren*). This distinction, he argues, demonstrates that the feelings are the manifestations of the virtues. The Song master commentator infers from this that the virtues are grounded in human nature, while the emotions of compassion and so on are their manifestations, and the mind is therefore the link between human natural coherence and our experience of this coherence in feelings.

> 惻隱, 羞惡, 辭讓, 是非, 情也. 仁, 義, 禮, 智, 性也. 心, 統性情者也. 端, 緒也. 因其情之發, 而性之本然可得而見, 猶有物在中而緒見于外也.
>
> Inner compassion, shame and revulsion, deference, and approval and disapproval, these are emotions (情 *qing*). Co-humanity, rightness, ritual propriety, and wisdom, these are nature (性 *xing*). The mind is that which unifies nature and emotions. The extremities (端 *duan*), these are visible feelings (緒 *xu*). Because it manifests (發 *fa*) in emotions, the root (本 *ben*) of nature can become visible. It is like things (物 *wu*) that are found within (在中 *zai zhong*), but their traces (緒 *xu*) are visible on the outside. (Zhu Xi, *Mengzi Ji Zhu*, 2A6)[12]

Zhu's hermeneutic treatment of the term 端 *duan* is quite telling here. While in the root text, 端 *duan* surely means something like "beginnings," and the feelings themselves are considered fairly straightforwardly by the *Mengzi* as themselves the emergent forms of virtue,

Zhu Xi's reading capitalizes on an alternative meaning of 端 *duan*, "extremity" or "end," and by virtue of this alternative interpretation, feelings are transformed from being the roots of virtue to virtue's endpoints or visible clues (緒 *xu*). Instead, what lies at the root of the feelings is nature, which, we remind ourselves once again, is in his works equivalent to the notion of coherence (理 *li*). The feelings, especially those feelings associated with moral behavior, are therefore in Zhu's thought manifestations of coherence. What ties these feelings to coherence is precisely the organ of the mind itself. Now, what presumably distinguishes these emotions from desires with respect to the natural coherence of persons is that people are born with these feelings, as the *Mengzi* passage attests and as Zhu Xi concurs. Since these emotions are the visible outgrowths of the roots of human nature, our possession of them does not depend on social conditioning or environing circumstances. By contrast, according to Zhu's account, desires, though they are possibilities of mental activity permitted by the coherence of our physical constitution, are not present at birth; the specific desires we have are acquired during the courses of our lives. This difference in the order of acquisition served as the justification for Song Confucians who followed Zhu to make a rather careful terminological distinction between feelings as they are enumerated in the preceding passage and desires.

But this narrative of human nature is duly complicated by the fact that the mind is considered here a physical organ, which means that the degree to which its feelings can be bound to virtues will hardly be a given but instead is contingent on the degree of cultivation a person undertakes and the effort he or she exerts in it.

> 學者為學, 未問真知與力行, 且要收拾此 心, 令有箇頓放處. 若收斂都在義理上安 頓, 無許多胡思亂想, 則久久自於物欲上輕, 於義理上重. 須是教義理心重於物欲, 如秤令有低昂, 郎見得 義理自端的, 自有欲罷不能之意, 其於物欲, 自無暇及之矣. 苟操舍存亡之間無所主宰, 縱說得, 亦何益, 銖.
>
> In learning, before inquiring into what constitutes true knowledge and vigorous action, a student should collect his mind and give it a place to settle. If in gathering it he places it in the midst of moral principle (義理 *yi li*), it'll be largely free of reckless thoughts, and after a while it'll

> lay light with material desire and heavy with moral principle—it's essential that moral principle outweigh material desire in the mind: it's like a scale that fluctuates between the low and the high end. And once he understands moral principle absolutely clearly, though he may want to stop, he won't be able to; as for material desire he of course won't have the time for it. But if in "holding it fast and letting it go, preserving it and losing it," he is without a master [i.e., a collected mind], even though we might explain [true knowledge and vigorous action] to him, it'd be of no use. (Zhu Xi, *Conversations*, 201:16 [Gardner 1990, 165])

We will in the next section move on to examine how in practice Zhu believed "preservation" of a virtuous mind could be achieved through contemplation and learning. For the moment, we see how he goes about arguing that, at least in the matter of natural human constitution, the feelings that most primarily motivate us to moral conduct, despite the fact that they surely result, like desire, in psychological turbulence, are fundamentally distinct from desires insofar as they are rooted in the stable virtues that are built into our coherence when we are born. And those roots are planted in the soil of the mind. The most precarious thing about human existence is that the connection of emotions to these roots can be severed, even though the roots themselves can't be eliminated. This severance can happen if the soil is not well tended, if the mind is not purposefully kept in as tranquil a state as possible through a trained disposition of cultivated reflection that allows the roots of virtue to manifest in interaction, at which point feelings can be abused by desires.

Proponents of the opposing Lu-Wang school of Confucian thought were, once again, troubled by the way that Zhu Xi thematized the relation between the mind, its feelings, and the moral principles in which they were rooted. As we have seen, Wang Yangming thought that speaking of natural coherence even as analytically distinct from human feelings that are aroused in the midst of an experienced situation creates a peril of a dualistic sort. This makes it sound like we may have more than one mind, one that knows moral principles and another that pursues desires. Putting Zhu's theoretical vision into practice, as we shall soon see, indeed requires that the moral principles found within natural coherence, despite the fact that we are born with them and they at times spontaneously manifest in our emotional responses and conduct, need to be thoroughly and consciously studied in order to be understood. This also makes it seem, Wang objects, that the moral principles that are supposed to be in us are still in some respect something different from us. After all, for Zhu Xi, feelings of compassion or deference mediate moral principles, they serve as the latter's conduits and evidence, but the feelings themselves are not the moral principles. Wang believed that our concrete experience both of feelings and of real goodness tells us a different story, and in his mind, a story much more faithful to the one we find in classical texts like the *Mengzi*. Wang thought that the difference between people who were compelled to act in moral ways as opposed to those who were not should not be represented as a difference between people who had actively learned about natural coherence as opposed to those who had not. Instead, that very difference could be accounted for in terms of people who themselves had concrete experiences of things like family care, deference, and compassion, and those who had not, for those concrete experiences were all that were needed in order for people to most deeply understand the virtues of their feelings. In that sense, moral experiences confer immediate knowledge that is not different in kind from the knowledge we derive from other sorts of affective experiences.

> 見好色屬知, 好好色屬行. 只見那好色時, 已自好了. 不是見了後, 又立箇心去好. 聞惡臭屬知, 惡惡臭屬 行. 只聞那惡臭時, 已自惡了. 不是聞了後, 別立 箇心去惡. 如鼻塞人雖貝惡臭在前, 鼻中不曾聞得, 便亦不甚惡. 亦只是不曾知臭. 就如稱某人知孝, 某 人知弟. 必是 其人已曾行孝行弟, 方可稱他知孝知弟. 不成只是曉得說些孝弟的話, 便可稱為知孝弟. 又如知痛, 必已自痛了, 方知痛. 知寒, 必已自寒了. 知饑, 必已自磯了. 知行如何分得開, 此便是知行的本體, 不曾有 私意隔斷的.

> Seeing a beautiful color is a case of knowing (知 *zhi*), while loving a beautiful color is a case of acting. As soon as one sees the beautiful color, one naturally (已自 *ji zi*, "in [the seeing] itself") loves it. It is not as if you first see it and, only then, intentionally decide to love it. Smelling a bad odor is a case of knowing, while hating a bad odor is a case of acting. As soon as one smells the bad odor,

> one naturally hates it. It is not as if you first smell it and, only then, intentionally, you decide to hate it. Consider the case of a person with a stuffed-up nose. Even if he sees a malodorous object right in front of him, the smell does not reach him, and so he does not hate it. This is simply not to know the bad odor.
>
> The same is true when one says that someone knows filial piety or brotherly respect. The person must have already acted with filial piety or brotherly respect before one can say she knows them. One cannot say she knows filial piety or brotherly respect simply because she knows how to *say* something filial or brotherly. Knowing pain offers another good example. One must have experienced pain itself in order to know pain. [Similarly] one must have experienced cold oneself in order to know cold, and one must have experienced hunger oneself in order to know hunger. How can knowing and acting be separated? This is the original state (本體 *ben ti*, "original substance") of knowing and acting, before any selfish thoughts have separated them. (Wang, *Chuanxilu*, 5:10 [Ivanhoe 2009, 140–141])

When the mind is aware and knows (知 *zhi*), it immediately acts (行 *xing*) on that knowledge without having to engage in any special sort of inquiry. This is what it really means, on Wang's view, to hold the conviction that the mind possesses natural coherence. It responds appropriately to its environing circumstances of its own accord because the feelings and virtues that enable it to know and act in the first instance are elements in its very constitution, not because those feelings mediate virtues that can or should be analytically abstracted from the feelings and matter of the mind itself. In other words, this is the real import, as Wang would have it, of believing in "innate knowing" (良知 *liang zhi*), the matter of the mind itself possesses the virtues that enable people to live ethically consummate lives.

This does not mean, of course, that conduct can never go wrong. The selfish desires implicated at the end of the previous passage are still very much capable of leading people astray. But in Wang's perspective, the mind really only is drawn in wayward directions when it fails to attend to its own knowledge and innate coherence and allows the rest of the body's organs to direct it.

何謂身心之形體? 運用之謂也. 何謂心身之靈明? 主宰之謂也. 何謂修身? 為善而去惡之謂也. 吾身自能為善而去惡乎? 必其靈明主宰者欲為善而去惡, 然後其形體運用者始能為善而去惡也. 故欲修其身者, 必在於先正其心也. 然心之本體則 性也, 性無不善, 則心之本體本無不正也. 何從而用其正之之功乎? 蓋心之本體本 無不正, 自其意念發動, 而後有不正. 故欲正其心者, 必就其意念之所發 而正之, 凡其一念而善也, 好之真如好好色, 發一念而惡也, 惡之真如 惡惡臭, 則意無不誠, 而心可正矣.

What do we mean by "person" (身心 *shen*, "embodied mind")? It is the way we refer to the physical operation of the heart-mind. What do we mean by "heart-mind"? It is the way we refer to the luminous and intelligent master of the person. What do we mean by "cultivating the self" (修身 *xiu shen*, "cultivating the person or *shen* body")? It is the way we refer to doing what is good and getting rid of what is bad. Is the physical self on its own (身自 *shen zi*, "the body itself") able to do what is good and get rid of what is bad, or must the luminous and intelligent master (灵明主 *ling ming zhu*) of the person first want to do so, and only then will one physically (形體 *xiang ti*, "with the form of the *ti*-body") start to do what is good and get rid of what is bad? And so, those who want to cultivate themselves must first want to correct their heart-minds.

Now the heart-mind in its original state is the nature. Since the nature is only good, the heart-mind in its original state is wholly correct. Why, then, must one make an effort to correct it? Since, as noted above, the original state of the heart-mind is wholly correct, it is only when thoughts and ideas begin to stir (自其意念发动 *zi qi yi nian fa dong*, "[when], on their own, wishes and habituated thoughts ensue in action") that there is that which is not correct. And so, those who wish to correct their heart-minds must correct their thoughts and ideas (意念 *yi nian*, once again perhaps "wishes and learned or habituated thoughts").

Whenever they have a good thought, they must really love it in the same way that they love a beautiful color. Whenever they have a bad thought, they must really hate it in the same way that they hate a bad odor. Then all of

> their thoughts will be sincere and their heart-minds will be rectified. (Wang, *Da Xue Wen*, 6 [Ivanhoe 2009, 168–169])

There is certainly an affirmation here that the mind is a physical organ, for the very definition of the person is given as an "embodied mind" (身心 *shen xin*). The mind is, however, again in resonance with the Confucian philosophical heritage, said to be the "lord" or "master" (主 *zhu*) of the rest of the body, for the remainder of the physical body on its own cannot distinguish between correct and errant forms of conduct. In addition, in Wang's thought, there is a discernible connection between desires and habituated thoughts (意念 *yi nian*) directing the body and selfish conduct. Merely bodily awareness inclines a person to make fundamental sorts of distinctions between their own body and its well-being, desires, and importance, and those of others. Rectifying this latter consequence demands the natural goodness of the mind to be ever involved in guiding our actions, for only the mind and its innate virtue of co-humanity can intervene to motivate us to "treat the entire world as one's own body."

> 大人者, 以天地萬物為一體者也. 其視天下猶一家, 中國猶一人焉. 若夫間 形骸而分爾我者, 小人矣. 大人之能以天地萬物為一體也, 非意之也, 其心之仁本若是, 其 與天地萬物而為一也, 豈惟大人, 雖小人之心亦莫不然, 彼顧自小之耳. 是故見孺子之入井, 而必有 怵惕惻隱之心焉, 是其仁之與孺子而為一體也.

> Great people regard Heaven, earth and the myriad creatures as their own bodies (體 *ti*). They look upon the world as one family, and China as one person within it. Those who, because of the space between their own bodies and other physical forms, regard themselves as separate [from Heaven, earth and the myriad creatures] are petty persons. The ability great people have to form one body with Heaven, earth and the myriad creatures is not something they intentionally strive (非意 *fei yi*) to do; the benevolence (仁 *ren*) of their heart-minds is originally like this. How could it be that only the heart-minds of great people are one with Heaven, earth and the myriad creatures? Even the heart-minds of petty people are like this. It is only the way that such people look

> at things that makes them petty. This is why, when they see a child [about to] fall into a well, they cannot avoid having a sense of alarm and concern for the child. This is because their benevolence forms one body with the child. (Wang, *Da Xue Wen* 1 [Ivanhoe 2009, 160–161])

Wang goes on to reject the idea that the mere fact that people belong to the same species provokes their natural benevolence into action, for we can, he insists, also feel compassion for animals, grass, and stones when they face the danger of destruction. The virtue of the mind's co-humanity (仁 *ren*), literally conceived, following one of the possible etymologies of the character, as the "twoness of human existence" is to treat the world as "one" (一 *yi*) with the self through one's conduct. But this treatment of the world as one with oneself is also dependent, it is important to note, on a change of regard for one's own body. To recall once again Deborah Sommer's classification of conceptions of body in Chinese thought from the opening chapter here, Wang claims that, in order to really act with co-humanity, the sage must look upon their body as the 體 *ti* body, the body that is in Sommer's rendition "co-substantial" with, and connected through interdependence with, the environment and not just as the individuated and personal 身 *shen* body. It is therefore also a reenvisioning of the body that makes a moral reorientation toward others and the totality of the natural world possible. But that reenvisioning is something the mind can accomplish without any special training, merely by having the experience of living in the world, which requires the constant cooperation of perception, feeling, and actional response.

Despite the pronounced differences in their theoretical articulations of the relationship between mental activities, feelings in particular, and natural coherence, there is an overriding sense in which the teachings of the Cheng-Zhu and Lu-Wang schools of Confucianism present a united front when it comes to emphasizing the significance of the human mind. Its own internal workings are the most reliable source of moral guidance. While surely learning, history, ritual, and good teachers are still considered invaluable assistants in the program of moral cultivation, they are not the moral foundations of human existence. Our natural and innate moral knowledge is the standard by which social goods are measured and are not themselves results of social construction. It is this conviction that carved out the space for moral reflection that was so vitally important to Song and Ming Neo-Confucians in their varied attempts to confront the historical and political challenges they faced.

Varieties of Learning for Oneself

In his historical study of the development of Song and Ming dynasty Confucian thought, Peter Bol makes an observation that helps contextualize the differences between Zhu's and Wang's pedagogical lineages. He notes that the former school, dubbed "Learning of the Way" or "Learning of Coherence," arose in resistance to the centralized educational policies and imperial examination system of the eleventh- and twelfth-century Song court, while, by the time Wang's "Learning of the Mind" school came to prominence in the fifteenth- and sixteenth-century Ming, it was the newly crowned educational orthodoxy and textual cannon of Zhu's school that was the target of their resistance.[13] There is some extent to which this insight allows us to see even these opposed wings of medieval Confucian thought as devoted to a common overarching cause. Both encouraged students—rather than merely to memorize a certain vast amount of literary materials in order to rehash them in ossified literary styles—to critically assess various interpretations of Confucian thought and, at the same time, to discipline their own minds in such a way that would ensure that reliable moral learning can be achieved. The imperative inherited from the very *Analects* of Confucius that, in order to perfect oneself morally, one had to engage in both learning (斈 *xue*) and reflection (思 *si*) was, therefore, in the process of being implemented during these centuries in novel ways. Nonetheless, these two schools had markedly different perspectives about what it meant to learn and what the process of learning entailed.

As we have seen, Zhu Xi argues that whether or not the mind is able to apprehend both its own innate coherence and the coherence of the natural order depends on the disposition of its constitutive 氣 *qi*. When the *qi* is in an agitated and turbulent state, its ability to perceive the holistic subtleties of natural coherence is occluded, whereas when the *qi* is calm but focused, its refined physical makeup can become translucent and suffused with the so-called luminosity of *li*. It is for this reason that Zhu did give credit to the Buddhist meditative practice of quiet sitting, since such practice manifestly and appreciably restores the mind to a condition that is both tranquil and attentive. But the value of this practice as a stand-alone approach according to Zhu is that, while it helps people see natural coherence in its pristine unity, it does not get us very far in comprehending how coherence orders specific relations between things in nature, between people in social relationship, and between society in its current state and its history. To be a complete human being means, in his interpretation of the Confucian heritage, to optimize our knowledge and conduct in all of these spheres of experience. We must therefore bring a mind divested of desires and therefore biases also to the reading of texts, the investigation of nature, and social action. This requires specific approaches in each sphere but a unifying mental attitude that attends all of them.

Zhu Xi, having established schools of learning as well as laying down a radically revised curriculum of study for students of Confucianism, devotes much of his time to giving practical advice about not merely what to read but how to read.[14] A recurrent theme in this advice is to keep the daily amount of material that students imbibe manageable, small enough to both commit to memory and reflect on carefully from hermeneutic and morally critical perspectives. He even counsels that the ranges of material to be studied should be adjusted for levels of learning and age. He strongly recommends that students read texts slowly and carefully dozens of times, consulting annotations and commentaries all the while, and pay more attention to context than character philology. He remarks at one point that only when a student fails to understand anything of a text on the fiftieth read should we worry that there may be something defective with his 氣 *qi*.[15] He acknowledges in places that we will find transcription mistakes even in canonical classical texts and sometimes their passages simply can't be understood. He further argues that the need to copy ancient bamboo strip texts facilitated better knowledge of them than is afforded by Song dynasty mass printing and distribution. Zhu castigates students who study classical texts just to pass the civil service exams so they can inherit posts that ensure them wealth and power. He avers, however, that once a text and its commentaries have been thoroughly understood, meaning that the coherence of their moral teachings has been thoroughly comprehended and incorporated into one's conduct, textual study can be dispensed with.[16] But, for our purposes, the most prescient things he has to say about the method of reading and interpreting involve how to gain what he calls "complete familiarity" (熟 *shu*) with a text and how the approach to accomplishing this aids the mind in apprehending the moral coherence classical texts communicate to us. The best way, he maintains, to make the mind consummately familiar with a text is to recite it aloud (讀 *du*) on every reading.

> 書只貴讀, 讀多自然曉. 今即思量得, 寫在 紙上底, 也不濟事, 終非我有, 只貴乎讀. 這箇不知如何, 自然心與氣合, 舒暢發越, 自是記得牢. 縱饒熟看過, 心里思量過, 也 不如讀. 讀來讀去, 少間曉不得底, 自然曉 得, 已曉得者, 越有滋味. 若是讀不熟, 都沒這般滋味. 而今未說讀得注, 且只熟讀 正經, 行住坐臥, 心常在此, 自然曉得. 嘗思之, 讀便是學. 夫子說: "學而不思則罔, 思而不學則殆," 學便是讀. 讀了又思, 思了又讀, 自然有意. 若讀而不思, 又不知其 意味: 思而不讀, 縱使曉得, 終是卼臲不安. 一似倩得人來守屋相似, 不是自家人, 終 不屬自家使喚. 若讀得熟, 而又思得精, 自然心與理一, 永遠不忘.
>
> The value of a book is in the recitation of it. By reciting it often, we naturally come to understand it. Now, even if we ponder over what's written on the paper, it's useless, for in the end it isn't really ours. There's value only in recitation, though I don't know how the mind so naturally becomes harmonious with the psychophysical stuff, feels uplifted and energized, and remembers securely when it reads. Even supposing we could read through a text thoroughly, pondering it over and over in our minds, it wouldn't be as good as reciting it. If we recite it again and again, in no time the incomprehensible becomes comprehensible and the already comprehensible becomes even more meaningful. But if the recitation doesn't reach the point of intimate familiarity (熟 *shu*), it won't be so meaningful at all. At the moment I'm not even speaking about the recitation of commentaries; let's simply recite the classical texts to the point of intimate familiarity. Whether we are walking or at a standstill, standing or sitting down, if our minds are always on these texts, we'll naturally come to understand them. It has occurred to me that recitation (讀 *du*) is learning

> (學 *xue*). The Master said: "Learning (學 *xue*) without thinking (思 *si*) is a waste; thinking without learning is dangerous." Learning is reciting. If we recite it then think it over, think it over then recite it, naturally it'll become meaningful to us. If we recite it but don't think it over, we still won't appreciate the meaning. If we think it over but don't recite it, even though we might understand it, our understanding will be precarious. It's just like hiring somebody else to guard our home: because he isn't one of the family, in the end he can't be used as we would use a family member. Should we recite it to the point of intimate familiarity, and moreover think about it in detail, naturally our mind and principle will become one (自然心與理一 *zi ran xin yu li yi*) and never shall we forget what we've read. (Zhu Xi, *Conversations,* 170:3 [Gardner 1990, 137–138])

In this passage, Zhu makes a clever association between the words for "learning" or "study" (學 *xue*) and "recitation" (讀 *du*), for the latter term, though it literally means to "read," has an etymological association of attending to the spoken word (言 *yan*) and so also generically means "to study." But most importantly, Zhu attests that reciting a text aloud over and over, coupled with an attentive reflection on its meaning, has a unique effect on the mind's *qi,* making it especially alert, increasing its retention, and eventually enabling it to unify the text's coherence (理 *li*).

This discipline of recitation that uniquely focuses the mind's *qi* also enables the mind to set aside its biases, since biases are also ultimately rooted in desire. This opens the mind to the many different possible interpretations of a text and in the end helps us to assess their relative value in determining what the text really means. While Zhu did establish a new curriculum and his commentaries themselves were eventually pronounced the only correct interpretation of the Confucian classics by the fifteenth century, the exegete himself is represented as encouraging his students to constantly challenge merely received understandings.

> 學者觀書, 病在只要向前, 不肯退步看. 愈 向前, 愈看得不分曉. 不若退步, 卻看得審. 大概病在執著, 不肯放下. 正如聽訟: 心先有主張乙底意思, 便只尋甲底不是: 先有 主張甲底意思, 便只見乙底不是. 不若姑置甲乙之說, 徐徐觀之, 方能辨其曲

直. 橫渠云: "濯去舊見, 以來新意." 此說甚當. 若不濯去舊見, 何處得新意來. 今學者有 二種病, 一是主私意, 一是舊有先人之說, 雖欲擺脫, 亦被他自來相尋.

The problem that students have with reading is simply that they wish to advance and are unwilling to retreat and reread. The more they advance, the more their reading lacks understanding. It'd be better if they were to retreat but fully comprehend what they read.

In general, the problem is that they stick to their opinions and are unwilling to give them up. It's just like hearing litigation: if beforehand the mind supports proposition B, it will simply search for the wrongs in A; and if beforehand it supports A, it will simply discover the wrongs in B. Better to put aside one's views toward A and B and slowly examine them both. Only then will one be able to distinguish right from wrong. Heng-ch'u said: "Wash away the old understanding and bring forth new ideas." This statement is extremely apt. If one doesn't wash away the old understanding, where will the new ideas arise? Students today have two kinds of flaws: one is that they let themselves be ruled by personal prejudices; the other is that they embrace received theories. Even if they wished to shake free of these, they'd still be troubled by them. (Zhu Xi, *Conversations*, 185:16 [Gardner 1990, 150–151])

And so, the only way to extirpate biases from one's interpretation of texts and adjudication of views is the conscious discipline of repeated recitation. This technique works far more surely than merely wishing biases away, because wishes do not calm the mind and make it receptive to meanings and transparent to coherence to the degree and in the way repeated recitation does. Reading, then, is not merely about meaning, it is also about cultivating the mind's 氣 *qi*.

Of course, coherence in Zhu's view is not just a matter of textual meaning and philosophical clarity but is also the basis of the natural order. A thorough investigation of the natural world will uncover its order. Zhu earnestly wanted to ground this conviction in the classics, and this was the primary reason for his elevation of a previously obscure chapter of the *Classic of Ritual* known as the *Great Learning* (*Da Xue*) as well as his own editions and reordering of the content of that text.[17] In his characterization of that work's depiction of complete knowledge, Zhu Xi famously writes:

> 所谓致知在格物者, 言欲致吾之知, 在即物而穷其理也. 盖人心之灵莫 不有知, 而天下之物莫不有理, 惟于理有未穷, 故其知有不尽也. 是以 大学始教, 必使学者即凡天下之物, 莫不因其已知之理而益穷之, 以求至乎其极. 至于用力之久, 而一旦豁然贯通焉, 则众物之表里 精粗无不到, 而吾心之全體大用无不明矣. 此谓物格, 此谓知之至也.
>
> What is meant by "the extension of knowledge that lies in fully apprehending the principle in things (格物 *ge wu*)" is, that if we wish to extend our knowledge to the utmost we must thoroughly probe the principle in those things that we encounter. It would seem that every man's intellect (心 *xin*) is possessed of the capacity for knowing (知 *zhi*) and that everything in the world is possessed of principle (理 *li*). But, to the extent that principle is not yet thoroughly probed, man's knowledge is not yet fully realized. Hence, the first step in the instruction of greater learning is to teach the student, whenever he encounters anything at all in the world, to build upon what is already known to him of principle and to probe still further, so that he seeks to reach the limit. After exerting himself in this way for a long time, he will one day become enlightened (用 *ming*) and thoroughly understand [principle]; then, the manifest and the hidden, the subtle and the obvious qualities of all things will be known, and the mind in its whole substance (體 *ti*) and vast operation (用 *yong*) will be completely illuminated. This is called "fully apprehending the principle in things." (Zhu Xi, *Da Xue Zhang Ju* 5 [Gardner 1990, 118])

Precisely because, as seen earlier, the coherence of the mind itself enables it to apprehend principle when its *qi* is tranquil and transparent, it is possible to purposely exercise this power in the pursuit of knowledge by prompting it to "investigate" or follow the patterns (格 *ge*) of things (物 *wu*).[18] The mind can become fully luminous itself when it accords with the luminosity (用 *ming*) of the coherence that can be found to order the natural world in its entirety. But such an enlightenment does not result from a sudden, mystical, and holistic vision gained through prolonged meditation or unexpected encounter, as in the Buddhist view. Instead, it results from careful, painstaking, detailed observation of natural phenomena. It reaches full culmination when accumulated knowledge attains the limits of all that is discoverable about the relations between things that reveals coherence in its interconnected totality.

Finally, Zhu insisted that the last step in the ideal program of study would be a reading of China's court-ordered dynastic histories, with an eye toward the application of the moral and practical lessons of history to issues of governing. Just as the individual was to translate the moral learning derived from the ancient works of Confucian philosophy into their own personal conduct, so was the ministerial advisor expected to draw lessons about the order of governing for today from the way that coherence had manifested itself in human society in ages past.

> 先看語孟中庸, 更看一經, 卻看史, 方另看. 先讀史記, 史記與左傳相包. 次看左傳, 次 看通鑑, 有餘力則看全史. 只是看史, 不如今之看史有許多嶢崎. 看治亂如此, 成敗如此, "與治同道罔不興, 與亂同事罔不亡," 知得次第.
>
> First read the *Analects*, the *Book of Mencius* and the *Doctrine of the Mean* (*Zhong Yong*). Then read one of the Classics. Then read the histories, which, at this point, will be easy to understand. Read the *Records of the Grand Historian* first. As the *Records of the Grand Historian* and the *Tso Commentary* are mutually inclusive, read the *Tso Commentary* next. Then read the *Comprehensive Mirror for Aid to Government*. And if you still have strength remaining, read the dynastic histories. Simply reading through the histories is not as good as reading through the twists and turns in them with an eye to the present, observing that this is what order and disorder are, this is what victory and defeat are, and that "following the path of orderly government is certain to lead to prosperity, while following the path to disorder is certain to lead to ruin." Do this and you'll understand the sequence of historical events.
>
> (Zhu Xi, *Conversations*, 195:8 [Gardner 1990, 160–161])

One reads first those works of Confucian philosophy he identifies, then the ancient Zhou dynasty classics idealized by Confucius himself, then the dynastic histories, particularly those of the Warring

States period, Han dynasty, and a review of developments from the Three Kingdoms period through the Sui and Tang dynasties, and then the fragmentation and lead-up to the establishment of the Song state itself. This is the program of reading, and its art, as we have seen, is repeated recitation. There are then three steps to Zhu's program of learning, namely, sitting mediation, the investigation of nature that unveils its coherence, and the discipline of recited reading. He frequently bemoans the cultivation of only one or two of these practices to the exclusion of the others, as he asserts that mediation without moral, natural, and historical learning will leave one unable to apply insight into fundamental coherence to everyday life, while reading and study unaccompanied by continuous reflection on coherence will leave one unable to judge the value and priority of what one learns.

The comprehensiveness and breadth of what one learns, and all the different ways that learning is pursued, however, are united by a heightened state of awareness that they are meant to further foster. As is his wont, Zhu employs an ancient term in a hermeneutically creative fashion to identify this disposition of mind. In its original context during the Zhou dynasty, 敬 *jing* was the attitude rulers were supposed to have toward their ritual obligations, an attitude of "reverence," or "veneration," or "offering" themselves completely up to the duties of his kingdom as the high officers of rites and intermediary with the great ancestors.[19] Zhu Xi associates this word with a mental state, which some of his early and most prominent disciples like Chen Chun, in his lexicon of Neo-Confucian terminology, define as straightening out the "internal" to line up with the "external" in conduct.[20] It is a mental state that can alternatively mean perseverance, calm, concentration, and seriousness.[21] Such a cultivated attunement of mind with what it focuses on prevents it from wandering and becoming distracted, and allows it to engage intently with the object of its concentration. It integrates both the stillness of meditative states and the activities of study and interaction with others with coherence and thus enables us to apprehend things as they are and be what we ought to be.

> 敬有死敬, 有活敬. 若只守著主一之敬, 遇事不濟之以義, 辨其是非, 則不活. 若熟後, 敬便有義, 義便有敬. 靜則察其敬與不敬, 動則察 其義與不義. 如 "出門如見大賓, 使 民如承大祭," 不敬時如何, "坐如尸, 立加 齊" 不敬時如何, 須敬羲夾持, 循環無端, 則內外透徹.

> There's a dead inner mental attentiveness (敬 *jing*) and there's a living one. If you simply hold on to inner mental attentiveness, concentrating on one matter, but fail, when some other matter arises, to rescue it with righteousness and to discriminate between right and wrong—this isn't living inner mental attentiveness. Once you're good at it, living inner mental attentiveness will always be accompanied by righteousness (義 *yi*) and righteousness always by inner mental attentiveness. In quiescence (靜 *jing*), you'll examine whether you're mentally attentive or not; in activity, you'll examine whether you're righteous or not. How can you "behave when away from home as though you were in the presence of an important guest or deal with the common people as though you were officiating at an important sacrifice" if you don't practice inner mental attentiveness? Or how can you "sit as though you were impersonating an ancestor, stand as though you were performing a sacrifice," if you don't practice inner mental attentiveness? It's essential that inner mental attentiveness and righteousness sustain each other, with one following upon the other ad infinitum. Then inner and outer will be thoroughly interconnected. (Zhu Xi, *Conversations*, 216:4 [Gardner 1990, 174–175])

There is then a distinction to be made between practices that represent inward cultivation and those that facilitate moral conduct, but they are tied together and mutually support one another only when 敬 *jing*, which Ivanhoe renders as "reverential attention" and Gardner translates as "inner mental attentiveness," is maintained throughout. And this conviction provides the basis for Zhu's selection of texts such as the *Zhong Yong* and *Mengzi*, which seem to focus on the priority of inner mental potentials and activities, as the first ones that should be mastered. In Zhu Xi's hands, Confucian learning becomes, before and above everything else, the nurturing of a certain disposition of 心 *xin*.

While in basic agreement with the Cheng-Zhu Confucian lineage that the cultivation of 心 *xin* was paramount in learning, Wang Yangming argues that Zhu has put the whole endeavor of "learning for oneself" in peril by making distinctions between "stillness" and "activity," and "inner" and "outer" in the first place. Wang writes that Zhu's demand for us to incessantly build up our store of empirical knowledge actually represents not only a distraction itself but also a fundamentally wrongheaded externalization of the mind's own naturally luminous coherence and our own direct access to it.

> 人惟不知至善之在吾心, 而求之於其外, 以為事事物物皆有定理也, 而求至善於事 事物物之中, 生意支離決裂, 錯雜紛紜, 而莫知有 一定之向. 今焉既知至善之在吾心, 而不 假於外求, 則志有定向, 而無支離決裂, 錯雜紛紜之患矣. 無支離決裂, 錯雜紛紜之患, 則心不妄動而能靜矣. 心不妄動而能靜, 則其日用之間, 從容閒暇 而能安矣. 能安, 則凡一念 之發, 一事之感, 其為至善乎, 其非至善乎, 吾心之良知自有以詳審精察之, 而能慮矣. 能慮則擇之無不精, 處之無不當, 而至善於是乎可得矣.
>
> It is only because people don't understand that the highest good is within their own heart-minds that they search for it on the outside. They mistakenly believe that each affair and every thing has its own fixed principle (定理 *ding li*), and so they search for the highest good within each affair and every thing. This is why they [become preoccupied with] disconnected fragments and isolated shards; confused and disheveled, they have no stable orientation. Now once one understands that the highest good lies within one's own heart-mind and does not depend on anything outside, then one's intentions will have a stable orientation and one no longer will suffer the misfortunes of being [preoccupied with] disconnected fragments and isolated shards and being confused and disheveled. Once one no longer suffers the misfortunes of [being preoccupied with] disconnected fragments and isolated shards and is no longer confused and disheveled, then one's heart-mind will not engage in wonton activity and one will be able to be calm. Once one's heart-mind no longer engages in wanton activity and one is able to be calm, then one's heart-mind will be relaxed and leisurely in its daily operations, and one will be able to be at peace. Once one is able to be at peace, then whenever a thought arises or an affair affects one, one's pure knowing will spontaneously inquire and explore as to whether or not this is the highest good, and so, one will

> be able to deliberate. If one is able to deliberate, then all one's decisions will be precise, all one's responses will be appropriate, and the highest good will thereby be obtained. (Wang, *Da Xue Wen* 4 [Ivanhoe 2009, 166])

There are two primary considerations at play in these commitments, and we shall deal with them in turn. In the first place, Wang famously criticizes Zhu Xi's understanding, both philological and practical, of the *Great Learning*'s formulation of 格物 *ge wu*. While Zhu had understood this as an imperative for us to "investigate things" or "apprehend the natural coherence in things," Wang takes it as one to be ever vigilant about the state of our own awareness in the circumstances in which we find ourselves. He argues for such an understanding on the basis of a philological reexamination of both terms in the expression.

> "格物" 如孟子 "大人格君心" 之 "格." 是去其心之不正, 以全其本體之正. 但意念所在, 即要去其不正, 以全其正. 即無時無處不是存天理. 即是窮理. 天理即是明德. 窮理即是明明德.

> The word *ge* in *ge wu* is like the *ge* in the line from the *Mengzi* which says: "Only a great man is able to rectify (*ge*) the ruler's heart-mind." It means to eliminate whatever is not correct in order to maintain the correctness of the original state (本體 *ben ti*) of the heart-mind. Whenever there is a thought (念 *nian*), one eliminates whatever is not correct in order to maintain what is correct. At all times and in every circumstance, one preserves Heavenly principles (天理 *tian li*, once again, "natural coherence"). This is what it means to fully realize principle. Heavenly principles are none other than the bright virtue, fully realizing Heavenly principle is nothing other than making bright one's bright virtue (明明德 *ming ming de*). (Wang, *Chuanxilu*, 7 [Ivanhoe 2009, 146–147])

Rather than meaning something like "investigating" or "apprehending the patterns in things," 格 *ge* in Wang's rendition means "rectifying" or "making correct" (正 *zheng*) one's thoughts (念 *nian*), and the correction of those thoughts effectively returns the mind (心 *xin*) to its supposedly "original substance" or "original state" (本體 *ben ti*). We will elaborate on this later. But for now, the term 物 *wu* in the pivotal text, in its own turn, must be clarified also.

> 是必實有其事矣. 故致知必在於格物. 物者, 事也, 凡意之所發必有其事, 意所在之事謂之物. 格者, 正也, 正其不正以歸於正之謂也.
>
> It requires one to always be working at some concrete task or affair. And so, extending one's knowledge must lie in rectifying one's thoughts [about things]. A thing or object (物 *wu*) is a task or affair (事 *shi*). A thought always arises in regard to some affair or other. The affair that is the object of a thought is called a thing. To rectify (格 *ge*) is to correct (正 *zheng*). It refers to correcting whatever is not correct and returning to what is correct. (Wang, *Da Xue Wen* 5 [Ivanhoe 2009, 170])

And, perhaps more clearly and certainly more poignantly, Wang insists that a thing is any situation or affair in which I happen to find myself, a family decision, a funeral, a conflict at the workplace, an argument among students, or whatever circumstance with which I am engaged. In every concrete situation that demands my attention and action, I am, on this account of 格物 *ge wu*, to be attentive to my state of mind, ensure that no selfish desires or limiting biases control my reflection, and then involve myself completely, or as he puts it, "to the full extent" of my attentiveness. If I am able to do this, because the original substance of the mind is, in its own reflection and activity, constituted of natural coherence, it will respond in a morally correct fashion to whatever is required of me.

> 身之主宰便是心. 心之所發便是意. 意之本體便是知. 意之所在便是物. 如意在於事親, 即事親便是 一物. 意在於事君, 即事君便是一物. 意在於仁民 愛物, 即仁民愛物便是一物. 意在於視聽言動, 即視聽言動便是一物. 所以某說無心外之理, 無心外 之物. 中庸言 "不誠無物," 大學 "明明德" 之功, 只是箇誠意. 誠意之功, 只是箇格物.
>
> The governor of the body is the heart-mind. What the heart-mind puts forward are thoughts (意 *yi*). The fundamental

> nature (本體 *ben ti*) is knowledge (知 *zhi*). Where there is a thought, there is a thing (物 *wu*). If one's thoughts are on serving one's parents, then serving one's parents is a thing. If one's thoughts are on serving one's ruler, then serving one's ruler is a thing. If one's thoughts are on being benevolent (仁 *ren*) to the people or caring (愛 *ai*) for other creatures, then being benevolent to the people or caring for other creatures are things. If one's thoughts are on looking, listening, speaking or acting, then looking, listening, speaking and acting are things. This is why I say that there is no principle (理 *li*) outside the heart-mind and no thing outside the heart-mind. The *Doctrine of the Mean*'s teaching that "without sincerity there is nothing" and the task of "making bright one's bright virtue" described in the *Great Learning* are nothing other than examples of making one's thoughts sincere. The task of making one's thoughts sincere is nothing other than "rectifying [one's] thoughts in relation to things" (格物 *ge wu*). (Wang, *Chuanxilu*, 6 [Ivanhoe 2009, 146])

It may not, of course, be easily apparent what all this has to do with learning. But once again, for him, learning means learning one's own mind. Wang's hermeneutically creative reading of the *Mengzi*, some examples of which we have already rehearsed, enables him to understand the classic as claiming that we, contrary to Zhu Xi's program, do not have to learn from books, natural observation, or history what to do in every circumstance. We don't train ourselves with these resources to acquire the knowledge of what is right or wrong and only then assess what needs to be done in our families, communities, and countries. The classics inform us only that the mind, the mind that deliberates, thinks, speaks, and directs the body's actions in our own experience and conduct, is already naturally moral. And so, "correcting" it means only to prevent it from being artificially limited by selfishness and bias, so that it can do what it is built to do, namely, to fully illuminate (明 *ming*) our experience and our behavior. This prevention of the mind from being dominated by desires and "preserving" it in its originally moral state does, surely, require constant effort, but not any pedagogical effort that is set in stone. Life immerses us in moral situations, and the mind is literally made to deal with them rightly, and so full attentiveness and engagement with its situations and circumstances will unfailingly prompt it, on Wang's provocative view, to do the right thing

These particular approaches to and understandings of learning in Zhu Xi and Wang Yangming are, then, markedly distinct, and so the conflicts of their respective lineages, both philosophically and historically, are drawn with discernible lines. These differences make it all too easy to miss a basic commonality between their convictions that represents precisely how medieval Confucian thinkers appropriated some basic Buddhist assumptions about the character of 心 *xin* into their own tradition, and why these appropriations were so significant. One of the persistent teachings in classical Confucianism that could, with some qualifications, be fairly generalized is that that learning and moral progress were long considered thoroughly relational affairs. The relationships between parents and children, students and teachers, history and the present, people in society that were solidified in rituals, and ancient sages and living noble men, all make learning, and even personal existence itself, a mutually transactional process. As we saw in the first chapter of this study, even for classical Confucian texts like the *Mengzi*, the inborn tendencies of human feeling that provided the roots of virtue required constant cultivation in order to be effective and constant learning in order to be correctly applied in conduct. The Neo-Confucian tradition, in its several major wings, did not, certainly, abrogate these relationships, did not devalue their importance, dissolve their respective hierarchies, or fundamentally change the character of classical orthodoxy even when they found it necessary to rearrange or innovate in curriculum or hermeneutically transform the priorities of certain practices and ideas. But, a constant refrain found in both Zhu and Wang as well as their respective preceptors is the consistent demand that students must "learn for themselves." Real sagehood and moral perfection is not acquired from parents, teachers, friends, books, or even social superiors. It is instead derived from one's own reflection, deliberation, and sincerity, and the basis of all of these habits and dispositions is the inborn, natural character of one's own mind, in its feelings and its abilities to think and judge. This common Neo-Confucian commitment, which sets one's own moral deliberations at the center of practice, coincides with the historical challenges these factions of Confucianism were born in and empowers their respective adherents to engage in trenchant, and often even institutionally decentered, social criticism of received authority. Indeed, in the classical Confucian tradition, the license of a child to remonstrate with their parents and the minister to do so with their ruler arises out of the duties that are circumscribed by loyal and dependable care (孝 *xiao*). Of course, the Neo-Confucians fully believe in and espouse 孝 *xiao*. But they would argue that even this virtue is born from the feelings and spontaneous responses that are built into the natural coherence of our own minds (心 *xin*). If it is indeed the case then that medieval Confucian philosophers were beholden to Buddhist metaphysical ideas, the mere fact of that influence is not as significant in itself as is the purpose to which Song and Ming disciples of Kongzi dedicated those Buddhist ideas.

6

Luminosity, Potential, and Personhood

The time has come to reflect on our journeys through classical Indian and Chinese theories of mind and personhood, and how the Buddhist tradition, which these two great cultural and philosophical heritages shared, was both influenced by and in turn exerted influences on these spheres of thought. Clearly we have made great generalizations in comparing and contrasting the various philosophical movements of these traditions, both in the choices about which materials to include and not to include as well as in the emphases that have been placed on what has been covered. Whatever conclusions are reached here are, of course, qualified by these limitations, and hopefully this will only prompt further debate and dialogue between scholarly and philosophical representatives of all these traditions. Nonetheless, in the great encounters that took place between the ever-transforming thought of Buddhism and South Asian Brāhmiṇical and Chinese Confucian ideas, some very conspicuous themes emerge whose philosophical significance justifies the foregoing investigations and deserves to be explored more fully and fruitfully.

In classical Brāhmiṇical schools, despite their fundamental internal differences from one another, ultimate selfhood or consciousness was thought to have a capacity that no other feature of either existence as a whole or any individual physical body possessed, and that was the power of "luminosity" (*prakāśatva*). While it was generally thought of the body's physical organs of external and internal sensation that they had special capacities to "penetrate" or "apprehend" other physical bodies owing to their possession of rarified "brilliance" (*sattva*) or their unstructured (*nirākāra*) transparency to things, these capacities of the organs to sense did not, it was thought, itself result in awareness. Instead, "luminosity" was thought to be the singularly unique essence of the spiritual self that, when it inhabited physical bodies, used them as its instrument to make the world manifest. The Buddhists, of course, rejected the notion of a spiritual self that transcended bodily existence, but they did at first, in slightly different vocabulary, characterize certain specifically enlightened states of awareness as exhibiting a "splendor" or "luminescence" (*prabhāsvara*). And, when this notion reached the hands of the Vijñānavādins, especially those that rendered this system into the Chinese world, the Buddhist conception of the luminescent, enlightened mind was transformed into the inalienable and basic form of all awareness, translated as 明心 *ming xin*, which accounted for the very condition for beings to become fully enlightened in their worldly lives and conduct.

The incredible currency that this idea gained, particularly in the medieval Confucian tradition's adoption of the notion as explaining our ability to learn, should prompt us to tarry with its significance. What does it mean for awareness or consciousness to be luminous? Luminosity, taken either as a strict description or a loosely connoting metaphor, speaks to a conviction that does not fit into the spectrum of familiar Western frameworks that represent consciousness as either merely "reflecting" or "mirroring" reality or constructing it according to its own inherent concepts or categories. It is certainly true, particularly with regard to the sense organs themselves, that notions of "mirroring" or "transparency" or "construction" of things in our experience are present in many different varieties in classical Asian systems. But these functions or relationships of the powers of the sense organs vis-à-vis the objects of our experience are, in the schools we have covered, clearly distinguished from the more fundamental luminosity of mind. The mind's luminosity does not simply reflect the world or arrange it according to its own principles but instead does something to nature that could not otherwise be done to it, namely, makes it fully manifest and allows every reach and feature of it, from its most elemental workings to its limitless breadth and duration, to be experienced, appreciated, fathomed, understood, put into words, and used. In Sanskrit terminology, without this luminosity, the world would remain in utter and pervasive darkness (*jagadāndhyaprasanga*).[1] The "luminous mind" that lies at the basis of our experience makes the world visible, tangible, thinkable, accessible, to the creatures that live in it. Without this luminosity, while the natural world would still undoubtedly be there, and would still bring about things, bodies, impulsive affects, and constant dynamic transformation, none of this would be revealed to anyone and would never serve anything that could deservedly be called a purpose. Only this brand of luminosity can make the natural world an experienced world, and such luminosity alone can make us not just physiological creatures but experiencing creatures. And only the complete enlightenment that results from total identification with this essence of luminosity can allow for optimal human experience and conduct. In their various fashions, the strands of thought we have covered have identified this luminosity of the mind with the ultimate core of our personhood. Despite their rejections of the notions of an eternal selfhood, the Buddhists also asserted this. We shall, therefore, spend some time in this chapter exploring this notion in more depth.

Now, at the same time, for all that was invested in the notion of mental luminosity and how it could be thought of as the irreducible core of human existence, no school of thought in the spectrum of classical Asian traditions ever denied that our capacity to fully manifest both the world and ourselves in knowing and conduct was crucially dependent on our physical existence and what potentials attended our physicality. In pre-Buddhist Chinese thought, understanding the specifically human bodily configurations of 氣 *qi* or "vital vapor" and the basic capacities of the heart (心 *xin*), itself a physical organ, could help us uncover both the original condition of human dispositions and the social and moral ideals toward which we ought to strive. In classical Brāhmiṇical thought, the energetic and dynamic configurations of *prakṛti* or "primordial matter" provide us with physiological and psychological dispositions, which define the full range of our possible inclinations, habits, and intelligence. In the South Asian traditions, the notion of *karma* (rendered into 業 *ye* in Chinese Buddhist texts) is not merely an abstract moral notion, but is physically created by intentional bodily "actions." Even in the earliest Vedic texts, *karma* is frequently referred to as a kind of fine "residue" (*anusāya*) and "remainders" or "leftovers" of the results of past deeds (*karmaphalaśeṣa*), making morality very much into a physical matter.[2] Of course, in Chinese Buddhist thought, only material 氣 *qi* combined with material *karma* and mind could make living bodies also sentient and possessive of certain character traits and moral inclinations. Though medieval Confucians rejected the Buddhist idea that certain desirous inclinations were inherited through *karma*, they reformulated the early Mencian conviction that moral motives were inborn and looked to a specially delineated conception of 理 *li* or "natural coherence" to crystallize the scope of our physical, learning, and moral capacities (才 *cai*). Whether we actually achieve variously idealized states of wisdom and behavior is, of course, contingent on the sincerity and intensity of our personal practice and cultivation. Buddhist views fit within this general framework quite easily, in the sense that they also believed that our natural, physical constitution told a great deal of the story of our present circumstances and ultimate possibilities. However, at least as they thematized the issues, Buddhist philosophers placed enormous emphasis in both South and East Asia on the dynamically complex and yet strictly causal nature of everything that comes about, which includes whatever occurs in the psychological lives of people and how our psychic stores of potentiality enabled the full range of human experiences, from those afflicted with extreme pain to the fully emancipated. Our cognitions arise and take their shape on the basis of previous causal conditions (*pratyaya*-s, 因緣) and in their turn serve as the causal conditions for future experiences. But, as noted earlier, Vijñānavāda Buddhists, in the historical development of their system, came to the conclusion that the possibility of enlightenment had to reside in a psychologically ultimate basis (根本 *gen ben*), immune from corruption, though not from concealment, by other experiences, and thus could serve as the finally originary cause (本源 *ben yuan*) of complete human perfection. This basis they identified as the "untainted cognition" (*amalavijñāna*, 阿摩羅識), and it was precisely in this untainted cognition that could be found the mind's "luminosity" (*prabhāsvaraṃ cittaṃ*, 清浄心). However, it must be remembered that the occurrence or the existence of such a causal basis of enlightenment was not, in the extended history of the school, construed in terms that made it in any way "supernatural" or transcendent of nature but instead one that lies at the very heart of the natural order. In the context of the larger South Asian philosophical tradition, this formulation placed the Vijñānavādins in the position of, on the one hand, denying the Brāhmiṇical assumption that the embodied individual could only be known and freed by a spiritual self that was not of the body and maintaining on the contrary that psychophysical phenomena accounted for everything in our experience. But on the other hand, in the Chinese context, this primordial and invulnerable potentiality for enlightenment, while surely at one with the 氣 *qi* that makes up the physical heart (心 *xin*), is, alternatively in Huayen and Chan, thought to be the very causal source (理 *li*) of the natural order and thus defining of the possibilities of its realization. It was also thought here to be the guarantor that we can slough off all the artificial habits that we have acquired and bring forth a genuineness that the merely impulse-driven body on its own never could. This new vision of the basic perfection of the human mind enabled the Confucian philosophers that followed them to theoretically safeguard the potential for their own moral and social sagehood from any corrupting influence. The Buddhists were, therefore, staunch naturalists, but naturalists with faith or trust (信 *xin*) that, in its original condition, an original condition that is ever accessible through practice, nature is suffused with perfection.

This will bring us to the concluding mediation, as it were, of the present study. It is a conclusion that is sometimes lost on Western readers, and occasionally is even misjudged by classical and modern Asian thinkers with respect to certain of their own traditions. But, in view of all that we have considered, the conclusion is a fully justified one. With regard to the possibilities of human experience, classical Asian philosophers and practitioners, and surely the Buddhists among them, were incorrigible optimists. They were not, by any stretch of the imagination, naïve optimists. South Asian Brāhmiṇical and Buddhist thinkers, after all, believed that the unavoidable frustration and loss of worldly life made the pursuit of release from rebirth in the physical realms the most noble of all human ideals. Buddhist thinkers were not only perhaps more attuned than others to the frailties, ailments, and imperfections of human beings but made great catalogues of and composed innumerable expositions on them. And, despite their high-minded ideals and mythical archetypes of surpassing virtue, Confucians incessantly ran aground on the intractability of ambitious rulers and the shifting tides of history and found themselves objects of sport and derision perhaps more frequently than ones of admiration and emulation, both inside and outside the halls of ritual and ministries. All the same, what is particularly philosophically compelling about the classical Asian traditions is that, despite their full and sustained exposure to the fragility and evils of human life, this exposure did not cause them to lose heart. After all, real insight for them revealed that the heart could not be lost. For most of the philosophers we have considered who represented these heritages, when observed and analyzed to its core, human nature was, when traced to its original state, perfect, and so, given enough time and effort, any human being could become perfect. Their visions of perfection are sometimes mistaken for pessimistic outlooks mostly because of the contesting ideals of those, for instance, who assume perhaps more exclusively hedonic, pragmatic, or fateful standpoints on what persons are and, given these standpoints, what people should pursue in their temporally and culturally bounded lives. Perhaps, however, it behooves us, in the face of the long-standing civilizational pedigree of these traditions, to reconsider their optimisms about human existence as a worthy philosophical challenge, even a provocation.

Luminosity: Making the World Manifest

A study such as this one, which crosses the divides of classical South Asian and East Asian worlds of thought on the bridge of Buddhism, will inevitably feature a discussion of the luminosity of the mind as a centrally significant point of comparison. A different study that might hypothetically restrict itself to comparing and contrasting, for instance, early Brāhmiṇical and pre-Buddhist Chinese philosophical schools would probably focus much more than this one has on the constitution and functionality of the bodily sense organs themselves. Such a study would doubtless be fascinating and worthwhile. It would uncover something only briefly noted several times in our foregoing chapters, namely, that both traditions identified six organs of sense, five external and one internal; that the sense organs work by virtue of their being made out of the same elements as the objects to which they are sensitive; and that feeling and deliberating are most often identified as being the capacities of the physical organ of the heart, the concrete "central organ" of the body. A great deal could indeed be written about the significance and implications of the fact that, just as many early Chinese thinkers, for various reasons, considered the heart (心 *xin*) the "ruler" or "nobleman" of the other sense organs, Indian philosophers of the earliest *Upaniṣads* as well as their numerous later scholastic commentators thought that the heart (*hṛdaya*) was the locus of the inner spiritual self (*ātman*), which, in one way or another, was the real source of the body's awareness and the driver, as it were, of the bodily chariot. The major point of contrast in such a study, nonetheless, would be the very issue of awareness itself. Early Chinese thinkers considered each of the sense organs to be its own unique "office" of "awareness" or "knowledge" (知 *zhi*), often though not always representing the heart as having the most powerful kinds of "knowledge." South Asian Brāhmiṇical thinkers, by conspicuous contrast, while willing to say things like the external sense organs and inner sense had the "semblance of awareness" (*cetanātva iva*) or that they were "instruments" (*kāraṇa*-s) of awareness, held as materialistic anathema the notion that these organs themselves could be called genuinely aware. For them, the "luminosity" (*prakāśatva*) of awareness was thought to be the exclusive essence or quality of the spiritual self. Thus, in pre-Buddhist Chinese thought, while the dynamic and responsive "vital vapor" (氣 *qi*) combined with the awareness of each of the sense organs made the physical body itself a conscious one, for South Asian Vedic traditions, the very materiality and ongoing transformations of the physical body were believed to be precisely reasons to infer that the body could not produce awareness, which requires retention and a continuous identity. South Asian Buddhism held to a basic tenet that what is all-too-often referred to as the mass noun of "consciousness" can only properly be understood in terms of the individual and causally conditioned instances of "cognizing" (*vijñāna*) that are always associated with and partially produced by the sense organs. They therefore formulated a model of bodily awareness that was relatively closer, though hardly identical, to classical Chinese sensibilities. However, it was the Vijñānavāda construal of the "luminescence" (*prabhāsvara*) of the mind in its most natural state as a necessary causal condition for not only the possibility of enlightenment, but for awareness in general, that carried the most weight with the articulation of Chinese Buddhist thought and also had the most philosophical influence on non-Buddhist Chinese traditions. This particular conception of the originally luminous mind was not by any means the earliest manner in which Vijñānavādins defined this idea of the *prabhāsvaraṃ cittaṃ*, as it appears to have been considered by the founding writers and commentators of this school to be the sustained result of the actually experienced moment of awakening rather than some originary state or kind of consciousness. But the full extrapolation and development of Cognition school Buddhism in China did accomplish this remarkable transformation of meaning, and thus the great emphasis we place on it in our own reflections here.

In our chapter on the Huayen and Chan traditions in China, we dwelt upon two quite novel ways in which this idea of the "luminous mind" (明心 *ming xin*) was expressed. Recall that pre-Buddhist Chinese philosophers tended to see the bodily 氣 *qi* as the basic material constituent of the physical heart (心 *xin*) and the heart in turn as possessed of, though hardly the only awareness of the body, its own peculiar kinds of awareness (知 *zhi*). The *Yuan Ren Lun* of Guifeng Zongmi, insists that even the most primordial physical configuration of "vital vapor" (元氣 *yuan qi*) in the unfolding of all natural evolution could not possibly have produced beings that possessed sentience in the first place had it not been itself evolved from a similarly primordial condition of mind (本心 *ben xin*). This primordial condition of mind also accounts for the possibility of enlightenment in embodied persons. Similarly, we bring back to mind the widely disseminated pre-Buddhist Chinese notion that, as noted, each sense organ, the eyes, ears, palate, and so on were their own "offices" (官 *quan*) insofar as they possessed their own unique kinds of awareness, which, while their stimulations are synthesized and categorized by the heart, still produce their various sorts of sensations whether the heart attends to them or not. By dramatic contrast, in the Chan Buddhist *Linji Yu Lu*, the mind is thought to be a "unitary, pure luminosity" (一精明 *yi jing ming*), but when it is found to be "at" or "in," or when it is made to "inhabit" (在 *zai*) the sense organs, only then does seeing, hearing, tasting, and so on take place, just as when it inhabits the hands and feet, grasping and moving can take place. It is thus solely because of the mind's awareness that is "apportioned" (分為 *fen wei*) among the "six organs of sense" (六和合 *liu zhi he*) that we can be conscious bodies and not merely, as we would otherwise be, just "lumps of red flesh." It was this notion of the unitary, luminous mind that accounted for our ability to understand the world, ourselves and to learn that was appropriated in such significant ways by the medieval Confucian schools and read back in such detailed ways into that tradition's ancient founding texts. The primordial luminescence of mind is therefore, in the transmission of Buddhism from South to East Asia, established as our most fundamental nature as persons and the ultimate aim of cultivating enlightenment in our daily activities, interactions, and communication.

In contemporary philosophical renditions, a number of attempts have been made to explain this notion of the luminosity of consciousness or mind in ways that may lend themselves to substantive dialogue with other modern Western categories. Chakravarthi Ram-Prasad, for instance, has written of Brāhmiṇical versions of the luminosity (*prakāśatva*) of awareness as being roughly the classical Sanskrit idiom for thematizing the "qualitative" aspect of our awareness, the Nagelian first-person idea of "what it is like" to have conscious experiences in contrast to third-person scientific descriptions of how awarenesses of various sorts are physiologically produced.[3] It has also been understood in a somewhat more phenomenological vein, for instance, by J. N. Mohanty, who aligns the idea with the givenness of consciousness to itself as a precondition for us to be conscious of any noematic content.[4] In another very recent representation, Matthew MacKenzie, largely following Ram-Prasad's framework, argues that the Buddhists are able to preserve the doctrine of the luminosity of cognitions even without making it the essence of consciousness by equating it with the "reflexivity" of awareness events, the auto-attention (*svasamvedana*) of awareness as being given with its mode and content in each event.[5] In more conventional Buddhist scholarship, particularly the writings that equate this notion of the luminous mind with other significant transitional conceptions such as the *tathāgata-gharba* or "womb of thusness," it is thematized as a Buddhist version alternatively of "essence" or "absolute idealism." All these avenues of access to the idea of the luminous mind have in different contexts and in varying degrees been helpful for facilitating understanding and cross-cultural reflection. There also may be some as-yet-unexplored resonances between classical Asian conceptions of "luminosity" and certain Deweyan ways of talking about "experience." For Dewey, "experience" is not merely the cognitive orientation of mind to the world as has been traditionally conceived in the West but includes unconscious, prereflective, and affective/aesthetic aspects of the nature of consciousness. He sometimes refers to the core of our "experience" as a "focus of immediate, shining apparency."[6] But perhaps the most significant patterns that have emerged from these attempts at explication help to illustrate that the notion of the luminous mind has two basic kinds of implications. These two kinds of implications I will characterize as, loosely speaking, metaphysical and consequential. We will now explore these in turn, and then ponder the somewhat dodgy question of whether these implications must be taken together or whether there may be value in distinguishing between them.

To generalize from all that has been laid out in the previous chapters as well as what has been said here, the metaphysical roles of the notion of the luminous mind can be thematized as follows. First, "luminosity" provides for the causal basis of awareness that arises in the multifarious physical bodies of creatures. Second, the notion makes of awareness a unitary phenomenon that can inhabit and integrate all of the body's experiences and activities in order to optimize its potential powers and virtues in the sagely or enlightened person. Whether in the guise of Brāhmiṇical theories that attributed cognitive luminosity exclusively to spirit or Vijñānavāda or Huayen models portraying it as the logical condition of sentience in physical beings or the medieval Confucian characterizations that align it with the mind's natural coherence, this notion of luminosity served as an explanatory model for the basic capacity of living creatures to be aware in both the most fundamental and broadest-ranging of possible senses. It thus took on cosmological and logical roles that undeniably invested it with great metaphysical significance for all these traditions. There were surely powerful and influential movements in classical Asian thought that made no recourse to such a notion of overarching or basic cognitive luminosity. Some, like the South Asian materialists, were perfectly comfortable saying that awareness was the product of a certain contingent and impermanent configuration of bodily matter. Others in the strongly naturalist early Chinese tradition also held normal states of awareness to be strictly psychophysical processes, and when they did speak of notions similar to cognitive luminosity, sometimes even invoking its vocabulary, reserved it for states of mind that resulted from various sorts of cultivation. For the philosophical movements that we have highlighted in this study, however, the signature feature of luminous awareness was that it was in various ways clearly distinguishable both from the matter of the individual body and the conditioned specificities that particularized any given instance of cognition. Without some such notion of luminosity, according to all these traditions, human experience and human personhood could not hope to be adequately explained or fully realized. It is, in the view of this study, impossible to identify a more significant philosophical commitment that was ever shared between the classical South and East Asian intellectual and spiritual worlds.

In addition to the specific metaphysical worldviews in which this idea of luminosity played pivotal roles, a somewhat more general perspective shared by all of these theories maps out a consequential implication of the notion. The consequence of awareness being literally luminous was that awareness, in its most primordial sense, does something to nature that nature could not otherwise accomplish on its own accord, namely, to literally bring it to light and enable it to be experienced by the creatures whose bodies it brings forth. That is to say that our awareness does not just passively mirror the natural world to different degrees of accuracy. Nor does it merely impose its own internal structures and accreted habits of categorization and action onto an otherwise unknowable world. Instead, our awareness reveals the world, makes it, of its own power, something experienced and lived in, shines upon it, not physical light but experiencing light. I thus label this aspect of the idea of cognitive luminosity the consequential one because, in addition to the metaphysical narratives that attempt to explain why such cognitive luminosity must exist as a unique and irreducible reality, its consequential facets attempt to demonstrate why luminosity is so important for us, so defining of us as persons, and so essential to the consummation of the human aspirations for wisdom and authenticity. There is, in the final analysis, no unsurpassable limit, no final roadblock, nothing in the world that can resist the luminosity of awareness; it will manifest things everywhere it is brought to shine and will bring to experienced life all things that would without it merely happen unbeknownst to anyone, and enable human beings not just to sense the natural world but also to speak of it, share it, and creatively transform it. This power of awareness dwells within all of us, and fully realizing its possibilities and optimizing them is what enlightenment is. Conversely, cultivating behaviors that limit this luminosity, hem it in, fixate it merely within self-interested boundaries, putting it only at the service of our passing and narrow desires, is to both hide and diminish the possibilities of our own most encompassing and enabling capacity. The luminosity of awareness then reveals the world, makes persons fully what they are, and makes the greatest of human ideals achievable.

But now, in view of both the metaphysical and consequential implications of the mind's luminosity, we must ask an exceedingly difficult question. Must we believe in the metaphysical irreducibility of the luminosity of awareness in order to discern the philosophical value in the axiological meanings and potentials that South and East Asian philosophers invested in it? Whether formulated in the Brāhmiṇical guise of the spiritual essence of selfhood, or the Vijñānavāda vocabulary of the unsullied germ of enlightened consciousness, or the Huayen depiction of the causal basis of awareness in nature, or the medieval Confucian conception of the mind's natural coherence, the notion of luminosity could not be analyzed into more fundamental components or traced to anything more primordial than itself. The *prakāśatva* or 明 *ming* of the mind was thought, even in its distinctive varieties of articulation, its own unique and ultimately indestructible essence or power, and it could not be accounted for by anything else in nature. This may be an especially provocative question in the context of a broad-ranging contemporary scientific consensus, which would not only reject the notion that awareness is one thing but would also insist that awareness itself is a product of natural, chemical, and physiological processes and subject, for its existence, persistence, kind, and degree, to the conditions of those processes. However, even limiting ourselves to classical Asian contexts, we have seen fraught metaphysical debates within and between traditions about how to most precisely define luminosity. Brāhmiṇical thinkers argued among themselves about whether consciousness could be considered the essence of the self or only a contingent feature of the self once it was embodied and in contact with sense organs. Buddhist philosophers rejected the Vedic insistence that luminosity was located in a spiritual self of any sort and, in turn, debated with one another about whether it was a feature of only specific states of enlightened awareness facilitated by practice or whether it was the causal basis upon which the possibility of enlightenment rested. In their turn, once they had appropriated the notion of luminosity, medieval Confucians tended to reserve its identification with natural coherence as a whole and postulated that the physical heart-mind must be made transparent to that coherence with methods of meditation and study that rendered the latter tranquil enough to be so transparent. These centuries-long contestations within and between Asian schools of thought about how to metaphysically characterize the luminosity of mind, though all held it in one way or another to be at the core of our personhood and the ideal of practice, would seem to indicate that the consequential implications of the idea could not only easily survive but be broadened to ever-more expansive goals of human conduct despite metaphysical disagreements about precisely what awareness, consciousness, and their luminosity amounted to. And yet, even this latter realization does not exactly get us out of the problem, since, to reiterate what has been said, despite their often-times radically different systems, Vedic, Vijñānavādin, Chan, and Neo-Confucian philosophers appear nonetheless to be at one in the perspective that, in the realm of nature, the luminosity with which awareness can reveal nature is a thing like no other and is not caused by anything else that nature brings about. Can this belief possibly be separated from holding fast to the consequential importance of the idea of luminosity, that it is really what makes us in the proper sense persons and that it calls us to the pinnacle of its own supposed perfection?

This question cannot be answered by some hermeneutically detached and abstract response that would attempt to bracket the metaphysical contours of luminosity and ponder whether anything of value remained. Quite the contrary, it can only be adequately answered by turning back to the textual traditions we have examined. South and East Asian thinkers alike fully acknowledged, despite their various metaphysics, that the luminosity of awareness operated precisely in conjunction with and through bodily processes, and could be manifested completely only by intentionally and meticulously cultivated bodily and interrelational practice. Luminosity may lie in some way at the most fundamental core of our personhood, but it does not by any means define it completely. Indeed, the luminosity of mind, when inhabiting and reflected through a human body, uses the external organs to sense, the internal organs to feel and think, the organs of movement to interact, the organs of speech to learn and teach, and finds itself in a world that it not merely reveals but enjoys. Moreover, as we shall also explore a bit further later, morality is of a piece with the physicality of the human body and its conduct. Enlightenment, in this respect, is not just a state of luminosity unto itself but a bodily pursuit, a training that will allow the mind to manifest the world untrammeled and enable the body to not only know rightly but act rightly. And whether that goal is reached depends entirely on the degree to which the body's own potentials can be actualized.

The Body, Nature, and Potentiality

There were specific reasons that the individual chapters of this study began with discussions of the concepts of nature and the taxonomies of the living body of these schools of South and East Asian thought. After all, this study is about personhood, and even traditions of thought like Sāṃkhya, which insisted that our true personhood (*puruṣa*) is pure spirit, offered an exhaustive account of material nature and the body in explicating human experience. Now, in the context of the immediately preceding section, some readers may be tempted to infer that the irreducible luminosity of mind that was believed necessary in order to make our bodies fields of experience in the first place still lands us in some species of "mind-body dualism." But things are not nearly so simple when it comes to classical Indian and Chinese thought. After all, we do find our existence as persons a physical and embodied one. Moreover, our moral potentialities are also everywhere recognized to be bodily, and the success of cultivating both action and wisdom depends on bodily practices, whether they be Brāhmiṇical *yoga*, Buddhist *vipassana* meditation, or Confucian recitation. And we are capable of fulfilling the ideals toward which these practices lead because our nature, rooted in the physical world, is perfection in *potentia*, and praxis is designed precisely to activate it.

As noted earlier, all the traditions we have covered in this study concur that the human body is enlivened by physical energies that are in dynamic interaction with the natural environment, 氣 *qi* in Chinese thought, and *prakṛti* in some South Asian schools, as well as vital bodily organs (*jivita indriya*) in others. This was the case despite the basic difference of views between classical Brāhmiṇical and Chinese thinkers about whether or not the physical body should be considered in any way conscious.

Indeed, even where ancient Vedic texts like the earliest *Upaniṣads* and continuing traditions like Nyāya held that the innermost self (*ātman*) was not as such a material or divisible thing, they did think its presence in a body, with its locus in the vicinity of the heart, accounted for the body's vital breath and life, perhaps because "breath" and "body" were two alternative ancient denotations of the very word *ātman*. Furthermore, both South and East Asian schools adopted taxonomies of the body that enumerated six distinct sense organs, the five organs of "external" sensation and one of "internal" sensation and deliberation, with the latter variously conceived as the multifunctional *antaḥkāraṇa* (inner agent), the singular *manas* (inner sense), or the physical heart (心 *xin*). The external organs among these were practically always represented as being in physical contact with things in the environment, and the organ of internal sensation responded to external sensation and accreted internal psychological dispositions and operated according to variously assessed capabilities of its own. The particular constitution of the body then is what thoroughly and robustly shapes experience as human experience, in terms of everything from our modes of sensuous life to our emotional responses and cognitive habits and reflections.

What is of very special importance is that many of these traditions also agreed that morality had a quite overtly physical dimension, not merely in the obvious sense that acts and their results are physical but also with regard to their respective accounts of moral motivation. In pre-Buddhist Chinese thought, 氣 *qi* was believed, as we have seen, to respond not only to the natural environment but to social creations like music as well, and its cultivation made moral behavior progressively easier for people. Even in Buddhist-influenced medieval Confucian thought, *qi*'s relative turbidity or tranquility accounted for different degrees of moral insight and capability. In classical Sāṃkhya, it should be recalled, the strands or energetic vibrations (*guṇa*-s) of *prakṛti* were not only basic measures of material density but were also irreducibly affective intensities, and the harnessing of the active (*rajas*) and brilliant (*sattva*) energies in the body could accrue a number of social and spiritual virtues. The mastery of such energies to various ends was precisely the rationale for the development of the multifarious techniques of *yoga*. Most conspicuously, the notion of *karma*—as the accretion of a very fine sort of particle residue that either itself formed a subtle "karmic body" (*liṅgam*), affixed itself to the transmigrating "self," or simply itself manufactured new bodies from one generation to the next—was successfully adopted in a Buddhist guise, as 業 *ye* in East Asian thought. According to the general theory of *karma*, the intentions that have been carried through in deeds accumulate and merge with other intentions and experiences in one's embodied psychophysical life, and their consequences to one's present or deferred actions cannot but ensue, in most cases requiring future lives. In future lives, the heritage of those accumulated intentional complexes must be "worked out," resolved, and ultimately dissolved in such a fashion as to enable one to know, behave, and even die selflessly, so that no lingering ego-limited and self-serving attachments whatsoever remain. Whatever varieties of metaphysical implications of such ideas may be found in these traditions, fraught though they especially are with problematics of class and gender, the shared conviction is nonetheless philosophically most significant. That core conviction can be articulated in the following way. No adequate consideration of moral motivations and outcomes can avoid fully accounting for one's embodied circumstances. Far from being some distorted conception of a passive fatalism, the broad contours of the idea of *karma* serve as an explanation of both our present lot as persons and imply one or another imperative program of moral rectification.

The Buddhist tradition in both South and East Asia embraces a fundamental commitment to a kind of naturalism, but the form of this commitment finds, in fascinating respects, different expressions in both of these contexts. Clearly, in the classical South Asian intellectual realm, the expression of this naturalism can largely be appreciated in the outright and consistent rejection of the Brāhmiṇical view that our most real and, more, eternal essence lies in a nonphysical "self" or "soul" (*ātman*), which can in no way be reduced to or identified with the body. From the Buddhist perspective, not only is it impossible to identify in our experiences anything more than an artificially manufactured and fraudulent conception of a stable and enduring identity, but such a notion of exclusively spiritual personhood is removed from all the embodied, psychological, social, and even utterly individually unique causal contingencies only within which the idea of a person can possibly be meaningful. Just as, in the Buddhist tradition, each awareness is specific to certain embodied experiences, so is the whole idea of experience itself only conceivable in the context of ongoing change, not of permanence and abstract cognitive stasis. Any account of human existence and experience then that departs from such grounding in the natural world will simply fail to adequately explain what serious reflection demands, namely, an understanding of who and what persons are. Now, by contrast, the Chinese philosophical environment presented an entirely different kind of naturalist challenge for the schools of Buddhism that flourished there. It was not an abstracted conception of self that Buddhists battled in the Central Kingdom but instead what they took to be an insufficiently causal representation of the natural order that would properly account not just for physical changes but moral deserts and transformations as well. From the Buddhist perspective, merely relying on ideas such as the orderly patterns or autocratic conferrals of "heaven" (天 *tian*) or the rarified "vital vapor" (氣 *qi*) to explain the world did next to nothing to elucidate how one group of beings rather than another possessed awareness or how one group of sentient beings could develop different bodily modes of awareness from others. Least of all could a generalized theory of Confucian natural order or Daoist differentiated energy take stock of why distinct human beings could acquire such profoundly different character traits, talents, potentials for knowledge and virtue, or be born to such different stations and suffer such variegated fates. Without an adequate causal theory, that is, none of these different levels and degrees of experience could hope to find a satisfying narrative that would justify them. And, after all, for a tradition like Buddhism, which was so fundamentally based on the idea that we could, through reflection and meditation, root out the causes of human suffering, without an adequate causal theory, our experience as persons in the natural world simply could not be fathomed, leaving us adrift in a world where, in actuality, we find ourselves precisely as effects of deeds already done within it. In both South and East Asian contexts, however, Buddhist philosophers find themselves defending not just a certain kind of naturalism but a naturalism that is morally and axiologically constituted out of discernible causes and conditions. It defies, in the classical South Asian world, an alternative naturalism that is accompanied by a conception of abstract spirit, and in the East Asian environment yet another brand of naturalism that struck them as too random and arbitrary to be true to our personal quest for genuineness.

However, it would appear that one of the most basic orientations of Buddhist thought, as it turns from battling South Asian varieties of naturalism to East Asian ones, itself undergoes a transformation. As can be discerned from our reading of the *Yuan Ren Lun* attributed to Zongmi, and in some ways reformulated into a more "existential" theme by Hongzhou Chan Buddhism, in East Asian contexts, Buddhism parlays this insistence on a causal view of nature into a philosophical mission to discern real human origins (源 *yuan*). This can even be seen in the transition of Vijñānavāda Buddhism from South to East Asia. In early Cognition school Buddhist treatises and commentaries, our stores of psychic seeds of both meritorious and deleterious *karma* could be located in an ever-transforming set of "base cognitions," and an enlightenment experience that rendered everything luminous could fundamentally alter the nature of that whole store. This view was articulated in an already well-established South Asian Buddhist tradition that, from the beginning, eschewed accounts of ultimate origin as *avyākṛta* or "inarticulable' metaphysical schemes that in the end could be grounded in experience or logic, and so there was no need to provide an explanation of where the "base cognitions" that prompt the formation of new human individuals first came from. But, in the hands of Buddhist commentators in China, the mixture of virtuous and unvirtuous "base cognitions" in the psychic lives of people simply could not elucidate our potential to achieve a kind of awareness that transcends the limited character traits we have inherited and apprehends all things in dynamic but inseparable unity. Such an elevated and encompassing potential could not, in the Chinese Buddhist view, be causally derived from any of the fragmented and incomplete inheritance of our experiences past and present. But, at the same time, we must possess that potentiality somehow, for otherwise, we could not hope to fully realize its promise. And, precisely because that potential cannot be supernatural, cannot be artificially dispossessed of the rootedness of the rest of our experiences in the world, it must be thought of somehow as a potential of our very nature. And if we find it a potential of our nature, it must be a potential available in the grander scheme of the natural order at large. The fulfillment of what we can become must be based in the conditions that make us what we are, and so in the Chinese Buddhist world, it becomes not just permissible but imperative that we grasp our origins, our 源 *yuan*.

If the aim of practice, in this case, is the perfection of human knowledge and conduct, and our nature and nature as a whole provide us with the capacity to realize that perfection, then there must be something about nature itself that is incipiently perfect. The incipience of the natural origin (本源 *ben yuan*) of perfection is indeed a daring idea. After all, nature brings about not only beauty but destruction, not only youth but disease, not only capacities for wisdom but also incapacitating infirmities, not only new life but inevitable death; it offers both the objects of our desires and the utterly unavoidable onset of our most dreaded fears. However, we must also bear in mind that Buddhist thought and practice demand precisely that we move beyond the ego-centered limitations of our assessments of nature and achieve that movement while still remaining persons. It is again not the accretion of our habits, both good and bad, that enables us to transcend those limitations and the self-conceit and egoism that invent them. Instead, what is called within the tradition simply "trust" or "faith" (信 *xin*) that such an independent potential for perfection is within us and so within our ken is called for. And given that the perfection being sought is a perfection of awareness, Chinese systems like Huayen are compelled to see within the unfolding of the natural order an originally rarified (細 *xi*) state of consciousness (識 *shi*) that, when it evolves and becomes differentiated among certain specific physical creatures, becomes coarse (麤 *cu*) in the embodied mind. So, in one theoretical stroke, as it were, we have an explanation for the causal source (理 *li*) of both the diffuse appearance of awareness among living beings and for the possibility that awareness can be perfected in real human insight. And, though employed to different reflective and social ends, it was this notion of the originary perfection of 理 *li* or natural "coherence" that medieval Confucian thinkers appropriated into their own social and political reformist agenda. The natural modes of awareness that ground our personhood then empower us with all the capacities (才 *cai*) needed to perfect our learning, conduct, and social aims. And so, to return to the issue that opened this section, the luminosity of mind, as it was reformulated in the Buddhist tradition and then absorbed into the broader Chinese philosophical context, while it does constitute its own irreducible class, is yet something that lies at the heart of nature itself; it both reveals the world in which we live and is only fully manifested and realized through our conduct within it.

The Provocation of Optimism

It was Schopenhauer, based on his own convictions combined with his reading of nineteenth-century Orientalist scholarship, who characterized the classical Brāhmiṇical and Buddhist movements as religions of "pessimism," which, to his eyes, was among their greatest of virtues. This label and assessment of some of the major traditions of Asian thought as "pessimistic" certainly did stick with Nietzsche, and with many other Western scholars and the students who have followed them. This judgment is, of course, based on the inference that, because in Brāhmiṇical and Buddhist practice, the ultimate aim of human life (*purūṣārtha*) is release from rebirth in the physical world, an aim for which only human beings are equipped, they fundamentally reject both the worldly value of human life and the hope for the betterment of human society. In fairness, modern Westerners were not the first peoples to arrive at such conclusions. The Confucian response to Buddhism in China, from at least the third century of the Common Era all the way through to the most prominent of medieval Confucian writers, was revulsion, though qualified in degree, at the monastic Buddhist rejection of family ties and full sociopolitical engagement. Many quite well-known possible rebuttals could be offered against this charge of Brāhmiṇical and Buddhist "pessimism." Among them could be the demonstration that, in classical Brāhmiṇical thought, release from rebirth was never considered the only legitimate aim of life, since pleasure, success, and social duty were entirely appropriate aims for different stages of psychosocial development. One may also point to the Mahāyāna Buddhist *bodhisattva* figures who refuse final *nirvāṇa* precisely to remain in the world and ensure the release of all suffering beings before themselves. Such possible responses are, as far as they go, surely convincing. But, in a certain sense, they are mitigated responses that still concede that, in the ultimate sense, for Brāhmiṇical and Buddhist praxis, release is still the most noble of all human pursuits, and thus there is just no way to avoid the hard nub that is found at the core of these traditions. That nub is the principle that the ultimate goal of being born as a human being is that it affords one the opportunity to never be reborn into the natural world of physical limitation and death ever again. And it is certainly the case that this is an accurate representation of the principle that enshrines *mokṣa* and *nirvāṇa* in these two heritages. So, in the end, for any contrasting philosophical view that is committed to the intrinsic value or betterment of worldly existence or the possible worldly redemption of human beings, this impression of Brāhmiṇical and Buddhist thought of being irreducibly "pessimistic" would seem to stand. However, as this study has demonstrated, when the major Asian traditions are considered on their own philosophical terms, it seems that the accusation that they are fundamentally "pessimistic" is not simply false in a qualified sense but is entirely false. Instead, these traditions are incredibly, even provocatively, optimistic, both about the character of human nature and the human potential for the complete perfection of moral conduct and wisdom.

As noted in the introductory section of this chapter, the optimism about human nature and possibility in the Brāhmiṇical, Buddhist, and Chinese traditions is hardly rose-colored or naïve. In classical Sāṃkhya, the *guṇa*-s that constitute one's psychophysical complex could compel one to apathetic and violent courses of conduct that were of the greatest imaginable extremes, and in Nyāya thought, the patterns of desire that one inherits from previous lives had the power to completely distort one's perceptions and prompt one to continue on a path of morally incorrigible conduct. From the very beginnings of the Buddhist tradition, there was a keen awareness of the frailty of human beings in the face of their overpowering attachments, both to the objects of their own longing and to life itself. Indeed one of the most heated debates within the Vijñānavāda school itself was over whether there was such a class of beings as *iccāntika*-s, creatures of "boundless desire" who could never be enlightened. Moreover, the Buddhist literature devoted to elevated forms of meditational practice featured both reflections and instructions on how to adopt a "right" assessment of bodily existence, subject as it is to aesthetic imperfection, disease, and death. In their own turn, Confucians from the earliest generations of lineage, including presumably the founder of the tradition himself, often failed to gain the kinds of ministerial positions they strove for, and even when they acquired them, found themselves vulnerable to betrayal, exclusion, disregard, punishment, expulsion, and even death in return for their moral and political advice. These vicissitudes prompted many Confucians through the centuries to lament and speculate on the reasons for the progressive decline of virtue in civilization, for instance, in early texts like the *Mengzi* and *Li Ji*, and the provenance of "fate" (命 *ming*) in determining everything from one's allotted number of years to the success or failure of their respective missions. The many centuries of evolution and dialogue among South and East Asian philosophical movements thus hardly lacked keen appreciations of the ephemeral conditions, evil motives, and tragic facets and outcomes of human existence, even to the point where, as we have seen, several of them enshrined release from worldly rebirth as the aim of practice more worthy than all others. This keen appreciation is precisely what prompted the "pessimistic" depiction of these heritages in the first place.

And yet, even in the presence of these stark acknowledgments of human weakness, very possible malice, and the progressive dissolution of everything they hold dear, Asian philosophers of the ancient and medieval periods believed, in various ways, that the core of human nature was either incipiently perfect or perfectible. They also were convinced that human beings, of their own accord, could bring themselves through meditation, learning, and great effort, to the culmination of knowledge and the heights of moral exemplarity. In ancient Brāhmiṇical thought, these things were possible both because at our core we are all luminous, pure personhood or spirit, and because the energies and karmic aggregations that allow for the formation of human bodies enable us to transform them into almost limitless powers. In early Buddhist thought, though our births as persons are taken to be evidence of still-strong remaining attachments, insights into inevitable truths about the world and progressive merit-making practices can dissolve all of these and eventually make us into embodiments of paramount compassion and wisdom. As we have seen, developments in South and East Asian Mahāyāna transformed this early conviction into the view that we are enabled to completely reorient our lives from ones driven by egoism to ones of selflessness precisely because we stand in possession of a basic kind of luminous awareness that, once in view and activated, can make us ourselves into Buddhas, transmitters of enlightenment, and lords of our respective environments. In pre-Buddhist Chinese views, a combination of the bodily configurations conferred upon us by 氣 *qi* and the natural abilities of the heart empower people to understand the world's processes, craft them to the benefit of human living and civilization, and in some cases make it possible even for the person "in the street" to become as perfect as the ancient sage-kings. When medieval Confucians appropriated the Buddhist notion of the luminous mind as being implicate in the overarching coherence of the natural order, they made it the basis for learning, moral criticism, and action even in the face of a society and polity that resisted these. To put this same basic point in the contrapositive, for all of these traditions, if persons were not in the most fundamental ways constituted of such elements and powers, their lives would presumably merely be driven by foregoing impulses, hemmed in by limitations on knowledge and conduct that would render them more or less on par with other species of animal life, and leave them no real avenue of hope for either optimal social success or genuine human contentment.

But putting things in this way, namely, in a manner that makes the highest human aspirations for goodness and wisdom contingent on our constitutive makeup, drives us back onto the ground of metaphysical speculation. Even if we were to relent in the aforementioned charges of dualism with regard to the distinctions in these traditions between luminous awareness and the body, by seeing the former in most cases as its own irreducible category within the natural order itself, we might still wonder if one or another of these classical metaphysical perspectives on personhood would have to be maintained in order for us to salvage the ethical and axiological beliefs and goals the traditions espouse. It seems that there is no other way, in the end, to answer this question except "yes." It seems that any philosophically formulated set of principles that leads to claims about what persons are capable of must somehow be grounded in a considered view of what sorts of beings persons are. This is even true for schools of thought that hold that persons are, while surely physical creatures, predominantly sociohistorical constructions that have some capacities in turn to influence the unfolding of history themselves, since such a narrative has a definitively constitutive dimension. It is surely the case that the metaphysical details of classical Asian accounts of personhood were open to contestation, amendment, and revision, as the considerable legacies of debates both between and within all of the relevant traditions clearly attest. Brāhmiṇical thinkers argued vehemently over how to understand the relationship between selfhood and body, and still do. Buddhist philosophers were given to calling one another names over issues such as whether there is really anything to the idea of Buddha-nature, and still do. Those with loyalties to the Confucian heritage still disagree starkly over whether the medieval Confucian adoption of Buddhist frameworks for understanding human existence was at all desirable or necessary. Appreciating these facts may justifiably lead to the conclusion that further revisions of these views in the light of new discoveries about nature, psychology, sociology, and the innovations in political society could easily be taken up and absorbed into these classical worldviews. If that were not possible, it is hardly conceivable that they could have survived through as much challenge, historical change, and even cross-cultural transmission as long as they have. Nonetheless, any philosophical view that defends the notion that human beings can, given a certain set of defined ideals, attain to the perfection of those ideals, must, it would seem, base that notion on what persons are in their physical makeup and potentialities of awareness.

Further reflection and debate about the parts and overarching conclusions of this study will doubtlessly complicate and enrich the presentations of the issues that are found here. But an effort has been made at the end of this work to state the case that, given the ideals that were articulated and at various stages made into orthodoxy in South and East Asian thought, these longstanding and widely influential traditions were, in the final analysis, profoundly and incorrigibly optimistic about the possibilities of human achievement. That optimism was directly due to their multifarious and fascinating representations of the disposition and constitutive makeup of the person. It has, after all, been quite easy for the philosophers and students of philosophy who came after him to render Schopenhauer's ironic praise of the Asian traditions as "pessimistic" into a less ironic derogation of their value. But the characterization of "pessimism" is only itself derived from a larger debate about the relative axiological status of various kinds of commitments about what proper human aims should be. In an era of history, our own, during which so much insight has been gained into the natural configuration and emergence of human beings, so much has been imbibed about the dependence of our respective identities on sociohistorical forces, and so much horrific destruction has been unleashed on the world by political forces and economic doctrines, a philosophically sophisticated optimism about human beings may, in large part, be difficult to uphold. Perhaps then a serious engagement with the philosophical traditions of South and East Asia, and certainly the intellectual and axiological products of their sustained encounter with one another, may help provoke us to rethink our appreciation of what we are, what lies within our grasp, and what we as communities of persons can hope to accomplish.

Notes

Chapter 1. Heart and Person: Early Chinese Thought

1. It must be acknowledged at the outset, though it will be obvious in what follows, that much of the content presented and claims made in this chapter are heavily indebted to the work of Deborah Sommer on conceptions of the body in early China and Jane Geaney on the senses and epistemology in the same period. While reorganizing their presentations to fit my intended framework and relying on their own characterizations, I will elaborate extensively when appropriate. The work of a number of other scholars will be used to articulate the social and moral implications of early Chinese conceptions of personhood in the second half of this chapter.

2. The term has been rendered into English in a wide variety of ways, ranging from "vital force" to "energy" to "pneuma." Capturing all of the early Chinese cosmological and physiological features of the notion with one English word indeed seems futile. I settle on the present, and certainly imperfect, rendering on the basis of the general sense of the term as "air" or "vapor" (氣 *qi*) and its dynamic and varied activities in the body that determine its degrees of vitality (see Sivin 1987, 46–53).

3. The fact that 心 *xin* both feels and thinks, as we shall see, has prompted many recent translators to render the term "heart-mind." I constrain my translation to "heart" in this chapter for two simple reasons. First of all, it is this bodily organ that was clearly believed by early Chinese philosophers to perform both functions. Second, given the facts that the other sensory organs were believed to have possessed the abilities to feel and think in their own specific ways and that the heart was, while certainly special, no exception to this rule does not justify whatever temptation we moderns may have to add the term "mind," either in its abstract senses or with some hinted implication of the "brain," to its concept.

4. Sommer 2008, 293–324.

5. Though frequent use of existing translations is made in this book, I will often insert parenthetical interpolations in the translations when I

feel that crucial terminology or phrasing relevant to the running discussion need to be clarified, as I do in this citation. All bracketed interpolations are original to the source texts.

6. An excellent detailed study of these issues can be found in Mark Csikszentmihalyi 2004.

7. This notion of the heart keeping tallies is a crucial one for understanding classical Chinese conceptions of the capacities of knowledge, and we will return to it later in detail.

8. Geaney 2002, 37.

9. Geaney 2002, 45. In her outstanding work, Geaney points out that, in the text of the *Xunzi*, the sense organs are also said to "discriminate" (辨 *bian*), which suggests not only that classical Chinese thinkers attributed to the sense organs themselves the ability to pick out things from their backgrounds and contrast them with one another, a function that names (名 *ming*) also serve, but that, as knowers, the sense organs and the persons they belong to are actively constitutive in their relations with things (2002, 34). This means that the features of things, while they certainly belong to the things, are also given their qualitative characters within the desiring, differentiating, and knowing acts of the specific bodily sense organs that engage with them.

10. *Xunzi* 22:5. In his summary of the scholarship on this issue, Kurtis Hagen (2007, 75–78) articulates the distinction between senses and judgment as one between the other sense organs "catching" things that correspond to their susceptibilities and the heart making judgments and decisions about them as well as conferring names on them. But some "sameness" has to be found in common experience in order to be believable and practicable by people in society.

11. 所以知之在人者謂之知;知有所合謂之智 (*Xunzi* 22:2). This sentence, from the beginning of the "Rectifying Names" chapter, has caused an interesting debate in the secondary literature. The translator John Knoblock thought the passage was distinguishing between the kinds of "awareness" both animals and humans possess and the kind of knowledge distinctive to human beings (1994, 3, 123). Geaney thought the line distinguished between "means of knowledge" that reside "in people" and another kind of knowledge that unifies things (2002, 194). Both readings seem to ignore the fact that the sentence occurs in a list of definitions that contrast lower forms of things to higher forms of things, for instance, between the mere "affairs" of people pursuing "benefit" and the "conduct" of people pursuing "rightness," or the "capabilities" of people just going about their business and the "capabilities" of people who can unite all their efforts, presumably under one overarching aim. I think the passage is distinguishing between two kinds of human knowledge, the first probably just the knowledge of the senses and the second the knowledge that results from comprehensive understanding.

12. Geaney 2002, 93.

13. *Zhuangzi* 4:8.

14. The felicitous translation of *ren* as "co-humanity" came from Peter Boodberg 1953, 7–32.

15. The translation "inclusive care" for *jian ai* originated with Chris Fraser. Fraser has also written that "self-interest" does play a recurring role in Mohist moral and political arguments, but he argues that the motive of self-interest only occurs within the nexus of other motivations and serves only as a "practicability" condition on certain moral and political theories (2008, 437–454).

16. There have been modern attempts to dull the Han dynasty cosmological readings of 別 by restricting its relevance to the functionalization of family roles in order to make the framework of those roles more fungible. See, for instance, Chan 2008, 148–150.

17. Ames and Rosemont 1998, 49.

18. The *Xunzi,* at one point, goes to great lengths to detail the appropriate expressions, dress, and even proper way to wear one's cap in specific social relations, and denounces those who depart from these prescriptions in the strongest of moral terms (see 6:15–17). The *Mozi* frequently makes sport of the Confucian conviction that dress betokens moral character.

19. Still noteworthy was the early twentieth-century poet Ezra Pound's reading of the word 信, which has it pictographically representing "a person standing next to their word" (1969, 22). This reading, of course, misses the fact that the 言 *xin* element of the character is its phonetic component and not technically a meaning component, the meaning, according to the *Shuowen Jiezi* having more to do with conduct. But, given the actual sense of the term, Pound's construal still has some appeal.

20. This has been most convincingly demonstrated by Dan Robins 2012, 60–91.

21. The description of the *Zhuangzi* as an "anthology" comes from personal conversations with Dan Robins. The fact that a number of different versions were floating around during the Han combined with the great heterogeneity of the philosophical materials in the received text make it much more likely a collection of materials compiled by editors than even a single text compiled by them. Such a narrative of composition does not in itself make the *Zhuangzi* unique, as many texts had their origins in such a process. Nonetheless, this felicitous description does drive the point home appropriately.

22. Sommer 2010, 212–227.

23. *Zhuangzi* 5:5.

24. See *Zhuangzi* 33.

25. The intertextual closeness between these two works has long been recognized. Ames has noted that about 15 percent of the opening *yuandao* essay of the *Huainanzi* can be found virtually unchanged in the *Zhuangzi* (1994, 215n36). Such overlap has led some scholars to hypothesize that at

least one version of the *Zhuangzi* was composed by the scholars of the Huainan court (see Roth 1991, 120ff). Roth calculates that the *Zhuangzi* is referred to or quoted five times more often than the *Laozi* in the text of the *Huainanzi*, and to him this demonstrates that these compilers were fundamentally influenced by the former though they did not consider it as canonical as the latter (1991, 94–95). The fact that the fifty-two-chapter version of the *Zhuangzi* in the historian Sima Qian's possession did not contain any of the "inner Chapters," combined with the aforementioned, seems to demonstrate that a lot of eclectic Han cosmological speculation went into both texts.

26. 以天為蓋，以地為輿，四時為馬，陰陽為禦 (*Huainanzi* 1:3).

27. *Huainanzi* 1:3.

28. *Huainanzi* 1:5, 7, 11.

29. *Huainanzi*, 1:3. Since the emotions, sense perceptions, and thought are generally believed to be coordinated by the heart, it would at first appear that the valorization of spirit over *xin* would follow along very similar lines in the *Huainanzi* as it does in the *Zhuangzi*, both in terms of their respective portrayals of personhood and of praxis. But in fact, a number of other passages make clear that the *Huainanzi* makes a more or less systematic attempt to recentralize the heart in relation to the other organs in the guidance of the person and simply credits the correct cultivation of the heart with the manifestation of spirit. Given the *Huainanzi*'s overt interest in government, this recentralization of heart in relation the body's other "officials" makes this departure at least understandable.

30. See *Zhuangzi* 1:5, 12:6. There is, of course, great ambiguity as to the text's views on immortality. The well-known story of the death of Zhuangzi's wife, quoted earlier, which occasions his explanation that death is merely another natural transformation of *qi* (18:2) and others like it seem to have convinced the authors of the 天下 chapter that the historical Zhuang Zhou, though he engaged freely in obscure speculations about the "goings and comings of heaven-and-earth's spiritual essence" (獨與天地精神往來 *tian di jing shen wang lai*), was undecided about immortality (33:6), and in its turn later Daoists believed that Zhuangzi was no true Daoist. But, given the general cosmological currency of the notion of the immortals (僊 *xian*) in classical Chinese thought, there is nothing particularly inconsistent in some passages of the *Zhuangzi* making the connection between the released spirit and such a deathless state.

31. *Zhuangzi* 6:3.

32. Zhuangzi 6:3.

Chapter 2. Two Brāhmiṇical Selves

1. I will note here that this idea of fixed "schools" of thought in the Indian tradition is not less problematic by any means than the cor-

responding one of fixed *jia* in ancient China. While the textual traditions of the Indian *darśana*-s are strongly associated with different institutional affiliations of study and debate, many of the received root texts of these heritages were composed quite late, many scholastic commentaries written by adherents of either opposing schools are by scholars who had no clear singular alignment, and doxographical literature in different centuries testifies to multiple varieties of philosophical persuasion. While Sāṃkhya as a system of thought tended itself to become less independently visible and was subsumed into and transformed by other worldviews, as Vaiśeṣika and Nyāya grew together only slowly through shared commentators and mutual defense, their distinguishability is sometimes problematic.

2. Unless otherwise indicated, all translations from Sanskrit texts are my own.

3. The temptation to translate *manas* with its technical cognate "mind" should be resisted. While colloquial variants of the term, like *manana*, do indeed mean "thinking" or "deliberating," the *manas* is fairly universally said in the classical Indian philosophical tradition to be aware of feeling states and affects, too, so its activities are not confined by any means to thinking alone.

4. A fascinating debate took place among mid-twentieth-century Indian scholars regarding how to interpret classical Sāṃkhya's *guṇa* theory in the light of modern conceptions. B. N. Seal argued for seeing the system as a kind of ancient Indian proto-physics, with the three *guṇa*-s representing different forms of mass and energy, whereas K. C. Bhattacharya saw the *guṇa* theory as representing the world in terms of irreducible kinds of energetic and phenomenological affect; see Mohanty 1992, 209–212. We may not in the end be compelled to choose between these alternative readings, since the classical texts appear to incorporate both basic physical energies and affect in the conceptual scheme of *guṇa*-s.

5. This argument would be famously employed by the Buddhists, Vasubandhu in particular.

6. *Sāṃkhyakārika* 11.

7. This is, of course, in sharp contrast to the view of the classical Indian materialists, who were said to believe that the chemical composition of the living body was able to produce awareness via a process of "fermentation" (*kiṇva*).

8. It should be noted that the exact same characterization could describe the much longer-lived system of Advaita Vedānta. Though this system's philosophical standard-bearer, the eighth-century prodigy Śaṅkarācārya, leveled many criticisms at Sāṃkhya metaphysics and modified it in important ways, he also insisted that *ātman* bore nothing in common to the heterogeneous physical world. The modifier that the school's name bears, Advaita or "without a second," therefore should only be understood to describe the internal unity of the self and not the oneness of self

and world. Indeed, it is quite possible to understand Advaita, accepting its revisions to Sāṃkhya's categories, as nonetheless a metaphysical variant of Sāṃkhya that merely objects to the latter's belief that there are multiple selves (see Krishna 1992, 56–65).

9. See Praśastapāda's *Padārthadharmasaṃgrah* 5:45.

10. To be somewhat more precise, impermanent substances are said by the Vaiśeṣikas to possess motion (*kriyāvat*), while permanent substances like *ākaśa* (the medium of sound), space, and time are said to be all-pervasive and thus do not move; see *Vaiśeṣikasūtra* 1:1:14–15. Incidentally, the term being translated as "substance" here is *dravya*, which has etymological associations with the basic "ingredient" of a thing, its individuality, and its serving as the basis (*āśraya*) of what can in this context be considered adventitious qualities (*guṇa*-s), and it is also classified into two kinds, indivisible and permanent and compounded and impermanent (see Halbfass 1992, 92–97).

11. *Nyāyasūtra* 3:1:6.

12. *Nyāyasūtrabhāṣya* 3:1–3. Recall here that, in the classical Chinese traditions, such a synthetic capability was accounted for in terms of the powers of the heart (*xin*), but the heart was not believed by classical Chinese philosophers to be, on its own, a "unitary self."

13. *Nyāyasūtra* 3:1:7–12

14. *Nyāyasūtrabhāṣya* 3:1:41. There are other epistemological arguments that are brought to bear on the distinction between the body and the self, including most interestingly what the locus of memories is, and invoking the fact that we do not come to discover our awareness through merely observing our bodies but rather by immediate awareness. While, in my view, these arguments feature a great deal more philosophical credibility than the aforementioned arguments, the Naiyāyikas do rely heavily on the former, and since it is not our present purpose to become overly detained by epistemological arguments here, we will leave them aside for now.

15. As we will see in the following chapter, the Vijñānavāda Buddhists would be willing to accept that the sense organs themselves, driven by both natural and karmic compulsions, could indeed produce cognitions independently of an agent. They would add that the sense of agency we are familiar with in our everyday experience is the result not of any real substance that serves as a real agent but of a psychological fabrication.

16. *Sāṃkhyakārika* 9.

17. *Nyāyasūtrabhāṣya* 3:1:17.

18. By contrast, Buddhist philosophers tended to believe that qualities and actions did, so to speak, "free-float," without needing to be based in a substance (*dravya*). Their criticism of standard Brāhmiṇical basing relations, which Advaitins sometimes echoed, was that the proposition that things needed to be connected through relational ties of various sorts fell prey to the logical flaw of "lacking a final basis" (*anavasthā*), the classical Indian logi-

cal equivalent of the infinite regress. However, Cognition school Buddhists greatly qualified this view, as we shall see in the next chapter.

19. See *Sāṃkhyakārika* 36 and 20.

20. *Tattva Kaumidī* 37.

21. *Nyāyasūtrabhāṣya* 3:2:4.

22. See Rukmani 1988, 367–376.

23. The Naiyāyikas and various schools of Buddhist philosophers would agree that there were such things as unconscious recesses of memory and vied for centuries of debate about how to account for the persistence of these memories and how they could be brought to consciousness. The notions of *ātman* and the contingencies of its states of awareness answered these questions for Nyāya. Many Buddhist schools struggled with this issue given their conviction that memories did not reside in any persisting substrate. As we shall see in the next chapter, the Buddhist school that probably offered the most successful answer to this question while maintaining their rejection of an enduring self was Vijñānavāda.

24. *Nyāyasūtrabhāṣya* 3:1:4–6.

25. *Tattva Kaumidī* 11.

26. As Larson, in his classic study of Sāṃkhya, notes, the school pays much more attention to the "proximity" between spirit and matter than to time in its account of their relation (1969, 188–189). One of the only overt mentions of time in the root text is in v. 33, where the temporal distinction between external organs, which operate only in the present, and internal organs, which operate in the past, present, and future, is made.

27. Vācaspati Miśra's *Tattvakaumudi,* 9, 15. This objection was not without force, for Vaiśeṣika texts made occasional but weighted reference to an idea known as *sattāsaṃbhandu* or "connectedness to reality" to explain how particularized instances of general substances or qualities could at least partially be effects of the latter. The extended debate between Sāṃkhya and Vaiśeṣika texts on their opposing views on causality receive an extensive and outstanding treatment in Halbfass 1992, 172–196.

28. *Nyāyasūtrabhāṣya* 3:2:27.

29. *Nyāyasūtrabhāṣya* 3:2:3.

30. As noted earlier, while Sāṃkhya, Yoga, and Vedāntic philosophers continued to fight against this implication, Tāntric and Kashmir Śaiva philosophers would, in the development of these traditions, deal with the implication by embracing it.

31. Ram-Prasad 2012, 129–146.

32. See Praśastapāda's *Padārthadharmasaṃgraha* 1:2:6. It is, of course, of very interesting note that the adherents and defenders of the so-called Vaiśeṣika school were not in agreement about what precisely *viśeṣa* was or whether or not the concept was even necessary to account for particularity or identity. Praśastapāda's near contemporary Candramati, we are told by

the Chinese Buddhist commentator Xuanzang, thought "particularity" only applied to all-pervasive and unitary substances like sound-space, physical space, and time, and much later Raghunātha Śiromaṇi would dispense with the category altogether. Nonetheless, the description of *viśeṣa* given by Praśastapāda seems to have been either assumed or largely agreed upon by most early Nyāya and Vaiśeṣika authors, and so it has an appropriate place in the present depiction.

33. See, for example, *Nyāyasūtra* 3:2:27 and 3:2:70–72.

34. *Nyāyasūtrabhāṣya* 3:1:14.

35. *Nyāyasūtra* 3:2:36–40.

36. Such a one-sided representation of the position of the Lokāyatikas or "Adherents of the Worldly" were doubtlessly unfair, given the latter's embrace of defined limits of violence, which included a prohibition on animal sacrifice, no-harm principles with regard to others, and an insistence, often couched in the form of criticism of the purported deceptions of the priestly class, that claims to knowledge be based on publically verifiable evidence and that positions of social authority be earned.

Chapter 3. Eliminating Identity and the Luminous Mind in Yogācāra

1. The difficulties surrounding this issue have had largely to do with the existence of widely variant dates given in the history of the Indian and Chinese traditions for the lives of Vasubandhu, the author of the *Abhidharmakośabhāṣya* and Vasubandhu, the author of the texts of Vijñānavāda; see Frauwallner (1951), Jaini (1958), and Anacker (1970). While the approach here will be textual only and will not address these matters, the variant dates and different perspectives and genres of these groups of texts do call into more serious question than has lately been believed that these texts share one author.

2. Tao Jiang (2005, 41–46) has provided an adept analysis of these difficulties, what he calls the Buddhist "problem of continuity," and I find his argument that the Vijñānavādins did the most philosophical work in addressing them compelling. It should be noted here also, as Jiang points out in accord with the earlier work of Lambert Schmithausen, that the need for some account of continuity within Buddhist explications of consciousness arose from the problem created by the notion that, once a meditative state that achieves enlightenment has been attained, it has to persist in the person even after they have exited that meditative state into the world of daily life (49).

3. The term *avidyā* is, of course, almost always translated as "ignorance." But I am more inclined to render it as the nominalized a form of "uncomprehending." *Avidyā* does not after all merely mean not knowing or not being aware of something but also denotes a lack of know-how,

not understanding, for instance, the principles of a Vedic ritual or medical science, or not knowing the means of how to accomplish one's end. Consequently, *avidyā* does not simply identify a passive state of lacking requisite knowledge but is instead a positive state in which one's inability to understand one's circumstances and how to conduct oneself appropriately leads only to further confusion and errors.

4. While his case for the reading that Vijñānavādins were "realists" more or less akin to Yogācāra Sautrāntikas like Diṅnaga and Dharmakīrti is overblown, Thomas Kochumuttom (1982) was not incorrect in emphasizing that the early advocates of the Cognition school, and the commentator Sthīramati in particular, did not disavow the existence of external things. I have in this chapter cited some of the examples of textual evidence for this that Kochumuttom highlighted. As many other scholars have observed, however, the tendency of the school in the direction of such disavowal did become much stronger by the time the Chinese commentators Xuanzang and Guoxiang composed their works. Since we are in this section focusing on the South Asian rendition of the school, I will limit myself here to the earlier textual materials for the moment.

5. Indeed, Waldron (1994, 220), in reviewing the Abhidharma precedents for understanding the Vijñānavāda conception of psychic seeds, calls the very word "seed" a "metaphor" for the "potentials and developments (*śakti* and *samārthya*)" of mental states.

6. Compare the arguments about memory in the *Ātmavādapratiṣedha* section of the *Abhidharmakośabhāṣya* with Ratnakīrti's seminal *Kṣaṇabhāṅgasiddiḥ Vyatirekātmika* 84:3.

7. Schmithausen (1987, 22) suggests, based on what he believes to have been the earliest textual occurrence of the term *ālayavijñāna* in the *Yogācārabhumi*, hypothesizes that the term carries the meaning of a "hidden" form of mind that remains in the limbs of a person and stores their foregoing propensities during meditative states, as opposed to *pravṛtivijñāna*, which are visible and manifest sorts of cognitions.

8. See Sthīramati's *Madhyānta Vibhāga Kārikā Bhāṣya Tikā* 1:2.

9. For instance, in his *Nyāyavārtika*, Uddyotakara argued that any distinction between the grasper and the grasped content of a cognition necessarily implied that the distinction had to be real lest it become meaningless. In his *Ātmatatvaviveka*, Udayana attempts to cement the possibility of self-knowledge with the argument that our awareness of ourselves is an act of internal perception and not, as the earlier Naiyāyikas had believed, the result of an inference. He therefore insists contra the Vijñānavādins that even the internal apprehension of a self, because of its incontestable certainty even within the Buddhist, is grounds for taking that self as real and not just an imagination.

10. We can see that this concern weighed heavily on Vijñānavāda thinkers among Indian and Chinese commentators alike. For example,

Dharmapāla and Xuanzang went to great exegetical lengths to formulate the argument that psychic seeds were really the "activity" of the abode cognition and so did not technically reside in it (see Jiang 2006, 64–68).

11. *Triṃśātika* 29 and *Trisvabhāvanirdeśa* 37.

12. I am, in much of what follows on Paramārtha, primarily indebted to the pivotal study of Radich 2008, 45–174.

13. Where citations from the Chinese canons are made in this work, I will identify them by the work's title followed by the register and line numbers.

14. Specifically, Theodore Stcherbatsky associates this occurrence of the term with *Aṅguttara Nikāya* 1:10 (1971, 225). Harvey (1995, 166) points out the relevant verses stretch from 8–11.

15. Harvey 1995, 170–173.

16. See the *Madhyānta Vibhāga Kārikā Bhāṣya Tikā* 1:23.

17. In his analysis, Radich (2008, 93–100) follows the traditional chronology of Paramārtha's writings and suggests that the connection between "untainted cognition" and the ultimate transformation of enlightenment already covered is motivated by general Buddhist concerns while the association of *amalavijñāna* with the "luminous mind" treated here is inspired by the need to identify special metaphysical doctrines of Yogācāra. He also deals with the common Buddhist proclivity to see Paramārtha as the proto-founder of *Tathāgata-ghārba* theories of Buddha nature by arguing that, while the latter group of theorists appropriated Paramārtha's teachings to forge this notion, there is no compelling evidence in writings reliably attributed to Paramārtha that he had any such doctrine as "Buddha nature" in mind.

18. Kalupahana 1992, 137.

Chapter 4. Mind, Nature, and Conduct: Two Approaches of Chinese Buddhism

1. Alan K. L. Chan 2014, 217–23.

2. Alan K. L. Chan (2014, 219), reports this through citation of the *Sanguo shi* or *History of the Three States*.

3. Such descriptions are even found in Wang's commentary on the Confucian *Analects* in describing Kongzi's most prized disciple, Yan Hui.

4. *Yuan Ren Lun* 708a7. There has, of course, been much discussion about how to best translate 理 *li*, and we will explore this issue in the next chapter a bit further. The most common modern renditions have been "principle" and "coherence," suggesting both that there is a fundamental order to nature and that comprehending this order is the ultimate task of both wisdom and science. The term had been used as early as Han dynasty philosophical texts and was appropriated by Song and Ming dynasty Neo-Confucians largely from Buddhist influences. The most ancient etymology of

the term from the *Shuowen Jiezi* suggests that it had to do with the patterns or texture of jade, with a word meaning "interior" (里 *li*) standing as the phonetic component of the character (治玉也從玉里聲). But the term also suggests causal patterns, and since the *Yuan Ren Lun* places such emphasis on Buddhist causal theory in the effort to understand human origins, I will for present purposes employ this rendition.

5. *Yuan Ren Lun* 708c17–18.

6. Indeed, in the text's very next passage, it is insisted that certain people have extraordinarily vivid memories of past lives, and such memories would, the *Discussion* infers, not even exist if beings spontaneously formed from *qi*.

7. No translation is given by Gregory of the last sentence of this passage, which concludes the polemic against Confucianism by asserting: "it is (thus) known that this specific teaching cannot explain the origin of persons" (是知專此教者, 未能原人).

8. *Yuan Ren Lun* 708c25–709a3.

9. *Yuan Ren Lun* 709a14–18. Always worthy of note, of course, is the way the term *karma* was translated into classical Chinese. In Sanskrit, *karma* is derived from a verbal root that means to "do" or "make," and so generically denotes an action or a deed, even though the conception of *karma* that is operative in the general theory of rebirth is largely focused on the intentions or desires (*kāma*) that motivate an act rather than simply the act's results or "fruits" (*phala*). In Chinese, the word that translates *karma*, 業 *ye*, denotes one's "occupation," which is thought to be the result in the present life of deeds done in past lives. In a strict sense, 業 *ye* should be a direct translation of the Sanskrit term *varṇa*, which idiomatically refers to one's occupational caste by denoting the "color" of one's ritual clothing, with one's caste membership believed to be a result of one's *karma*. I call attention to this here not to critique the translation but rather to bring to the reader's mind the fact that, in deliberating about *karma*, Chinese Buddhist philosophers were perhaps primarily thinking through its results.

10. 故知佛教法中, 小乘淺淺之教, 已超外典深深之說, 都由不了此身本不是我, 不是我者, 謂此身本因色心和合為相. "All this comes about from (beings) not understanding that the body is from the very outset not the self. 'Is not the self' refers to the fact that the body originally takes on phenomenal appearance because of the coming together of form and mind" (色心和合 *se xin he he*). *Yuan Ren Lun* 709b04–06 (Gregory 1995, 142).

11. *Yuan Ren Lun* 709c08 (Gregory 1995, 159). Yet another translation issue is worthy of recognition here. Classical Chinese Buddhists translated the Sanskrit word *vijñāna* with the term 識 *shi*, which, given the fact that its primary meaning component is 言 *yan* or "word," usually denotes forms of discursive knowledge, such as discernment, memory, belief, and so on. The point here is that 識 *shi*, at least in its most literal sense, can more easily be rendered "consciousness" because it generally refers to a kind of knowledge

that persists. By contrast, in its most literal sense, the Sanskrit term *vijñāna*, as we saw in the previous chapter, denotes an individual and very specific "cognition" that may or may not take on a dispositional sort of continuity. This important difference, while it certainly does not itself account for the distinctions between Indian Vijñānavāda and Chinese *Wei Shi* and the schools most influenced by the latter, it perhaps sheds a little light on some of those distinctions.

12. *Yuan Ren Lun* 709c19.

13. This definition was, of course, established by the seminal founder of Mādhyamika thought in India, Nāgārjuna. In his *Mūlamadhyamakakārikā* 24:18, Nāgārjuna declares the meaning of "emptiness" to be equivalent to the meaning of "conditioned co-arising" (*pratitya-samutpada*) and therefore excludes any theory of self-causation. The early texts of Vijñānavāda famously make an addendum to this definition, claiming that emptiness has both a negative and a positive sense, with the negative sense corresponding to the absence of a distinction between self and objects within consciousness, and the positive sense being the existence of that absence in consciousness. One of the finest discussions of the differences between these Mādhyamika and Vijñānavāda conceptions of emptiness can be found in Garfield 2002, 128–151.

14. *Yuan Ren Lun* 709c26. Yet another translation is worthy of attention. The Sanskrit term often rendered as "emptiness" (*śūnyatā*), though it is often colloquially understood as the "absence" or "nonexistence" (*abhāva*) of something in a particular place, attaches the abstract ending *-tā* onto the word *śūnya*, where the latter word describes the shape with which the number "zero" is written. By contrast, the Chinese term 空 *kong*, while it does have a variety of associations with "hollowness" or "emptiness"—as these can be observed, for instance, in a "hole" or "cave" (穴 *xue*) as well as existential senses of "emptiness" like "vanity"—also can refer to the empty and open "air" or "sky" and so does not exclusively have a privative meaning but also can suggest expansiveness and limitlessness. The Sanskrit term *śūnya*, while it is sometimes linked to these latter meanings in texts, does not have such positive literal meanings itself. In the present argument in the *Discussion*, it is at any rate the privative meaning of 空 *kong* that is being employed.

15. See Welter 2008.

16. See Yanagida 1983, 187. It was Yanagida who coined the phrase "encounter dialogue" to identify the literary genre in Chan that dramatized enlightening interchanges between teachers and students.

17. Hershock 1996, 64. The conception of enlightenment as "unprecedented" experience in Chan pedagogy is also featured in the literature and meditative practice of 公案 *gong an*, which, of course, predominates in the Rinzai order in Japan. The characters 公案 *gong an* mean a "public precedent" that is recorded in either the extended or short interchange of the teacher and student; but the point of the practice for the student is to

get beyond or not buy into the premise of the 公案 *gong an* being studied (see Foulk 2000, 40).

18. Faure 1991, 299.

19. This basic motif of the mind, in its ideal operation, not being interrupted from its "movement" or "procession" (道 *dao*) dates back, for Linji's lineage of Chan, to the *Platform Sūtra of the Sixth Patriarch,* a school whose historical cause had been championed by the eminent Tang dynasty monk Shenhui (神会) and which, through the teachings of Mazu Daoyu, had embraced the notion that it was the "ordinary" mind, not the mind immersed in meditation, that should be restored to untrammeled activity.

20. See McRea 2000, 47–48.

21. McRae 2000, 48.

22. *Linji Yu Lu* 501a05–08, 501a09–10 (Sasaki and Kirchner 2009, 246, 247). Though I am referencing the translation in these notes, the translations of the terminology and expressions in the present and following paragraphs are my own.

23. *Linji Yu Lu* 501a10–13 (Sasaki and Kirchner 2009, 247).

24. *Linji Yu Lu* 501a13–15 (Sasaki and Kirchner 2009, 247).

25. *Linji Yu Lu* 501b03–09 (Sasaki and Kirchner 2009, 251).

26. *Linji Yu Lu* 0498c19–22 (Sasaki and Kirchner 2009, 201). Each of these "environments" is associated with a basic natural element, namely, earth, water, fire, and air, respectively, and part and parcel of dissolving attachments to these emotions is the knowledge that the elements themselves are fleeting and changing, and therefore not to be fixated upon.

27. *Linji Yu Lu* 0497c11 (Sasaki and Kirchner 2009, 166).

28. *Linji Yu Lu* 0498a02–b01 (Sasaki and Kirchner 2009, 188).

29. *Linji Yu Lu* 0498a02–b01 (Sasaki and Kirchner 2009, 188).

Chapter 5. A Space for Moral Reflection: The Confucian Rapprochement

1. One of the most articulate examples of this line of thought can be found in Hansen 1992. The first two chapters of this study offer an extended argument that, while the structural similarities of Sanskrit with European languages give rise to analogous philosophical worldviews in India and the West, the unique nature of the ancient Chinese language did not saddle Chinese thought with mind-body dualism and all its attendant problems. What we have in the case of Buddhism and by extension Neo-Confucianism then, according to Hansen, is not so much a "Sinicization of Buddhism" but rather an artificial and philosophically unsalvageable "westernization" of Chinese thought.

2. Bol 2008. Bol's perspective informs a great deal of my presentation in this chapter.

3. Bol 2008, 159.

4. The issue about how to best translate 理 *li* in the present Neo-Confucian context presents a slightly different problem than it did for us in the previous chapter with regard to the works attributed to Zongmi. There, given the term's etymological association with "patterns" and its particularly Buddhist embeddedness in the context of being a causal ground, and sometimes a kind of template for how the parts of individual material things (事 *shi*) were integrated into a whole, the terms "causal principle" or simply "principle" make somewhat more sense. However, when it comes to medieval Confucian thought, Willard Peterson has persuasively argued that—given the concept's association with how things work, the logic that links ideas together, and the comprehension or understanding of ideas—the translation "coherence" makes more sense (1986, 13–32). Peterson's rendition is thus followed here.

5. Bol 2008, 171.

6. This chapter makes references only to the first volume of the 1986 Beijing compilation *Zhuzi Yu Lei* (*Conversations of Master Zhu Arranged Topically*, hereafter identified as *Conversations*) and follows the translations of Daniel Gardner (1990) unless otherwise indicated. The present citation comes from *Conversations* 3:8 and Gardner 1990, 92.

7. See *Conversations* 130:13 and 140:14.

8. Bol 2008, 165. Bol notes that Zhu Xi's most illustrious disciple, Chen Chun, who compiled the first official lexicon on the Cheng-Zhu "school," only qualified this identification by pointing out that *li* primarily refers to the holistic and unitary coherence that all things possess, while *xing* refers to the *li* that governs the constitution of individual things and creatures. Chen adds, significantly, that, because the word 性 *xing* is partly built from the radical for "mind" (*xin*), it also alerts us to the fact that "coherence" can be most fully apprehended by the human *xin*.

9. *Conversations* 155:1.

10. *Conversations* 200:3.

11. The Chinese text, in both of the relevant instances, actually reads "three minds" (三心 *san xin*), presumably referring to the mind of *dao*, the merely human mind of desires, and the "one" mind as an overarching unity that is under general discussion in the passage. But Ivanhoe's translation here avoids any unnecessary confusion by not introducing this enumeration in the original.

12. The translation of this passage is my own.

13. Bol 2008, 184.

14. As is well known, Zhu elevated previously neglected texts like the *Zhong Yong* and *Da Xue* to prominence, rehabilitated the *Mengzi*, and insisted that the these texts, along with the *Analects*, be read before the seminal five classics and the official dynastic histories.

15. *Conversations* 169:3 (Gardner 1990, 135–136).

16. *Conversations* 192:8 (Gardner 1990, 157–158).

17. Zhu famously changed the priority of two steps in the learning process enumerated by the *Da Xue* and actively changed the meaning of one of them. At the opening of the *Great Learning*, an organic relationship is laid out that connects a harmonious state to ordering one's own family to individual moral self-cultivation, and in the original text, the most fundamental practice in personal cultivation is "making the intentions sincere" (诚意 *cheng yi*). But Zhu makes this step subordinate to the "investigation of things" as discussed later (see Ivanhoe 2000, 50; and Bol 2008, 137–138.

18. As we shall discover shortly in Wang Yangming's criticism of Zhu's conception of knowledge, the term 格 *ge* has an abundant number of connotations and can mean everything from "correcting" or "regulating" to "studying" to "attacking" or "blocking." Early etymologies of the term identify both its phonetic particle as "wood" (木 *mo*) and its meaning as following the patterns of wood in construction. There is thus some etymological affinity between the words 格 *ge* and 理 *li*, the latter of which, it may be recalled, is connected with patterns in jade. As Bol points out (2008, 155–156), this notion of 格物 *ge wu* as understanding how anything, from a natural object to a relational virtue like family care, works "on the outside and inside" is explicitly defined by thirteenth-century inheritors of Zhu's teachings such as Rao Lu just as Gardner has translated the expression, namely, "fully apprehending the coherence" of things. The meaning of the terms has, of course, been contested by proponents of the two wings of Neo-Confucianism since.

19. Ivanhoe 2000, x–xi.

20. Bol 2008, 212.

21. Ivanhoe 2000, 49.

Chapter 6. Luminosity, Potential, and Personhood

1. Mohanty 1992, 33.
2. See Malamoud 1996, 7–22.
3. Ram-Prasad 2007, 154.
4. Mohanty 1992, 26–32.
5. MacKenzie 2012, 181–198.
6. Dewey quoted in Alexander 2013, 50.

Bibliography

Alexander, Thomas A. 2013. *The Human Eros: Eco-Ontology and the Aesthetics of Existence*. New York: Fordham University Press.

Ames, Roger, T. 1994. *The Art of Rulership: A Study in Ancient Chinese Political Thought*. Albany: State University of New York Press.

Ames, Roger T., and Henry Rosemont Jr., trans. 1998. *The Analects of Confucius: A Philosophical Translation*. New York: Ballantine Books.

Anacker, Steven. 1970. "Vasubandhu: Three Aspects: A Study of a Buddhist Philosopher." PhD diss., University of Wisconsin.

Bol, Peter. 2008. *Neo-Confucianism in History*. Cambridge: Harvard University Press.

Boodberg, Peter. 1953. "The Semasiology of Some Primary Confucian Concepts." *Philosophy East and West* 2.4: 7–32.

Chan, Alan K. L. 2014. "Embodying Nothingness and the Ideal of the Affectless Sage in Daoist Philosophy." In *Nothingness in Asian Philosophy*, ed. JeeLoo Liu and Douglas L. Berger. 213–29. London and New York: Routledge.

Chan, Sin Yee. 2008. "Gender and Relationship Roles in the *Analects* and the *Mencius*." In *Confucian Political Ethics*, ed. Daniel Bell. 147–174. Princeton: Princeton University Press.

Csikszentmihalyi, Mark. 2004. *Material Virtue: Ethics and the Body in Early China*. Leiden: Brill Academic Publishing.

Deurlinger, James. 2003. *Indian Buddhist Theories of Persons: Vasubandhu's 'Refutation of the Theory of a Self.'* London and New York: Curzon.

Faure, Bernard. 1991. *The Rhetoric of Immediacy: A Cultural Critique of Chan/Zen Buddhism*. Princeton: Princeton University Press.

Foulk, T. Griffith. 2000. "The Form and Function of Kōan Literature." In *The Kōan: Texts and Contexts*, ed. Stephen Heine and Dale Wright. 15–45. Cambridge: Oxford University Press.

Fraser, Chris. 2008. "Mohism and Self-Interest." *Journal of Chinese Philosophy* 50.3: 437–454.

Frauwallner, Erich. 1951. *On the Date of the Buddhist Master of the Law Vasubandhu*. Rome: Serie Orientalia, III.

Gardner, Daniel K., trans. 1990. *Learning to Be a Sage: Selections from the Conversations of Master Chu, Arranged Topically*. Berkeley: University of California Press.

Gardner, Daniel K., trans. 2007. *The Four Books: The Basic Teachings of the Later Confucian Tradition*. Indianapolis: Hackett Publishing Company.

Garfield, Jay L. 2002. *Empty Words: Buddhist Philosophy and Cross-Cultural Interpretation*. Cambridge: Oxford University Press.

Geaney, Jane. 2002. *On the Epistemology of the Senses in Early Chinese Thought*. Honolulu: University of Hawai'i Press.

Gregory, Peter N., trans. 1995. *Inquiry into the Origin of Humanity: An Annotated Translation of Tsung-mi's Yuan Jen Lun with a Modern Commentary*. Honolulu: University of Hawai'i Press.

Hagen, Kurtis. 2007. *The Philosophy of Xunzi: A Reconstruction*. Chicago and La Salle: Open Court Press.

Halbfass, Wilhelm. 1992. *On Being and What There Is: Classical Vaiśeṣika and the History of Indian Ontology*. Albany: State University of New York Press.

Hansen, Chad. 1992. *A Daoist History of Chinese Thought*. Oxford: Oxford University Press.

Harvey, Peter. 1995. *The Selfless Mind: Personality, Consciousness and Nirvana in Early Buddhism*. Richmond, Surrey: Curzon Press.

Hershock, Peter. 1996. *Liberating Intimacy: Enlightenment and Social Virtuosity in Ch'an Buddhism*. Albany: State University of New York Press.

Ivanhoe, Phillip J. 2000. *Confucian Moral Self-Cultivation*. Indianapolis: Hackett Publishing Company.

Ivanhoe, Phillip J., trans. 2009. *Readings from the Lu-Wang School of Neo-Confucianism*. Indianapolis: Hackett Publishing Company.

Jaini, P. S. 1958. "On the Theory of Two Vasubandhus." *Bulletin of the School of Oriental and African Studies* 21: 48–53.

Jha, Durgadhara, trans. 1963. *Padārthadharmasaṃgrah of Praśāstapāda with Nyāyakandali of Śrīdhāra*. Benares: Benares Sanskrit University.

Jha, Ganganath, trans. 2004. *The Sāṃkhya Tattva Kumāḍi: Vācaspati Miśra's Commentary on the Sāṃkhyakārikā*. Delhi: Chaukambha Sanskrit Pratishthan.

Jiang, Tao. 2006. *Contexts and Dialogue: Yogācāra Buddhism and Modern Psychology on the Subliminal Mind*. Honolulu: University of Hawai'i Press.

Kalupahana, David J. 1992. *A History of Buddhist Philosophy: Continuities and Discontinuities*. Honolulu: University of Hawai'i Press.

Knoblock, John, trans. 1994. *Xunzi: A Translation and Study of the Complete Works*. Stanford: Stanford University Press.

Kochumuttom, Thomas A. 1982. *A Buddhist Doctrine of Experience: A New Translation and Interpretation of the Works of Vasubandhu the Yogācārin*. Delhi: Motilal Banarsidass.

Krishna, Daya. 1992. *Indian Philosophy: A Counter-Perspective*. Delhi: Oxford University Press.

Larson, Gerald James. 1969. *Classical Sāṃkhya: An Interpretation of Its History and Meaning*. Delhi: Motilal Banarsidass.

Li Qingde, ed. 1986. *Zhuzi Yu Lei*. Beijing: Zhonghua Shu Chu.

MacKenzie, Matthew. 2012. "Luminosity, Subjectivity and Temporality: An Examination of Buddhist and Advaita Views of Consciousness." In *Hindu and Buddhist Ideas in Dialogue: Self and No-Self*, ed. Irena Kuzentsova, Jonarden Ganeri, and Chakravarthi Ram-Prasad. 181–198. Hampshire: Ashgate.

McDermott, A. C. Senape. trans. 1970. *An Eleventh-Century Buddhist Logic of 'Exists': Ratnakīrti's Kṣaṇabhaṇgasiddhiḥ Vyatirekātmika*. Dordrecht: D. Reidel Publishing.

McRae, John R. 2000. "The Antecedents of Encounter Dialogue in Chinese Ch'an Buddhism." In *The Kōan: Texts and Contexts*, ed. Stephen Heine and Dale Wright. 46–74. Cambridge: Oxford University Press.

Malamoud, Charles. 1996. *Cooking the World: Ritual and Thought in Ancient India*. Cambridge: Oxford University Press.

Mei, Yi-Piao, trans. 1929. *The Ethical and Political Writings of Mo-Tse*. London: Probsthain Press.

Mohanty, J. N. 1992. *Reason and Tradition in Indian Thought*. Cambridge: Oxford University Press.

Peterson, Willard. 1986. "Another Look at *Li*." *Bulletin of Song and Yuan Studies* 18: 13–32.

Pound, Ezra, trans. 1969. *Confucius: The Unwobbling Pivot; The Great Digest; The Analects*. New York: New Directions.

Radich, Michael. 2008. "The Doctrine of *Amalavijñāna* in Paramārtha (499–569) and Later Authors to Approximately 800 CE." *Zinbun* 41: 45–174.

Ram-Prasad, Chakravarthi. 2007. *Indian Philosophy and the Consequences of Knowledge: Themes in Ethics, Metaphysics and Soteriology*. Hampshire: Ashgate.

Ram-Prasad, Chakravarthi. 2012. "Self and Memory: Personal Identity and Unified Consciousness in Comparative Perspective." In *Hindu and Buddhist Ideas in Dialogue: Self and No-Self*, ed. Irena Kuzentsova, Jonarden Ganeri, and Chakravarthi Ram-Prasad. 129–146. Hampshire: Ashgate.

Robins, Dan. 2012. "Mohist Care." *Philosophy East and West* 62.1: 60–91.

Roth, Harold. 1991. "Who Compiled the *Chuang Tzu*?" In *Chinese Texts and Philosophical Contexts: Essays Dedicated to Angus C. Graham*, ed. Henry Rosemont Jr. 79–128. La Salle: Open Court.

Rukmani, T. S. 1988. "Vijñānabhikṣu's Double-Reflection Theory of Knowledge in the Yoga System." *Journal of Indian Philosophy* 16.4: 367–376.

Sasaki, Ruth Fuller, and Thomas Yuho Kirchner, trans. 2009. *The Record of Linji*. Honolulu: University of Hawai'i Press.

Schmithausen, Lambert. 1987. *Ālayavijñāna: On the Origin and Early Development of a Central Concept of Yogācāra Philosophy*. Tokyo: International Institute for Buddhist Studies.

Sivin, Nathan. 2007. *Traditional Medicine in Contemporary China*. Ann Arbor: University of Michigan Press.

Slingerland, Edward, trans. 2003. *Confucius: The Essential Analects: Selected Passages with Traditional Commentary*. Indianapolis: Hackett Publishing Company.

Sommer, Deborah. 2008. "Boundaries of the *Ti* Body." *Asia Major* 21.1: 293–324.

Sommer, Deborah. 2010. "Concepts of the Body in the *Zhuangzi*." In *Experimental Essays on Zhuangzi*, ed. Victor Mair. 212–227. Dunedin: Three Pines Press.

Stcherbatsky, Theodore, trans. 1971. *Madhyānta-vibhāga / Discourse on the Discrimination between Middle and Extremes*. Calcutta: Indian Studies Past and Present.

Thakur, A. L., ed. 1967. *Nyāyasūtra* with *Bhāṣya* of Vātsyāyana, *Nyāyavārtika* of Uddyotakara, *Nyāyavārtikatātparyatikā* of Vācaspati Miśra and *Parisuddhi* of Udayana. Darbangha: Mithila Institute.

van Norden, Bryan, trans. 2008. *The Essential Mengzi: Selected Passages with Traditional Commentary*. Indianapolis: Hackett Publishing Company.

Waldron, William. 1994. "How Innovative Is the *Ālayavijñāna*? The *Ālayavijñāna* in the Context of Canonical and Abhidharma *vijñāna* Theory. Part I." *Journal of Indian Philosophy* 11: 199–258.

Waldron, William S. 2003. *The Buddhist Unconscious: The Ālaya-vijñāna in the Context of Indian Buddhist Thought*. New York: Routledge.

Watson, Burton, trans. 1963. *Hsun Tzu: Basic Writings*. New York: Columbia University Press.

Welter, Albert. 2008. *The Linji Lu and the Creation of Chan Orthodoxy*. Cambridge: Oxford University Press.

Yanagida Seizan. 1983. "The 'Recorded Texts' Sayings of Chinese Ch'an Buddhism," trans. John R. McRae. In *Early Ch'an in China and Tibet*, Whalen Lai and Lewis Lancaster. Berkeley: University of California Press.

Ziporyn, Brook, trans. 2009. *Zhuangzi: The Essential Writings with Selections from Traditional Commentaries*. Indianapolis: Hackett Publishing Company.

Index